COLLINS

COMPLETE GUIDE TO
PHOTOGRAPHY

COLLINS

COMPLETE GUIDE TO
PHOTOGRAPHY

Your Key to Taking Good Pictures

MICHAEL FREEMAN

HarperCollins*Publishers*

COLLINS COMPLETE GUIDE TO PHOTOGRAPHY

Most of the material in this book was originally published in *Collins Photography Workshop Series*, but is here completely revised and updated.

First published in 1993 by
HarperCollins Publishers

This book was created exclusively for
HarperCollins Publishers by Nigel Osborne
Design: Nigel Osborne and Anne Clue
Editor: Richard Dawes

For HarperCollins Publishers
Project Editor: Barbara Dixon
Art Editor: Caroline Hill

A catalogue record for this book is available from the British Library

ISBN 0 00 412918/0

Typeset by Wearset, Boldon, Tyne and Wear
Printed and bound in Italy by Amilcare Pizzi, S. p. A.

The author and publishers gratefully acknowledge the assisstance of **Canon (UK) Ltd, Hasselblad (UK) Ltd, Minolta (UK) Limited, Nikon UK Limited, Olympus Optical Co (UK) Ltd, Pentax UK Limited.**

CONTENTS

INTRODUCTION

Photography has always been bound up with the new – new ways of making images, new ways of seeing the world. Its invention was a startling technological advance for the mid-nineteenth century, and ever since, one new development after another has helped to extend the kinds of images it can produce. Faster films made it possible to capture movement, smaller cameras could be carried and used more often and in more places. Colour film, longer lenses, wider lenses, filters and high-speed films all added to the range, and photographers have always seized on the opportunities to take pictures that were special to each new development.

Little wonder, then, that almost all of us have an appetite for new images in photography. Because of this, it is one of the most exciting media to work in. Now more than ever, for a fresh wave of technology, mainly electronic, has made picture-taking simple and reliable. On the face of it, this may sound a little less exciting than, say, the invention of colour film or the first extreme wide-angle lens, but it has probably done more than anything else to encourage an interest in making images – and among more people than ever before.

Electronics, advanced optics and advances in film chemistry have done two things for photographers – they have made high-quality images absolutely normal, and they have taken most of the need for technical skill out of the users' hands. These two things are, in fact, connected. Automation in cameras, and particularly in making a good exposure, simply guarantees that most of the pictures will be technically perfect. Even though much of this is no more than mistake-proofing, the final result is better-quality images (after all, even professionals sometimes make basic errors). Better optics make for sharper images, with richer contrast and colour saturation. Better film does much the same, and the choice of films makes it possible to shoot pictures in a variety of situations, from city streets at night to underwater.

Now, while there is no doubt that improvements in image quality benefit everyone, the idea of cameras by-passing the photographer in adjusting focus, exposure and so on occasionally meets a little old-guard resistance. The arguments generally run along the lines of making it too easy and ignoring important skills, and speak of gadget overkill.

In fact, the point-and-shoot principle is a triumph for technology. Not because a modern camera is a stunning piece of apparatus, but because it makes picture-taking easy. It may once have seemed that mastering the technology of cameras and lenses was a vital part of becoming a photographer. If you knew how to calculate the depth of field, use a motor-drive and work out the contrast range in strange lighting conditions, then you were somehow qualified to take pictures. Being skilled at operating the hardware was rather like being able to tune the engine of your car. You were an expert.

That idea no longer makes any sense. Provided that you don't get bogged down in the choice of modes that the more expensive models offer, a camera is now more than ever a very efficient tool for capturing an image of what you see. This makes what goes on behind your eye much more important than your skill in working the controls. It may not please enthusiasts who are happiest treating cameras as machinery, but it's very good news for everyone else.

For a start, it removes the exclusivity that serious photography used to enjoy. By serious, I mean photography with the intention of expressing an idea, informing, or exploring the creative possibilities in an image. In the past, you needed fairly professional equipment to tackle this. Indeed, there used to be simple, unimportant cameras for rank amateurs, and real cameras for those who considered themselves photographers. Now, however, even the point-and-shoot compact at the bottom of the range delivers top-quality images. The better models just cover more picture-taking situations, with more lenses.

Not only does the new technology of photography allow everyone the opportunity to take good, interesting pictures – it has also opened up the possibilities of fresh images. Indoors and night-time shooting, for instance, is a relatively new area. At one time, the slowness of films – and lenses – put a time limit on natural, unobtrusive photography. Without flash, colour photography virtually stopped around dusk. Fast colour films have extended photography's range. This is only one example, and there is more technology to come, much of it digital and very radical.

This all means that photographers now produce more exciting images than ever before – experimenting with new styles, ignoring old prejudices, taking pictures in more corners of human life. Better still, you are a photographer because of your eye, judgement and ideas rather than because you might know how to mix a developer solution. This book has the same bias – towards the visual rather than the mechanical – and is written to help you see and think about images.

Essential Equipment

The intention of this book is to provide a different way of looking at a very familiar subject. A large part of the difference is the emphasis on image. But as photography uses more equipment than most other media, it is important to give this aspect of the craft serious attention. Even though the critical factor in a photograph is nearly always the way you see the subject, the camera, lens and film must at least be right for the job, and you must know how to use them. Nevertheless, equipment used without talent or imagination can at best produce only a technically correct image.

The basic mechanical unit of photography is the camera body. It is this that governs the format of the photographs, and indeed most models are designed to accept only one size of film. For most photographers, this means 35mm film, although medium and large-format cameras remain popular among professionals, mainly for studio and other kinds of controlled work.

Although you would be hard put to distinguish what camera was used just by looking at a printed photograph, the characteristics of a lens are usually spread all over the picture. It is normally the lens that determines how sharp the image appears, how much of it is in focus, the contrast, the impression of perspective, and more.

Film, which at least for now is the recording medium that most cameras use, has undergone some remarkable technical progress. There is now a greater choice of film types than ever before, and the variety is increasing all the time. The major film manufacturers are continually improving the performance of existing basic films, while at the same time producing new emulsions aimed at special needs (such as for portraits in dull weather, or for landscapes with specially intense blue skies). The film chemistry that makes this possible has to do with new grain structures, better dyes and more efficient colour couplers.

Use the best equipment you can afford right, but remember that there is far more to a good photograph than the hardware.

35MM COMPACTS

The majority of 35mm cameras that do not have through-the-lens viewing are compacts. That is, cameras that are small and portable, designed to be used simply and without fuss, for snapshots. In the camera market as a whole, this kind of camera has always been the most popular, appealing mainly to people who want to take pictures of family, friends and holidays. Older designs were too limited to produce good-quality images, but now the electronics that were first applied to 35mm SLRs have been used to make many compacts worth considering for serious photography. One advantage is that many of these cameras are small enough and light enough to encourage

The sophisticated Minolta Riva Zoom 90EX offers several advanced features in addition to a zoom facility that ranges from a moderately wide-angle view of 38mm to a telephoto view of 90mm. Eye-start automation activates the exposure system when the camera is brought to the eye, and a further feature is that images can be superimposed in the same frame.

users to carry them more of the time – and so miss fewer opportunities for pictures.

Field of view
The traditional disadvantage of having to focus without seeing the effects has been overcome in many models by means of autofocus, but there is still a practical limit to the range of lens focal lengths. Telephoto lenses are difficult to use because they frame such a small area of the whole view. Non-reflex cameras are best used for wide-angle to normal angles of view, and most are fitted with a lens of this type.

Types of 35mm non-reflex
As with SLRs, the different types of non-reflex cameras vary mainly in the automation. The simplest are fixed-focus compacts, inexpensive, lightweight, with a moderately wide-angle lens that will provide an adequate depth of field for most views. These are snapshot cameras, but if the lens quality is high, no less useful for candid photography. A step up from these are manual focus compacts. The choice of focus is often in the form of zones, so that the dis-

tance does not need to be measured.

However, only a few of the cheapest compacts now use fixed focus or zone focusing. Fixed focus works well enough with a wide-angle lens and provided that your expectations are not very high, for a substantial enlargement may show up loss of focus at wide apertures. Very few non-reflex cameras now use the traditional rangefinder focusing system, which inexperienced photographers find very slow to use, but it remains a feature of the redoubtable Leica, which is discussed on the opposite page.

Autofocus
The small extra cost of autofocus – and its great convenience – has made it the standard focusing system in compact cameras. Autofocus overcomes the difficulty of focus-

Compact cameras with autofocus and a zoom facility, such as the Olympus AF Zoom, usually offer a continuous focal-length choice of from around 40mm to around 80mm – useful for most subjects. Most have reliable exposure systems but little scope for manual override.

ing accurately without actually being able to see through the lens. Most middle-range compacts have autofocus and a moderately wide-angle lens, or two lenses (typically moderate wide-angle and normal).

Zoom facility

The most technologically sophisticated type of 35mm non-reflex is the autofocus zoom compact. Autofocus having already made the lack of reflex viewing less important, it has since made zoom lenses practical. The zoom range is typically from moderate wide-angle (such as 35mm) to moderately long (such as 80mm). Although the lens cannot be removed, these cameras rival some 35mm reflexes.

None of the compacts except the Leica looks professional, and there are many situations in street photography when this is an advantage as they do not draw attention to themselves.

Canon's Sureshot Telemax is a twin-lens model which gives a choice of a 38mm wide-angle lens or a 70mm short telephoto. However, as with other twin-lens compacts in the mid-price range, it is not possible to zoom between these two focal lengths. The camera also incorporates a flash system which can be turned off.

PROJECT: Candid photography

The 35mm non-reflex cameras come into their own in situations that allow little or no time to think or to adjust controls. The project for this camera is candid photography, similar to what is usually described as street photography but with an important difference. Even the Leica does not accept long telephotos, and most compacts have moderate wide-angle or normal lenses. This means being close to your subject more of the time, and this alone makes it important to practise shooting quickly and decisively. If you have an autofocus or fixed-focus compact, you do not have to think about focus, and this saves time.

The viewing system is clearly very different from that of an SLR, and generates a particular way of working. The viewfinder gives direct vision, which is clearer and brighter than the equivalent reflex view, and uninterrupted by the shutter. In some cameras, the viewfinder frame is slightly larger than the film frame, so that you can see things entering the frame a fraction of a second early. If your compact has a built-in flash, make use of that for some pictures, although the lighting quality will be limited.

The top-of-the-market, push-button Pentax Espio has a 35-70mm zoom lens, a wide range of flash functions and a multiple-exposure control, among other automated features. Its advanced shutter control includes a facility for programming shooting at intervals of three minutes or one hour. It is an attractive and versatile camera.

At the top of the range of compact cameras, and in a class by itself, is the Leica – the first 35mm camera ever built. It is unobtrusive, rugged and extremely well made, has interchangeable lenses and, in the later models, some automatic features. A power winder is available for some models. Almost alone of compacts nowadays, the Leica uses rangefinder focusing. This works on a principle similar to the way in which we judge distances with our eyes. A second view, from a smaller window to the right of the viewfinder, is projected onto the eyepiece by prisms and lenses. When the user has focused the rangefinder image, the system measures the angle between the two views and so determines the distance. The Leica is very much a professional piece of equipment – a consideration reflected in its high price.

35MM SLRs

Among serious photographers, the 35mm single-lens-reflex is by far the most widely used type of camera, and over the years has received an enormous amount of techno-logical innovation. Much of this has made life easier for photographers and has extended the opportunities for shooting. Sophisticated automatic metering, automatic fill-in flash and fast autofocusing are all a real help in guaranteeing accurate shots. They are particularly useful in situations that you might miss, or where you might react too slowly, if you tried shooting man-ually. At the same time, however, some of the clever technology of recent years has simply complicated the process of seeing and taking pictures.

Types of 35mm SLR

Manufacturers tend to use jargon, inventing different names for similar parts and func-tions, so there may appear to be more types of 35mm SLR than there really are. Essentially, there are two categories – auto-focus and manual focus – and three grades, determined by sophistication and price: basic, mid-range and professional. An example of each is shown *below*. Autofocus needs a fast and accurate method of measuring sharpness (or distance) and a motor for the lens that will respond quickly. Both of these elements have improved greatly in recent years, and autofocus is increasingly standard in 35mm SLRs.

Manual control

The simplest design of SLR camera is the kind with the minimum of automation, leav-ing the user to make the decisions about shutter speed, aperture and focus. In the past, this was the state of the art of 35mm photography, but has been overtaken by programmed models. A large number of professional photographers use manual SLRs because there is less to go wrong and because they are familiar enough with cam-era settings not to need much automation.

Mid-range cameras are usually pro-grammed and automatic. They are designed not to bother the photographer with deci-sions while shooting, but instead to offer a choice of options, usually in a window dis-play. These options, or "modes", are for dealing with different situations. So, for example, in a shutter priority mode, the shutter speed remains fixed at one setting chosen by the photographer, while the aperture is altered automatically to suit the exposure. This mode would be useful for shooting action, for example. On the other hand, to keep the greatest possible depth of field, an aperture priority mode would keep the aperture fixed and vary the shutter speed. This automation makes programmed cameras battery-hungry.

The Pentax K1000 offers basic SLR features usable by any photographer. Minolta's mid-range X-700 is a proven tool for the keen amateur who is comfortable with manual focus. The Nikon F3 has aperture-priority and manual exposure modes and a wide range of shutter speeds.

Pentax K1000

Minolta X-700

Nikon F3

Professional SLRs

Professional photographers stand slightly apart in the camera market, and there exists a category of 35mm SLR aimed at them. Professional cameras are distinguished by a few obvious features: the automation is not cosmetic, and there are manual overrides to the automation and some simple back-up systems, usually mechanical. Construction is stronger and the cameras more rugged. They are highly adaptable, and accept a wide range of accessories, with means of interchanging screens, sometimes viewing heads, and so on. They are also expensive. Professional/amateur distinctions are, however, blurred by two things. First, a manufacturer's professional model is also the top of the range, and this status makes it attractive to serious amateurs. Second, many professionals have turned to smaller advanced-amateur models, sometimes to the surprise of the manufacturer.

The basic camera functions – what is actually necessary to expose a frame of film – are limited and do not change, whatever the model. They are simply these: shutter operation, aperture setting, exposure measurement, film transport and focus. The first three of these, grouped together, make up a kind of overall function: exposure control. All of these can be automated, but equally, there is nothing particularly difficult about operating them manually. In many ways, you will get the best out of this book and its projects if you rely least on automation and more on manual control.

Spot meter and flash/continuous-light incident meter

Strong neutral-density viewing filter gives near-monochrome view, to aid basic composition

Portable flash units with extension leads to allow off-camera dedicated use

Polaroid 35mm instant film and processor, for checking camera settings and composition before final shooting

Over-size plastic filters: graduated and other

Fishing-tackle accessory box with sync leads, spare batteries and rubber base pad for tripod head

Cable release

Basic repair kit (jeweller's screwdrivers, pliers, tweezers)

The professional photographer will take a full location kit above on a 35mm shoot. Many amateurs, too, prefer to be equipped so as not to miss any chance of a shot.

The Canon EOS 1000N has many features of interest to the beginner, including an innovative soft-focus mode. Built-in flash adds to the versatility of Minolta's well-designed Dynax 3xi. Four metering modes, plus stop-down metering, and six exposure modes are offered by Canon's sophisticated EOS-1.

Canon EOS 1000N

Minolta Dynax 3xi

Canon EOS-1

Shutter

The focus plane shutters in 35mm SLRs travel across the rectangular film gate either horizontally (the more traditional method) or vertically. In some models, flexible drum-mounted curtains are used, in others a set of blades. Modern improvements include high-strength light-weight metals such as titanium, textured ribbing to the curtains or blades, electromagnets for instantaneous release, high-voltage drives and more efficient shutter brakes. All these improvements are aimed at faster operation, which allows not only higher top speed ($\frac{1}{4000}$ second is not uncommon) but also flash synchroniza-

tion at higher speed settings ($\frac{1}{60}$ second used to be the normal limit, but faster speeds are now common). When selected manually, shutter speeds are stepped in one-stop increments, but models with electronic automatic exposure can set the speed variably in aperture-priority mode.

The normal means of releasing the shutter is the button-like release on the camera's top plate, but electronic operation in many models makes remote triggering straightforward. Traditionally, the wind lever on the top plate tensions the shutter, but many of the latest electronic cameras dispense with this arrangement.

Aperture

The aperture diaphragm is sandwiched between the groups of elements in the lens, but its controls in a fully-automated camera are likely to be in the camera body as well as in a ring surrounding the lens barrel. The metal-blade design of the diaphragm is consistent and traditional; when the aperture is selected manually, the settings are usually marked in full *f*-stops on the ring, with clicks at $\frac{1}{2}$-stop intervals. Linkages in the form of pins and levers pass information mechanically between the aperture diaphragm in the lens and the camera controls. Normal viewing is at full aperture, so

In the center-weighted average metering system below, the entire picture area is read and the light values averaged – with the center of the frame given extra emphasis. The very top of the frame, normally occupied by the sky in outside views, is under-rated.

The strong center-weighted metering system below gives a strong weighting to the central 12-15 per cent of the picture area. This area is usually delineated in the viewfinder by a 0.5in (12mm) diameter circle engraved on the focusing screen.

In the spot-metering system below, all the meter's sensitivity is concentrated in about 3 per cent of the picture area. On the focusing screen is a small central circle defining this area.

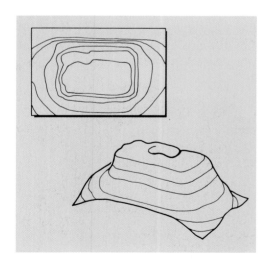

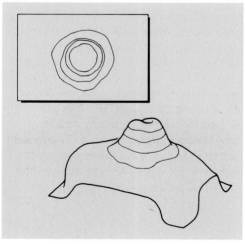

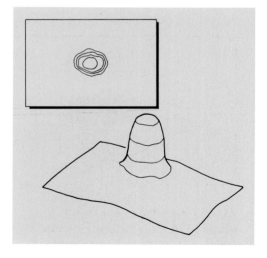

The center-weighted averaging metering system is the most commonly used in 35mm SLR cameras.

The strong center-weighted metering system gives a marked bias to the center of the picture area.

Spot metering is a system designed for use with small subjects placed centrally in the frame.

that one linkage is reserved for stopping down the diaphragm to the working aperture a moment before the shutter opens. Another linkage may be needed for the depth-of-field preview button. For metering purposes, a lever must indicate the aperture setting, while cameras that allow automatic control of the aperture (in shutter-priority mode) must have yet another linkage for changing the setting. Four linkages are normal on an automated camera.

Exposure measurement

Even a bare-bones manually operated SLR contains a through-the-lens (TTL) metering system. The internal differences between cameras are mainly in the location of the sensors and from which part of the light path inside the camera they take their information. More obvious from the user's point of view are the differences in the parts of the image that are being measured. There

are a number of possible sensor locations inside the camera body, but most are now usually below the reflex mirror or in the prism head. Sensors in the prism head can read the viewfinder display; a sensor element at the base of the camera can read either directly from the film surface or from a secondary mirror hanging behind the main mirror. Some models contain a combination of methods to allow for the different metering modes.

The most straightforward metering pattern gives greater value to the center of the picture, where most photographers place the center of interest. The exact pattern varies from overall with a center bias, to just the center alone. There is often a circle engraved on the focusing screen to show the limits of this central area. On a different level of sophistication are patterns that synthesize readings from several areas of the image. The result depends on a set of rules

drawn up by analyzing a large number of exposure situations, and stored in the camera's memory.

Exposure control

The last three functions, when interlinked, allow exposure to be set directly, without requiring decisions by the photographer. Overtly sophisticated, high-tech models make a show of allowing the photographer to select various modes; in essence, this means letting the user choose priorities. All of these exposure systems work well, but it is essential if you own one that you know what the methods are. No exposure system is appropriate for all situations. Indeed, it is

The cross-section of an autofocus SLR below shows the location of the metering cell and autofocus module. The viewfinder is surprisingly bright, although 40 per cent of the light entering the lens does not reach the screen.

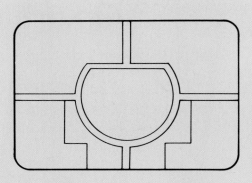

In the metering pattern above, referred to as synthesized metering, the camera reads each subdivision independently, compares the relative values and sets the exposure according to a programme.

In addition to the specialized metering screen illustrated left, for some cameras other viewfinder screens are available for compositional and focusing purposes. These include the popular screen with a split image within a microprism collar, both of which assist focusing. Other screens include the grid screen for architectural photography; the cross-hair screen for extremely precise focusing ; the calibrated micrometer for copying and close-up work; and the microprism spot screen, which scrambles any image which is out of focus.

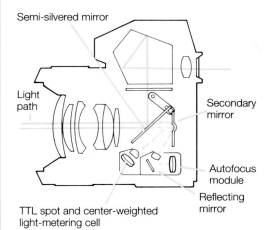

Semi-silvered mirror

Light path

Secondary mirror

Autofocus module

Reflecting mirror

TTL spot and center-weighted light-metering cell

often more important to know how to override an automatic system.

Film transport

Traditionally, the wind lever draws the film from its cassette across the film gate and from there onto the take-up spool. Many models, however, will accept a motor-drive or power winder, and a few have these motors built into the camera body. The drive moves the film as soon as an exposure is finished, so that the camera is ready for the next shot very quickly; there is no loss of concentration; and the camera can easily be triggered by remote control or according to a timer.

Focus

Sharp focus is one of the basics of photography. To make it easy to achieve, the operation of the focusing gears in the lens barrel is made as smooth as possible; light transmission through the reflex mirror, focusing screen and pentaprism is kept as high as possible; and various devices are incorporated into the focus screen.

Autofocus is now standard on many cameras, and becoming more so as manufacturers are able to make it more efficient, faster and take up less room in the camera. Operation is fast and accurate with most subjects, but sometimes autofocus responds poorly to low-contrast scenes. If the part of the picture that you want to have sharply in focus is off-center, you will usually have to aim at it, lock the focus, and then recompose the shot. One new automatic solution is to monitor the movements of the photographer's eye from inside the viewfinder, and in that way find (and focus on) the main point of interest.

PROJECT: Active subjects
The purpose of this project is both as a test for how familiar you have made yourself with the basic equipment, and as a demonstration that complete planning is just not possible in much of photography. As a back-up to the main sequence, I have included a series of wildlife shots because, given an accessible location, it may be relatively easy to predict some fast activity. In this case, the birds are fighting for nesting places, and although there is no possibility of getting really close and moving around yourself, this kind of situation is predictable.   Preparation is very important for this project; if your equipment is not ready to go, you will miss the shots. It involves nothing very complicated, simply having the camera loaded with the right film, batteries in working order, suitable lenses and spare film.

Look first at the sequences of frames. In the fire-fighting scene, 8 frames have been selected from 134 (nearly four rolls) for reasons of space; nevertheless, they are representative, and include two short bursts. The shooting took about 45 minutes, although the urgency had gone after about half an hour. By contrast, the sequence of birds

Some of the most exciting pictures that you can take with a 35mm camera are in unpredictable, short-lived circumstances, and the only way of being able to capture them is by being prepared and by being able to shoot quickly and confidently. Admittedly, we are plunging in at the deep end with the fire-fighting sequence shown here, but it seems better to use a real example of an active and urgent subject than to make do with something quieter.

squabbling was shot over about ten minutes from one fixed position with a long telephoto. In both cases a motor-drive was used, but was only necessary in a few short bursts of action during the fire. In neither case was the motor-drive set to "continuous"; quickly repeating pressure on the button was enough.

Key points

- The shutter speed is important and, generally, the faster the better. A suitable film speed is essential, allowing for the maximum aperture of your lenses, and it is sensible to have a choice – for instance, ISO 64 and 200, or ISO 100 and 400.

- Uncomplicated equipment is best, to avoid getting lost in a confusion of lens changing. The birds needed a long lens only; the fire was shot on just three lenses: 24mm, 35mm and 105mm, and all but a few frames on the first of these.

- Action usually looks best if it fills the frame, so either be close yourself or use a lens that is long enough.

- The main ability in this type of photography is fast reaction, based on familiarity with your equipment. Ideally, you should be able to shoot intuitively, without having to think about the settings. Also important is anticipation. If you can sense what is going to happen, you can get into a better position and perhaps change lenses.

OTHER FORMATS

Medium-format SLR

Film format determines camera design, and the size above 35mm, rollfilm, has produced a variety of medium-format cameras, some with quite different operating features. The film is large enough to permit several formats, from 6 x 4.5cm (2.3 x 1.8 inches) to 6 x 17cm (2.3 x 6.7 inches), and some camera models are designed for shooting on more than one format, accepting different sizes of film magazine. A common designation for this size of film is 120, although it also appears in two less well-used forms: 220 rollfilm and 70mm.

Reflex viewing

The most sophisticated designs of rollfilm cameras are the SLRs, which use reflex viewing systems that are more or less similar to those in 35mm cameras, though considerably more bulky. The *raison d'être* of these cameras is a relatively large format (nearly four times that of 35mm) that still allows rapid shooting of sequences, so that their appeal is very much towards professionals and serious amateurs. Rollfilm cameras are not particularly good for street photography, for example, but they are excellent for subjects that benefit from being reproduced in fine detail. Among the "classic" range of rollfilm subjects are portraits, landscapes, certain types of nature (flowers and approachable subjects rather than shy, fast-moving animals), most still-life subjects, and close-ups.

Rollfilm SLR designs vary much more than among 35mm cameras, and there is no standard model. Nor are there as many makes. Nevertheless, allowing for different picture formats, most models are modular and feature both interchangeable lenses and interchangeable film magazines. Penta-prisms are normally available for eye-level viewing, but as the style of use tends towards the planned and considered rather than quick-reaction shots, it is normal to use most rollfilm SLRs with a plain focusing screen, shaded only by a hood. The image is reversed left to right when seen like this. This can be disorienting if the subject moves or if the camera is panned, but in most situations it makes no difference to the composition.

Film backs

Interchangeable backs are a design feature that can be put to good use by shooting different films on the same subject. A dark slide at the front of the film magazine shields the film from light when removing it from the camera body, and backs can be changed in mid-roll. One common practice is to keep one magazine loaded with colour and a second with black-and-white (or reversal film in one and negative in another). Also, in situations where a 35mm user might carry a second body loaded with

The models below *represent the most common sizes of medium-format camera. The Hasselblad is 6 x 6cm (2.3 x 2.3 inches), the Mamiya 6 x 7cm (2.3 x 2.8 inches) and the Bronica 6 x 4.5cm (2.3 x 1.8 inches)*

Hasselblad

Mamiya

Bronica

high-speed film just for low-light shooting, a spare film magazine is less costly and relatively less bulky.

Format variations are mainly a matter of personal preference. The smallest size – 6 x 4.5mm (2.3 x 1.8 inches) – is the most economical, but there is correspondingly less of a size advantage over an equivalent 35mm SLR. The traditional format for this film is 6 x 6cm (2.3 x 2.3 inches) but the more usable picture proportions of 6 x 7cm (2.3 x 2.8 inches) are now more common. One feature of the film size is that it allows cropping without a great loss of picture quality. To some extent, the practice of cropping a shot after it has been taken rather than composing it precisely in the viewfinder has become common because the traditional square frame is not the easiest shape for designing within.

When a rollfilm SLR like the 6 x 6cm model right *is used with only the focusing screen, the image is reversed left to right* below. *A pentaprism attachment is needed to rectify the image.*

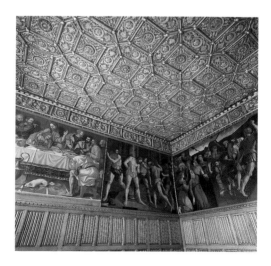

Standard lens for
6 x 6cm format is 80mm

Film winding knob

Image is reversed left-to-right on focusing screen

Film magazine

SLR eye-level

The Pentax 6 x 7cm (2.3 x 2.8 inches) camera is designed on a different principle, and are, as far as the format allows, scaled-up versions of the standard 35mm SLR design, with eye-level viewing through a roof prism, and virtually all the controls in similar positions to those on an SLR. Necessarily, it lacks the modular construction and interchangeable backs of other medium-format SLR models, but in place of these features it is much more convenient for hand-held shooting.

The design of this eye-level camera invites comparison with smaller 35mm SLRs. Apart from bulk, the method of holding is not the same, and the left hand has to be used much more as a support for the base and lens. The depth of field, even with the wide-angle lenses, is by no means as great; a natural consequence of the larger format that requires longer focal lengths to give equivalent angles of view. As with all rollfilm cameras, the range of holdable lenses is curtailed at the upper, telephoto, end. Focal lengths that give substantial compression of perspective and strong magnification, such as 800mm, are too heavy to hold and must be tripod-mounted.

Medium-format non-reflex

Enjoying a revival in spite of their lack of sophistication, medium-format viewfinder and rangefinder cameras offer easy portability without any frills. The very basic nature of their design may contribute to their appeal. There are several makes, and even more formats than among SLRs (without the need for reflex viewing, it is relatively simple to make the picture area larger on the film). The smallest format is 6 x 4.5cm (2.3 x 1.8 inches); 6 x 17cm (2.3 x 6.7 inches) – which by the extreme length of the image counts as a special film for panoramic cameras – is the largest.

The principal advantage of these cameras is that they weigh little more than a 35mm SLR – less if you take the lightest or include a motor-drive on the 35mm camera – yet give the image qualities of a large negative or transparency. In particular, they are good for any kind of technically uncomplicated shot, such as landscape or even candid photography of people. Street photography is possible with a rollfilm viewfinder camera, and offers the unusual interest of an unexpectedly large image; if the model you use has a wide-angle lens (most do), this will give you the opportunity to crop the image when printing.

There are natural limitations, and these do restrict the uses to which you can put this design of camera. The lack of reflex viewing, which allows a leaf shutter inside the lens to be used rather than a bulky focal plane shutter with a mirror, makes it impossible to check the depth of field accurately. Where depth is important, in still-life photography and other types that involve close shooting distances, the only solution is to follow the depth of field scale on the lens very closely – neither convenient nor completely safe. Remember that, compared with 35mm cameras, the focal lengths of equivalent lenses are longer, and this is one of the factors that make the depth of field shallower. This, and the greater opportunities for making focusing mistakes with a larger-format camera, is one of the reasons why wide-angle lenses are commonly fitted. Most models have fixed lenses, and several are sold as "wide-angle cameras".

Parallax error

Parallax error is another potential problem, and because these cameras are larger than 35mm models, the distance between the lens and the viewfinder also tends to be greater. With a camera that does not incorporate parallax correction in the viewfinder, there is a way you can compensate for it if you are using a tripod. The method is first to compose the shot as you want it through the viewfinder, and then to raise the central column of the tripod by exactly the distance between lens and viewfinder – a few inches or centimeters only. Naturally this is a little cumbersome, and if the viewfinder is off-center you will also need to make allowance at the sides.

View camera

Despite its reputation as professional equipment, the view camera is the most simply

The Mamiya RZ67 is a versatile 6 x 7cm camera which has as standard a 110mm f2.8 lens and offers manual and aperture-priority exposure modes. It takes 6 x 4.5cm and 6 x 6cm film backs.

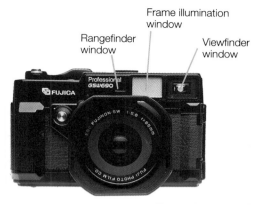

Rangefinder window

Frame illumination window

Viewfinder window

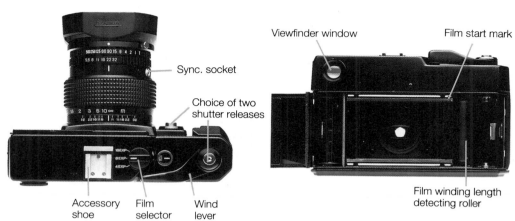

Sync. socket

Choice of two shutter releases

Accessory shoe

Film selector

Wind lever

Viewfinder window

Film start mark

Film winding length detecting roller

The 65mm lens on the 6 x 9cm camera above gives a field of view across the diagonal of the frame of 76°, the equivalent of a 28mm lens on a 35mm camera.

Rollfilm viewfinder cameras like the 6 x 9cm model shown below are designed to be carried very simply, and can be used with no or very few accessories.

Field tripod in carrying case

Cable release

Exposed film wrapped with desiccant

Selenium-cell light meter

Hip pack

Exposure data record

Spirit level

designed of any camera. In essence it is a flexible light-tight box, consisting of a rigid panel at the back to hold a sheet of film, another rigid panel at the front that carries the lens, with both panels connected by concertina-like bellows that extend and compress for focusing. Because view cameras do not, as a rule, contain features of convenience, such as reflex viewing, instant return mirrors or even means of transporting film, they have remained this simple. You can learn more about the principles of photography by practising with a simple view camera than you can by using any other piece of equipment.

Large-format cameras like the Wista Field below left and the monorail model below right – the latter is designed for studio use only – take sheet film.

There are two basic types of construction. The traditional one, and still used, particularly in outdoor photography, is the flatbed, so-called because the mechanical support for the camera is a flat base. Wood construction with metal fittings is common; this is lightweight, and therefore useful for carrying, and the tolerances are not so close as to make metal absolutely necessary.

Monorail

The second type of construction is the monorail, very much a studio camera. Instead of a flat base, the support is a well-machined rail, circular, rectangular or even triangular in cross-section. The parts of the camera – front and rear standards, lens shade, and even supports for close-up subjects held in front – attach to this rail and slide along it.

There are several different sizes of view camera. The original nineteenth-century models varied considerably, but the common film formats now are 4 x 5 inches (102mm x 127mm) and 8 x 10 inches (203mm x 254mm).

Lenses for view cameras

Most view cameras do not come with a lens, and large-format lenses are produced by independent manufacturers. Users of 35mm cameras become accustomed to classifying lenses by their focal length, but usually this means the perspective effect (so, 28mm denotes wide-angle with its stretched perspectives; 300mm denotes a lens that compresses the planes of the subject and magnifies the image). With a view camera, however, the different formats available, sometimes on the same camera by means of

a change of film back, means that one lens can have different pictorial effects. The rule of thumb whereby the diagonal of the film frame is the same as the focal length of a standard lens still applies, so that for the 4 x 5 inch camera a 150mm lens would be considered standard. For an 8 x 10 inch camera a 300mm lens is the equivalent.

Another consideration that does not occur with fixed-body cameras is camera movements. This extremely useful facility embraces the variety of shifts, tilts and swings of the lens panel and film back that make it possible to correct converging verticals, change the shape of the image and alter the distribution of sharpness.

The series of photographs right *shows the camera movements involved in correcting converging verticals in the depiction of the house shown on this page. In step 1, with zero movement, aim the camera up to include the whole building. In this shot the verticals will converge towards the top, as in the upper shot.*

Vertical lines converge upwards

Less illumination because close to edge of image circle

Top of image "stretched"

Vertical lines appear vertical

In step 2, level the camera; the verticals will appear vertical but the top of the building will be out of frame.

In step 3, shift the lens panel upwards until the entire building appears once more in view. This time the verticals will be corrected, as in the lower shot right. Both images were made with a 90mm wide-angle lens on a 4 x 5 inch view camera.

ACCESSORIES

What items count as accessories depends very much on your point of view. Here, we include everything beyond the basic configuration of camera body, motor-drive and lenses, with the exception of a few categories that are treated separately. These are: camera supports (pages 26-8), close-up equipment (pages 164-7), filters (pages 170-5) and on-camera flash (pages 230-33).

Essential accessories

The most basic accessories, such as cable releases, sync. leads or cords, tape and spirit level are essential; others are decorative or destined hardly ever to be needed. Accessory lists undoubtedly induce gadget mania, but where you draw the line between the useful and the trivial is entirely up to you. The best that can be done here is to lay out a reasonably comprehensive array, tempered by my own opinions of what may conceivably be useful. Your choice should depend on the kind of photography that you really expect to be doing and, under most circumstances, the

The small set of equipment below is what one photographer considers essential additions. Its weight – an important factor – is almost exactly 1 lb (0.5 kg).

Stop-watch for time exposures

Spirit level fits into camera's accessory shoe

Flexible-necked flashlight

Cable release with locking collar

Small C-clamps

Thread adaptors for tripod head

Adjustable-angle accessory shoe

Adhesive putty in spare film can

Sync. lead connectors (can be unscrewed)

Sync. leads

2-way and 3-way sync. adaptors

Remote triggering lead

Tape

Threaded clamp

Ball-and-socket accessory shoe

Rubber protector pad for camera base when on tripod

less equipment you take, the better. I think that the one reasonable exception that justifies carrying everything you can think of is when a location shot has to be set up and planned, so that it is important to be prepared for any eventuality.

Prism-etched disc fits over lens to convert camera's TTL meter for incident readings

Reflex-viewing spot-meter with 1° angle of acceptance with a measuring range of EV1 to EV22 at ISO 100. Memory allows recall of highlight, shadow and average data

Meter booster for more sensitive readings directly off the film plane or viewing screen

The value of the light meter – those shown above are all hand-held – is that they allow different types of light measurement to supplement the reflected-light readings from the camera's built-in metering system.

Miniature receptor for use on meter in close-up work

Multiple-function meter allowing both reflected-light and indicator readings, for continuous light and flash. Acceptance angle for reflected-light readings, without plastic dome, is 40°.

Selenium-cell meter capable of reflected-light readings with an acceptance angle of about 40°, and of incident readings with indented plastic dome fitted

CAMERA SUPPORTS

However proficient you become at hand-held shooting, a solid, locked camera support is still the most secure method. It is essential for certain conditions: low light levels and small-aperture shooting that call for shutter speeds below the safest hand-held speed, with large format cameras and with macro set-ups that require exact positioning it is an advantage when you want precision in the composition or in the placement of subjects. For instance, a loosely locked tripod head in portrait photography makes it possible to shoot without having to spend the whole time looking through the viewfinder. This will let you talk to the subject, often necessary to help create the right atmosphere.

The normal support is the tripod, which can be used in most situations. There is a surprisingly big difference in stability between a tripod used well and one set up inefficiently.

Using a tripod

A few principles concerning the use of a tripod are worth bearing in mind.
- Low is more stable than high.
- Make sure that the floor or ground surface itself is stable. Sand shifts, as do loose floorboards.
- Adjust the legs so that the platform (the immediate base for the tripod head) is level. Do not rely on levelling by means of the tripod head only.
- If you can, place the center of the erected tripod under the center of gravity of the camera and lens. If this is not possible, place one leg so that its line is under the center of gravity (normally forward).
- Shelter the tripod from wind.

You can test the stability of your support by gently tapping the end of the lens. Look for visible movement of the equipment, and repeat this when looking through the viewfinder. It is possible to add stability by lowering the center of gravity and increas-

To make the best use of a tripod, follow the sequence on these pages. Remember that the thickest sections of the legs are the strongest, and that the adjustable center column, if there is one, reduces the stability considerably. It raises the camera above the stable point where the legs meet, so only use it after you have reached the maximum height with the legs alone.

First extend the leg that will point downhill on a slope. If you want full height, extend this leg fully. Holding the tripod approximately straight, extend the two other legs in turn. With each, extend the thickest section fully before the next. Tighten each collar fully.

Make fine adjustments to the thinnest section of the legs only to level the tripod platform (not at this stage the head). Use a spirit level if possible (some tripods incorporate one), or judge the level by eye.

ing the base area. The two easiest methods of lowering the center of gravity are to lower the height (by shortening the legs or by spreading them at a greater angle) and to suspend a weight from the center of the tripod (a camera bag works well, but beware of it swinging).

Maintenance

Maintain the tripod in good condition. Prime weaknesses to watch for are loosening of the joints at the top of the legs (this increases the risk of torque, or twisting) and corrosion and dirt inside the leg telescope adjustment. Regularly tighten the joint nut or screws, and occasionally take apart and clean the leg sections. For loosening a stiff joint, use WD-40 or a similar anti-corrosive penetrating spray lubricant.

Long-focal-length lenses are both long and heavy, and therefore need skilful tripod management. Professional photographers take this requirement seriously, particularly at major newsworthy events, which leaves no room for mistakes. In the picture above a platform on top of a heavy-duty tripod allows the photographer to align three telephoto lenses for shooting at different focal lengths and at different film speeds.

If you need still more height, raise the center column and lock it. An angled center column is particularly unstable, making it critical to have a levelled platform.

Finally, fit the camera and adjust its position on the tripod head. Now you have a fully extended tripod in its most stable configuration. The exception to this set-up is when you are using a long, heavy lens that places the center of gravity out from the center of the tripod. In this case, place one leg so that it points along the lens axis.

When shooting in awkward camera positions, it is often better not to place all three tripod feet on the floor. By shortening one leg you may be able to put it on a raised surface such as a shelf, step or window-ledge. For this kind of shot it helps if the legs can be splayed at angles wider than normal. Some makes of tripods have adjustable stops for this purpose; others, like the one shown right, have a fully adjustable leg-locking bar. If you have another person to help you, first loosen all the movements on the tripod for maximum free play, hold the camera firmly in the position you want, and then place and lock the legs.

To hold a heavy camera in a potentially unstable position like that shown in the photograph below, a fully adjustable tripod is essential. The model illustrated features leg angles that are adjustable by means of leg-locking bars. Stability can be increased by adding clamps to the legs.

Collars lock at any position by tightening screw

Extra clamped leg increases support area of base

Leg-locking bars

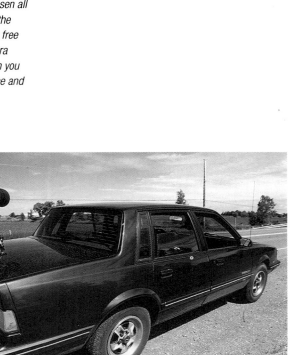

Raised surfaces have the big advantage of needing only a short tripod extension. With a heavy lens like the 600mm telephoto shown left, this short tripod can be conveniently left attached and folded back when not in use by loosening the tripod head. Used like this, the camera and lens are carried on the back seat of the car and can be set up for shooting very quickly – in less than half a minute.

CASES AND CARRYING

If you practise hand-held photography regularly you will work out, over time, your ideal set of equipment and ways of carrying it. Most photographers have idiosyncrasies in this area, but not only are the contents of camera bags rarely similar; bags are chosen to meet individual requirements and so also vary widely. On this and the following page are shown two bags filled with different selections of equipment. While the choice of items is not necessarily typical of a working photographer, it is not unusual either. The bag shown on this page, made to the photographer's specifications, is designed to carry two 35mm SLR cameras and about half a dozen lenses, including a long telephoto. In use, one of the cameras is normally carried outside the bag. Everything shown here weighs 20 lbs (9 kg) in total.

Notebook and pen. The main reason why professional photographers keep notes is not to record camera and lens settings but for caption information.

Street map

105mm f1.8 fast short telephoto: a portrait and low-light lens

Hand-held light meter, used principally for its incident-light-reading capability. A valuable exposure check in difficult metering situations

Neutral graduated filter, mainly for use with the wide-angle lens to darken skies

Cokin 52mm filter holder

Swiss Army knife has enough tools and attachments for some emergency repairs

Spare meter batteries for cameras

Principal camera, with motor-drive and medium telephoto (180mm f2.8), loaded with regular daylight film

Mesh cloth has several uses, including padding the interior of the bag, as a cushion for resting camera on available supports, and for general cleaning and wiping

Small, robust flashlight

Marker for numbering film cassettes

Film pocket with six cassettes of professional Kodachrome 64, one of medium-high-speed ISO 200 film, one of high-speed P800/1600

Two essential filters: a magenta correction filter for average fluorescent lighting, and an 80B blue correction filter for tungsten light. Both for use with daylight film

Second camera, fitted with 35mm f1.4 lens and loaded with high-speed film

55mm f3.5 macro lens does double duty as standard focal length and close-up lens

400mm f5.6 telephoto, the longest lens here, fits easily into a separate lengthwise zippered pocket. When not in constant use, it is wrapped in cloth bag

24mm f2 wide-angle lens in zipped leather pouch. An alternative to divided compartments in a camera bag is to protect each lens individually. Although sometimes a little slower for access, this allows lenses to be dropped into the bag without being careful that they are in a certain place

The bag shown below holds the minimum useful selection of equipment, arranged so as to be easy to carry and take out for use. There is only one camera and two lenses, one of which is a zoom to take the place of three regular focal lengths. Used by a woman photographer, the bag is actually a handbag. It was chosen in preference to a custom-made camera bag precisely because it does not advertise the fact that the carrier is a photographer. This both minimizes the risk of theft and proves very effective in street photography, where there is an over-riding need to be discreet if it is not possible to remain completely unseen.

Provided that you can find a high enough surface, a soft camera bag like the one shown right allows very slow shutter speeds to be used, and is particularly useful with telephoto lenses, which are difficult to hold steady.

Rest the weight of the lens here

An internally-focusing lens is best; changes in focus do not push the lens barrel forward

Push the front of the lens beyond the bag so that no straps or folds obscure the view

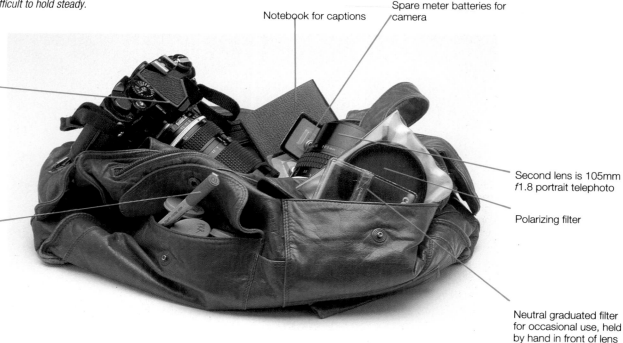

Notebook for captions

Spare meter batteries for camera

Small, basic SLR fitted with 35-70mm zoom and autowinder

Second lens is 105mm *f*1.8 portrait telephoto

Polarizing filter

Marker pen doubles for notes and numbering film cassettes. Cans are unboxed to save space and time, and marked to identify film type. Pocket contains three cassettes of professional Kodachrome 64, enough for limited shooting

Neutral graduated filter for occasional use, held by hand in front of lens

Like the 35mm SLR, the rollfilm camera, particularly the square-format Hasselblad below, *forms part of a modular system in which there is a wide choice of lenses, filters, focusing screens and other accessories. In addition to being used extensively in studio photography, medium-format cameras are very useful for outdoor assignments, and are especially favoured for landscape work, which calls for a sturdy carrying case.*

250mm telephoto lens with bellows lens shade

Spot meter

Magnifying hood for focusing screen

21mm extension tube

Close-up and light-balancing filters

Camera, film back, standard 80mm lens

Quick-coupling plate on large ball-and-socket tripod head

120-size rolls of film wrapped in plastic with silica gel

Spare focusing screen

Frame viewfinder for quick shooting

Aluminium case

Superwide 38mm fixed-lens camera with ground-glass screen and viewing hood attached to film gate

Wratten gelatin filters (fit in bellows lens shade)

Masks for using bellows lens shade with different lenses

Spare magazine slides

The medium-format (6cm x 6cm/ 2.3 inches x 2.3 inches) equipment shown above *is selected for landscape photography with a tripod rather than for hand-held use. The equipment includes a choice of three lenses – standard (80mm), wide-angle (38mm) and telephoto (250mm). The aluminium, gasket-sealed case is rugged and designed for backpacking, but access to the equipment is slow. Note also that the rollfilm is poorly protected from humidity and light in comparison with 35mm film cartridges, particularly after exposure. Here the rolls are wrapped in a plastic bag with a sachet of desiccant. The tripod has a head of the ball-and-socket type, with a quick-coupling plate. Also included is a selection of filters.*

FOCUS

Focus is inextricably linked to sharpness. Practically everybody has such a well-developed intuitive sense of what is sharp in an image that you may imagine there is little to say about it. However, recognizing sharpness in a picture is one thing, but achieving it in all conditions requires a command of certain techniques, and some of these need plenty of practice. Probably the worst technical error you can make in photography is an unfocused image; the margins of error that we are prepared to accept as viewers are remarkably narrow, and much less than, for instance, those acceptable in satisfactory exposure. You cannot salvage a picture that is out of focus.

Sharpness

Sharpness is not an objective quality. Instead, it is a personal assessment made intuitively on the basis of several factors. The two principal ones are resolution and contrast; both can be measured objectively, but each can be independent of the other. It would be easier to manufacture a higher resolution lens with less contrast.

Resolution is the ability of a lens to distinguish detail. A basic method of assessing this is in terms of the number of distinct parallel lines in one millimeter that can be recorded; the more sophisticated modern method is modulation transfer function (MTF), which is a measure of the change in spatial frequency (the number of light waves per millimeter) when light passes through a lens. Contrast is the difference in brightness between adjacent areas of tone; the bigger the difference, the greater the

Although follow-focus (turning the focusing ring to keep the image of the subject constantly sharp) is often touted as the basic method of dealing with an approaching subject, in fact it is difficult and rarely suitable. However, the situation right is suitable, because the movement is predictable and repeated (different cyclists following the same path), the distance travelled by the cyclist is very short, and the camera is on a tripod. Key techniques here are to have a known starting point for the focus (the base of the tree on the left), and to practise on the first few cyclists.

contrast. High resolution and high contrast together create the sensation of sharpness.

In the vast majority of situations facing the camera, there is absolutely no doubt what to focus on, just as most photographs have distinct subjects. To a large extent this is the nature of the way people take photographs, first choosing an object and then making it the center of interest. Nevertheless, one condition that makes for some difficulty is when the subject is changing position. If the depth of field is limited, as it is with a telephoto lens used wide open, the margin for error is very restricted. Moving subjects need experience and technique, but any practice that you put into accurate focusing with them will enhance the speed at which you can focus on easier, static subjects.

PROJECT: Focus on movement

Choose a situation and location which present you with a moving target that is approaching (either directly or diagonally). The easiest, though probably not the most interesting, might be close to a road with constant traffic. Something a little more worthwhile should not be too difficult to find, however. Make sure that there is a succession of moving targets, so that you can take plenty of repeat shots and improve your timing.

In the photograph right, which was shot with a 600mm telephoto at maximum aperture, the out-of-focus foliage makes a casual frame, conveying the appropriate impression of a shy creature glimpsed fleetingly through a chance gap. The effect, of course, would not be the same if everything were sharp.

The first step in this project is simply to make one completely accurate exposure. If the subject is moving fast, you may be surprised at how difficult this is. A basic method is to focus in advance and shoot as the subject moves through the focus point. You may find at the first few attempts that you have a tendency to let the subject move into and then a fraction beyond best focus. This is why practice is essential, to get a feel for the timing. After this, work on making more than one sharply focused shot in an approach sequence. The measure of your success is the number of good shots that you make in a set distance.

PROJECT: Selective focus

This is a fairly loose exercise, to practice whenever you are working with a telephoto lens at a wide aperture. In situations like that involving the zebras, there is no alternative to having some parts of the picture frame significantly out of focus. The exercise is experimenting with where to place these unfocused elements, noting the different effects they have on the design of the picture. They can, for instance, act as a kind of frame, or as a colour or tonal wash; they can help to make the main subject stand out, and they can enhance the sense of depth.

The same lens and aperture setting as for the picture above was used for the photograph right. The framing here was chosen as an alternative to including an uninteresting horizon, and the wash of colour created by the strongly unfocused foreground helps the unity of the shot by limiting the setting to a single hue.

SHUTTER

The shutter has two functions, which often conflict. One is to regulate the amount of light – a duty it shares with the aperture. The other is to freeze the image sharply. These functions become opposed when the image is moving and the light level is relatively poor. Even though the aperture usually allows some adjustment and a faster film can be substituted, there are occasions when the only practical way of giving enough exposure is to slow down the shutter speed, and this may result in a speed too slow to freeze the movement.

Freezing

Put at its simplest, the first basic skill in using the shutter is being able to judge the slowest shutter speed that will do the job. In most situations this depends on how active the subject is, but at the slower shutter speeds camera shake sets the limit.

Several variables are involved in selecting shutter speed:
- how fast the subject is moving
- its angle of movement to the camera: head-on, side-on, or diagonal
- the distance from the camera
- the focal length of the lens.

In addition, the following factors set limits to the speed that is actually possible.
- the need for good depth of field, and so for a small aperture
- the acceptability of graininess from a high-speed film
- the amount of acceptable blur
- the amount and direction of light

This seems to have the makings of a complicated sum, but it can be simplified at a stroke. What is ultimately important is how much the image moves inside the frame. The only practical measure of this is experience, because the circumstances hardly ever arise where you would have time to make calculations. In effect, you must practise assessing movement in the viewfinder.

Distance and direction

The distance between the camera and the subject and the angle of motion are the major factors in determining the least shutter speed needed to freeze movement. Provided that you do not change to another lens, the apparent movement of a distant object will clearly be less than that of something nearer, just because the image will be smaller in the picture frame. Equally, the greatest apparent movement is perpendicular to the view – that is, across the picture. The least apparent movement is when the subject is approaching the camera directly; then, the only important movement is in the parts of the subject, such as the arms and legs of a runner.

Panning

When there is continuous movement and it happens across the field of view (it most often does; head-on views are a special case), the usual technique is to follow it with the camera. The name for this is panning, and there is normally nothing complicated in keeping the target in frame. However, the conditions of the picture may change and the extra complications in panning are the control adjustments that you may need to make simultaneously.

Panning is usually associated with telephoto lenses (there are very few occasions when you will be close to something moving past you without the distance between you and the subject changing very much), and these lenses, because of their bulk and length, are more difficult to operate than lenses of short focal length. Hence, if you are anticipating a panning sequence rather than reacting to a sudden opportunity, it is an advantage to use a tripod. This technique frees at least one hand to operate focus or exposure controls.

A word about the tripod head. Ideally, there should be enough friction to support the camera and lens without putting any strain on your hands, with enough free play in the important direction to allow the target to be followed without drag. As most panning sequences involve horizontal movement, it usually helps to loosen the rotating axis fully, keeping the friction on the other movements. One danger in tripod panning is that if the tripod itself is not level, the vertical and horizontal lines in the picture will become increasingly askew as the camera is rotated. If you can prepare the set-up and know the route that the moving subject will follow, check the levelling first with a dry run. There will be too much to do when you are actually panning the subject to correct tilted verticals.

Another reason for checking out the path of the pan is that it may involve changes in focus and exposure, and also some obstructions. For focus shift under these circumstances, refer back to pages 32-3. Any changes in lighting along the target's route will require adjustments to be made to the exposure controls; preferably the aperture, as the shutter may need to be at a certain speed to cope with the movement. If you can leave this to the camera's automatic exposure system, all the better. However,

For the pair of photographs of the aircraft coming in to land above, the camera was mounted on a loosened tripod head, which was turned slowly to follow the right-to-left movement of the plane across the sky. In any

attempt to capture diagonal movement the focusing is the critical control, so that the exposure should be set beforehand, as was the case with these pictures. Alternatively, automatic exposure should be used.

this is not a good idea if there are any big differences between the subject and its background. In the case of the aircraft shown on this page, simple automatic exposure may result in an image that is too dark. The alternatives are either to use matrix metering or preset manual exposure.

A technique that can be introduced into a panning sequence is a slight intentional blur. Select a shutter speed just fast enough to render most of the subject sharp – in the example right $1/125$ of a second with a 400mm lens. The idea of panning is to keep the subject more or less in the same position, and as a result the blur chiefly affects the background, which is conveniently streaked in the direction of the movement.

The motion-blurred shots here were photographed at ¼ of a second top and ½ a second right at apertures of f22 and f32 respectively. Conveniently, they were shot later in the afternoon, when the bullring was in shadow and the light levels were too low for sharply frozen pictures with the f5.6 telephoto lens. The comparison picture center was shot at ¹/₁₂₅ of a second at f5.6.

Blurring

The sharply frozen image will always remain the reference standard in photography, but there is still room for experiment. Unsharpness due to motion blur has a very different appearance from that caused by lack of focus and is to many people more acceptable. It is not so much soft as streaked, and, if nothing else, it communicates movement graphically.

On occasion, the benefits of strengthening the impression of movement may overcome the drawbacks of blurring details. If and when you decide to use motion blur deliberately, consider just how important is the information content of the picture, because this is what you will reduce.

Abstract blur

While there are widely accepted guidelines for handling blur creatively, personal taste influences the matter so strongly that these are questionable. The very elimination of identifiable detail may make the image more intriguing, or it may reduce it to just a pattern of streaked tones and colours. There is nothing intrinsically wrong with going to this latter extreme, but if you do, you should realize that the abstract design must then be strong enough to carry the picture on its own, without the help of a recognizable subject.

PROJECT: Fireworks

A few subjects only sensibly reveal themselves on film by means of motion blur. One is a firework display. Even to the human eye, it is the rapid movement of points of light that conveys the impression of lines and patterns (just as the rapid sequence of still frames in a movie appears to be continuous action). A sharply frozen photograph would look like nothing more than bright points. Unless there is a considerable amount of drifting smoke, illuminated by the explosion, the shutter speed will have no significant effect on the brightness of the picture; it will simply determine the length of each streak.

Use speeds of between ½ a second and a few seconds and, of course, a tripod. A wide-angled view simplifies the problem of framing the display. With a telephoto, as used here, loosen the tripod head slightly, following the rocket trail upwards, and when it reaches its highest point, quickly lock the head and open the shutter.

PROJECT: Time and motion

Any subject that has distinct blocks of tone or colour, and an outline that is easy to recognize, can be degraded by blurring without losing its identity. As an example of this, I have taken a bullfight, which contains heavily stereotyped photographs of forms: black bull, toreador, red cloak. A sharp, high-information-content version is included for reference.

For your own project find an equivalent situation – equivalent, that is, in the recognizability of the images, and in the isolation of the subject. Some contrast with background is often an advantage in the ultimate clarity of the image, and a bland, featureless background is at least predictable in contrast to the subject.

With the bullfight, the motion-stopping shutter speed is $\frac{1}{250}$ of a second or $\frac{1}{500}$ of a second. To introduce blur, speeds of ¼ of a second and 1 second were used. One advantage of working at these speeds is that the aperture can be very small, and so the depth of field can be great enough to cover any likely changes in focus during the exposure. The principal drawback with an SLR is that the viewfinder is blind during the exposure, making it quite difficult to follow movement. In these examples, the exposures were made at moments when it was expected that the action would take place in one spot.

The results, of course, will prove unpredictable, but that is part of the entertainment of using motion blur. As with many techniques that display strong visual signatures, its interest soon palls with repeated use.

PROJECT: Free shooting

As part of any regular photography, such as in the street, try shooting a variety of moving subjects at long exposures. The cleanest streak trails will occur when the subject is light against a dark background, but try the opposite as an experiment. Also try both panning with a long exposure to create more sharpness in the main subject than in the setting, and keeping the camera steady so that movement is rendered blurred against a sharp background.

A typical firework burst, photographed with a 180mm lens at 1 second on ISO 64 film. For further details on the technical considerations involved in shooting firework displays, see Project: Fireworks above.

APERTURE

The lens aperture diaphragm shares with the shutter the control of the amount of light reaching the film. Also in common with the shutter, there is a second major function; in the case of the aperture this is control of the depth of field.

Shutter–aperture relationship

In order to make camera operation relatively easy, there is a reciprocal relationship between shutter speed and aperture. Just as shutter speeds are graduated in steps that double or half the time (and so the exposure), the main steps in the aperture control are separated by the same amount. Each stop down from the widest aperture halves the area of the circular opening. In practice, one stop down to a slower speed accompanied by one stop down to a smaller aperture makes no change to the exposure.

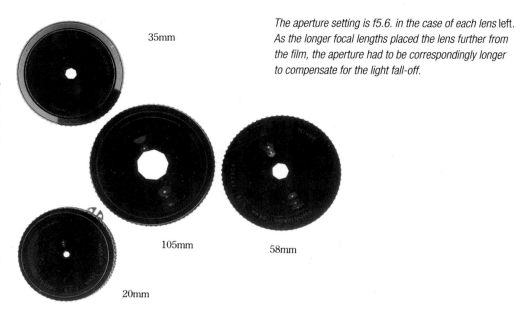

35mm

105mm

58mm

20mm

The aperture setting is f5.6. in the case of each lens left. As the longer focal lengths placed the lens further from the film, the aperture had to be correspondingly longer to compensate for the light fall-off.

In the aperture diaphragm a set of curved blades close and open in synchronization to give different sizes of an approximately circular aperture right. Each main step doubles or halves this opening, so doubling or halving the exposure. These steps are f-stops, and are calculated by dividing the lens's focal length by the effective aperture. (The effective aperture is slightly larger than the physical diameter of the diaphragm, because the front elements of most lenses converge, thereby reducing the size of the light beam that will actually fill the size of the aperture.) The standard numbering sequence of f-stops proceeds in steps that halve the illumination, and is as follows: f1, f1.4, f2, f2.8, f4, f5.6, f8, f11, f16, f22, f32 and so on. In this sequence the numbers are increased by the square root of two.

f8

f11

f16

f22

The two shots below *were taken within seconds of each other with the same 600mm lens and from the same position. In the upper picture, the f16 aperture details more than is wanted, but the f4 aperture used in the lower shot opens up the view by throwing the foreground so far out of focus that it behaves more like a mild diffusing lens than as an obstruction.*

Close-up photography is often characterized by images like the pair *below, in which there is a strong visual separation between a subject and its background. Here this helps to define the orchid against what would otherwise be distracting vegetation. Note how the depth of field at the same shallow aperture (f5.6 on a 200mm lens) is less when the camera is moved closer.*

BASIC EXPOSURE

Most photographers use an SLR with TTL metering, and you should become proficient in using the camera's light-reading system to determine exposure. Using the center-weighted metering system employed in most SLRs, the techniques available are:

- Direct reading, no compensation. This is ideal for average lighting conditions and when you want an average exposed result.
- Direct reading with compensation. With experience, this can work remarkably well. The principle is to take the reading, then judge how much darker or lighter than average you want the result. This technique is used in the examples shown on these pages.
- Aiming off, to exclude unwanted areas from the metering area.
- Substitute readings. Aim the camera at a different view which, in your judgement, is the same brightness as the part of the picture you want to measure. This is useful when the subject is too small for the camera's TTL metering area.
- High/low readings. Aim off to read the bright part of a scene and then the dark part. Average the two readings.
- Spot readings. Fit a telephoto lens and use the camera like a spot meter. Good for reading small areas.

Incident readings

Apart from these methods, which in most conditions are sufficient if not always ideal, incident readings can be taken. These measure the light itself, not how it is reflected from a subject.

We will concentrate, however, on what you can do with the basic center-weighted TTL reading in the camera. First, you should familiarize yourself with exactly what area in the frame your camera is measuring. The instruction booklet should tell you, but you may need to consult the manufacturer.

Remember that the TTL reading you get is the one that will reproduce the metered area as an *averaged* tone. Look at the area and decide if that is how you want it to appear. You will obviously not want white snow or a black fur coat to appear grey, and will need to compensate according to your judgement in a number of situations.

Contrast range

As a rule of thumb, the contrast range that negative film can record satisfactorily is about 7 stops, but for transparency film it is only about 5 stops. If the brightness range of the scene exceeds this, something has to go. With transparency film, try always to hold the highlights; washed-out bright areas usually look worse than underexposed shadow areas. If in doubt, use more film.

For simplicity, the basic metering situations have been subdivided into nine, and examples of each are discussed below.

PROJECT: Metering

Locate your own examples of each of these nine different metering situations, and use the recommendations here for calculating the exposure. Then, in order to have a basis for comparison and a means of assessing your accuracy, make exposures above and below the prime exposure. In other words, bracket each shot, ½ a stop over and ½ a stop under. It is essential that you keep a written record of your exposure measurements for this project.

To familiarize yourself with your camera's light meter, choose a scene which, seen through the viewfinder, is divided sharply between two contrasting tones. Move the camera around, taking readings, until you find the edges of the metering area. In the example below, also featured on the following pages, the central 12mm circle engraved on the focusing screen of a Nikon conveniently marks the area from which 80 per cent of the measurement is taken. Other averaging TTL systems may not be so precisely marked, but the purpose of this exercise is to understand the metering bias of your camera. Once you know this well, you can aim off to take readings from parts of the scene, or take substitute readings of a completely different view.

In a simplified form, most scenes in front of the camera fit one of the stylized conditions shown right. High-contrast conditions are the main source of exposure difficulties. Each of these situations is dealt with in detail on the following pages.

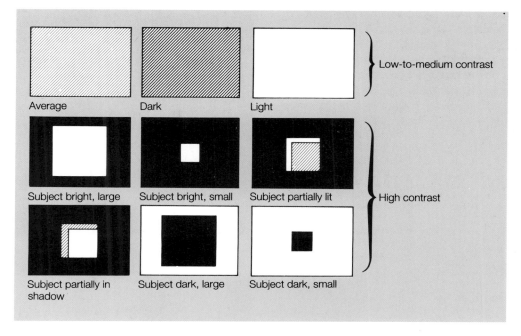

Average   Dark   Light   } Low-to-medium contrast

Subject bright, large   Subject bright, small   Subject partially lit   } High contrast

Subject partially in shadow   Subject dark, large   Subject dark, small

Low contrast, average subject

This is about as close as you can expect to come to an even tone in normal shooting conditions. The contrast is low to the point of drabness. There are no particularly bright or dark areas to worry about, and no reasons to want any other than an average reproduction. An average TTL reading is ideal. Incident and spot readings would be the same.

It is obvious that the central metering area is completely typical of the entire scene. Reproduced as an average exposure, it will look like this, and the only possible variation is whether to suggest a bright cloudy day (add ½ a stop) or an approaching storm (reduce ½ a stop). Typically, average scenes like this offer the least latitude in exposure

A random selection of spot readings shows consistency to within ⅓ of a stop. There is no reason for taking any measurement other than the camera's average TTL reading

High contrast, subject bright and dominant

The first step is to identify the subject – that is, from the point of view of exposure. Exclude the deeply shadowed frame and sky from the reading by aiming off so as to meter only the pale buildings. The indicated reading would give a fairly dense exposure. For a more average, if slightly less richly coloured version, compensate by increasing the exposure by ½ to 1 stop.

As a dense black shadow, this area of the picture plays no part in the exposure calculations, and does not need to be measured

The dark blue sky should not influence the exposure measurement

This brightest face of the building is the key tone. Any exposure calculation must hold this tone as a just-readable white. Too much exposure would give it a washed-out appearance

Although a straightforward TTL reading would be influenced to an excessive degree by the sky and shadow, aiming the camera

slightly off will give a usable reading of the essential parts of the scene. This will still need compensation to avoid underexposure

High contrast, subject bright and small

A reading of the darker part of the gold bank sign would be accurate, but only possible to make with a spot meter, a spot-reading alternative in the camera's TTL system (available on a few models), or by changing to a long telephoto. Failing all of these, make a substitute reading of some other surface that seems to be of average reflectance and is in the same sunlight, and then bracket.

15·ᴄG·63

The key tone naturally is within the small area of the subject. A spot-meter reading would be ideal; allowance would then be made to avoid underexposure

The area occupied by the subject is too small for the metering circle, even if the camera is aimed off in order to make the reading

The moderately bright sky just above the horizon is the only anomaly in this otherwise low-contrast scene

The key spot reading in this scene is coincident with the camera's metering circle

Low-to-medium contrast, dark subject

Apart from the skyline, the contrast in this scene is also below average, and the center-weighted area will give a typical reading. However, this is a pre-dawn scene, and there is good reason for wanting it to look dark, as a night view should. Hence, the indicated reading should be reduced by 1 or 2 stops. The same compensation would apply to, say, a black automobile or a close portrait of very dark skin.

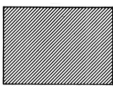

The camera's TTL reading is accurate for the entire scene, as long as the metering circle does not include the sky

Low contrast, bright subject

Again, contrast is low, but an average TTL reading, if followed, would make this headstone appear grey rather than white. Compensate by increasing the exposure by about 1½ to 2 stops. More exposure than this will cause the texture of the stone to disappear.

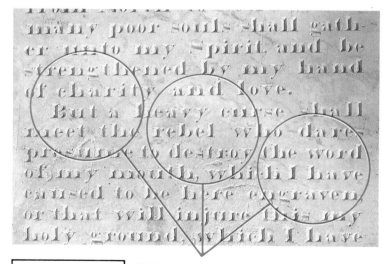

Within the area of this inscribed headstone, any reading will give the same result. The three circles represent different aiming points for the camera's TTL metering circle

The contrast range between these two extremes is 6 stops

High contrast, subject dark and dominant

This high-contrast scene actually allows considerable latitude for interpretation. Nevertheless, the objective ideal would be an exposure that leaves some tone in the foggy sky, and shows the barest hint of detail in the silhouetted bell. One method is to aim the camera so that the metering area takes in the light sky and dark bell in equal proportions. This is essentially a quick method of approximating a high/low reading. Again, where there is uncertainty about exposure, bracket.

Given that the metering circle covers both dark and light areas about equally, a straightforward TTL reading would, in this case, probably be accurate (but bracketing would be advisable). On the whole, an incident reading would be safer

The contrast range between subject and background is 8 stops

High contrast, subject dark and small

There is no point attempting any kind of reading of the boat, or of a substitute dark area. The most easily available reading is of the bright sunlit water. Take this reading and compensate by adding about 2 or 2½ stops. Less exposure will give more texture and colour to the water but may absorb some of the outline of the boat. More exposure will tend to introduce flare and a greyness to the boat's silhouette.

The easiest practical method here is to read the background and then open up the aperture by 2 to 2½ stops so that it is just held below the point of being washed out

High contrast, subject partially lit

Any direct TTL reading here, center-weighted or spot, has no value. Take a substitute reading of another sunlit area and bracket. In this example, many other photographs had been taken in full sunlight before, when the basic setting was familiar – $\frac{1}{250}$ of a second at f5.6 with ISO 64 film. As the highlights are more important for outlining the shapes of the figures than for showing their own detail, the exposure given was deliberately 1 stop over – $\frac{1}{125}$ of a second at f5.6.

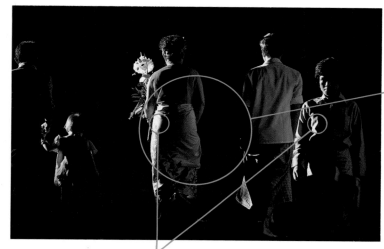

The metering circle in this case is useless

The key tones are these rim-lit highlights outlining the figures. Not only are they too small even for a spot-meter reading, however, but the movement leaves insufficient time. A substitute or incident reading would be the only reasonable alternative in this situation

The brightest part of the scene needs to be held. Too much exposure would wash it out

A snap judgement from the TTL reading would be to reduce the indicated exposure by about 1½ stops

Ideally, this large shadow area should be sufficiently well exposed to show some detail – about 1 or 1½ stops above the threshold of dense shadow

High contrast, subject partly in shadow

Here the bright areas have priority, but the shadow areas also need to be held. Spot readings of the brightest and darkest parts would be ideal, but if only the TTL measurement is available, you could take a direct center-weighted reading and reduce the indicated exposure by about 1½ stops, bracketing for safety.

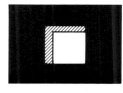

CHOOSING AND USING FILM

Within the last few years there have been some remarkable advances in film technology which have set the scene for a continuing programme of development. This has resulted in a greater choice of film types than ever before, quite apart from all the competitive brands, and the variety is increasing all the time.

Improved performance has been achieved through such methods as the use of flat grains of silver halide instead of the traditional compact shape of crystal. As long as these grains are aligned in the emulsion

The basic choice of film types is seen below: colour transparency (slide), colour print and black-and-white print film.

so that they face the incoming light, they respond more efficiently; for the size of grain, the silver halide is more sensitive to light. Another basic improvement in colour film is a new type of colour coupler, the chemical which forms a coloured dye. In this, the molecules are packed more tightly than usual, making it possible to have a thinner emulsion, which in turn reduces the amount of light scattering. The result is a sharper image.

Another outstanding development is "pushable" colour film. Photographers, particularly professionals, have always been accustomed to pushing the processing of films as one method of gaining more speed. Usually, though, this has been something of an emergency measure, used when a faster film was not at hand. The price was loss of image quality, the more so with colour film than with black-and-white. The new films, fast to begin with, are actually designed in

such a way that the photographer can choose the film speed setting, from ISO 400 up to ISO 3200. This flexibility widens enormously the scope of low-light photography.

Film choice

In colour photography, the first choice to make is between negative and transparency film. The required end product determines which of these you choose, but the decision may need a little thought. If one form of the final image is of overriding importance, the choice will be obvious: for example, professional photographers who sell photographs for publication use colour transparency film,

In the DX coding system the speed of a film is indicated by a rectangular metallized pattern on the film cartridge, which is read by a strip of contacts inside the camera's film chamber. Automatic cameras transfer this information direct to the metering system.

A typical clip test of transparency film above, push-processed by 1 stop. About 8 or 9 inches (20cm) from the beginning of the roll are pulled out of the cassette in darkness, cut off and processed specially. Note that the laboratory has first pulled out a couple of inches in daylight and marked the film for identification.

also known as slide film, because the separations for printing are made from these. If photographs are wanted for both slide shows and prints, prints can be made from transparencies, but then slides can also be made from the negatives produced by print film. If what is required is a top-quality print and the ability to fine-tune this, then colour negative film is the obvious choice.

Colour transparency film

Transparency film delivers its image in what is effectively a single stage, through a reversal process in which the initial negative image is discarded and the unexposed parts of the film are developed to colour. The film that is exposed in the camera carries the final picture. Although it can be printed by means of Cibachrome, Ektachrome and other positive-to-positive processes, a transparency looks its best and shows off its colours at their most brilliant and saturated when light is shone through it, and this usually means projected in a darkened room.

By producing an image directly, without the intervening period of grace to tune the colours and density in the darkroom, colour transparency photography makes tougher demands on colour accuracy. If a colour negative has a slight cast in the direction of one hue, it is no great problem to compensate for this in the printing. The same colour shift in a transparency, however, is there for ever. Shooting with transparency films teaches colour precision at the time the exposure is made, since mistakes cannot be corrected.

Colour negative film

Like colour transparency film and black-and-white negative film, colour negative film is undergoing a considerable technological overhaul. Much of this is due to the strong competition, with Kodak's dominance no longer certain. The majority of casual amateurs shoot colour negative film, and the market is enormous. But however much concern professionals and serious photographers have for black-and-white and colour transparencies, colour negative film is where the volume business is for the film manufacturers. As a result of this demand, there is an extensive choice of brands across a limited range of film types.

Printing

Improvements have tended to follow the needs of the snapshot market, but this has benefited all photographers. Two of the things that distinguish casual snapshot photography are that the prints are nearly always machine-processed by a high-volume laboratory, and there is a high incidence of under-exposure. Custom printing is for the enthusiast. Successful colour negative films need to be easy to print even if the way in which they were taken was not perfect. In particular, one of the demands is for richer colours, and the main technological improvements have been to give better colour saturation without increasing overall contrast. This is not so straightforward, as simply increasing the dye concentration in each emulsion layer makes the contrast higher as well. New types of colour couplers, which form the dyes, have been produced, and an orange mask has been produced to keep unwanted colours out of some of the layers to avoid degradation. This is in addition to the use of thinner and fewer layers, the purpose of which is to increase sharpness.

Kodachrome 64, a good general-purpose slow film, shows off its best characteristics in images like the one left, *with its fine detail and saturated hues.*

The slow speed of Kodachrome 25 – the slowest of any transparency film – restricts its use to bright lighting and situations where the camera can be supported. Nevertheless, it is unsurpassed for still-life, architectural photography and other subjects that need the finest detail in the image to be recorded. In the photograph left *of a group of unfinished Shaker oval boxes, a tripod was used for a $^1/_{15}$ of a second shutter speed.*

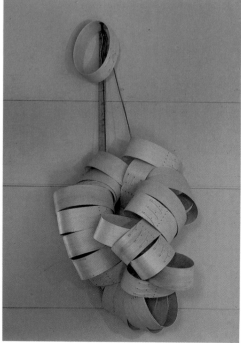

SLOW OR FAST FILM

Whether we look at black-and-white or colour films, the most obvious distinction between the different types is their speed ratings. The present system of film speed rating, which in recent years has almost entirely replaced the ASA and DIN systems, is known as the ISO (International Standards Organization) system. In its full form the ISO rating gives the old ASA rating and then the DIN rating – for example, ISO 100/21° for a film with an ASA rating of 100 and a DIN rating of 21°. In practice this is abbreviated to ISO 100.

Popularly referred to as "fast", "medium" or "slow", the speed of a film is a measure of how sensitive it is to light. Other considerations apart, the more sensitive a film emulsion is, the easier it is to use; shutter speeds can be high enough to overcome problems of camera shake or the blurring of a moving subject, and aperture settings can be small enough to give good depth of field. Front-to-back sharpness and frozen movement are not always desirable in a picture, but for most photographers in most situations they are important enough to make good film speed vital.

Slow films

In the range of colour transparency film speeds, slow is around ISO 50 and medium around ISO 100 (Kodachrome 25 is available but it is something of an exception). In image quality, these films are the standard, designed for as much sharpness, as fine a grain structure and as saturated a range of

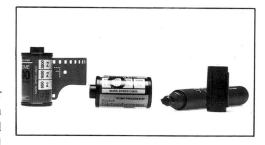

Fast films like Kodak's P800/1600 offer a choice of speed rating at the time of use. The panel is for marking before sending the film for processing.

Candlelight was the main illumination for the atmospheric shot below. It was taken with ISO 400 film, a maximum aperture of f2.8 and a shutter speed of ¼ second, and the camera was mounted on a tripod.

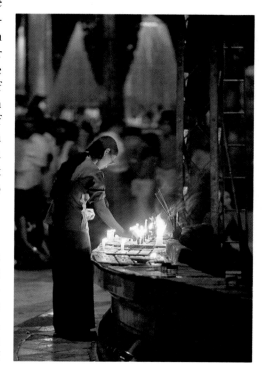

colours as possible, while still keeping a film speed that is practical. From every manufacturer, the films that are faster than these have poorer image quality and are compromises. Two of the major manufacturers, Fuji and Agfa, make ISO 50 and ISO 100 emulsions; Kodak still produces professional ISO 64 film, but is relying on improved technology to allow its Ektachrome 100 to carry most of the sales. In fact there is not a great deal of difference between the slow and medium-speed films: the grain is slightly finer in one, while the other offers an extra stop of exposure.

Fast films

The choice of fast transparency film has changed considerably in recent years, and is now: ISO 200 films from Kodak and Agfa offering a small speed advantage over the majority of fine-grain films; ISO 400 films from all manufacturers; and ultra-fast films that perform at their best around ISO 800 to 1000 but which can be given altered processing to take them up to ratings of ISO 1600 and, if need be, beyond that.

Fast film meets the needs of photographers who want to shoot, without tricky slow exposures, in low light. With this as the accepted priority, no one expects a high order of saturation and sharpness. Grain is the biggest problem, and this is the reason for the existence of three groups of film speed. The ISO 200 films, for example, have their adherents despite what is now a very modest speed, because they still have the edge in graininess over the ISO 400 films. If the light levels will just allow the use of an ISO 200 film, the grain advantage is a good argument for carrying at least one extra roll of this medium-fast film.

TUNGSTEN FILM FOR INDOORS

The question of colour balance rarely comes up when we consider how scenes look to the eye. The overall lighting has to be strongly coloured to be intrusive, and under most of the lighting that we are accustomed to – from daylight to tungsten bulbs and fluorescent strips – white objects appear more or less white, greys seem properly grey, and other colours look as we expect them to. In fact, the colour of even daylight varies considerably, although we tend not to notice because the human eye and brain adapt very well to the changes. Film does not adapt so well, however, and the dyes that are used in colour film must

A reverse use for tungsten-balanced film is to create an unusual twilit atmosphere. In the example below, a waterfall in a rain forest in the Philippines, both daylight left and tungsten-balanced right films were used. In some ways, the blue version on unfiltered Ektachrome 50 is more appropriate for the cool, dark scene.

Kodachrome 64

Ektachrome 50

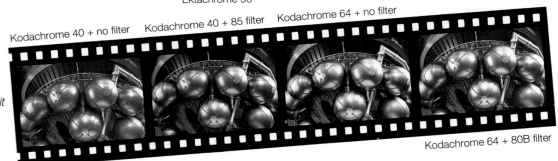

Kodachrome 40 + no filter   Kodachrome 40 + 85 filter   Kodachrome 64 + no filter

Kodachrome 64 + 80B filter

Mixed lighting may sometimes be handled better on tungsten-balanced film than on daylight emulsions. The scene above was lit by a mixture of daylight through tinted windows, vapour discharge lamps and an unfiltered 1000-watt tungsten lamp. The most accurate film was the filtered Kodachrome 40.

be balanced for a particular kind of light. The films we have looked at so far are balanced for daylight or, more specifically, for the colour of midday sunlight in a clear sky. On the scale of colour temperature, which is described more fully on pages 178-9, this is rated at 5500 K.

Tungsten lamps

Electronic flash units are designed to produce this same colour temperature, so that daylight-balanced films can be used. The other major source of artificial light used in photography is tungsten, and most lamps made for the purpose produce a light that is much more orange than daylight, at 3200 K.

The portrait below of an artist who paints electrolytically on titanium was photographed on both daylight-balanced Kodachrome 64 and tungsten-balanced Kodachrome 40. The lighting was 3200 K photographic lamps. The unfiltered Kodachrome 64 gives an orange cast – although by no means unusable – which the addition of an 80B conversion filter reduces. However, there is a greenish cast due to reciprocity failure at the ½ second exposure. The Kodachrome-balanced film gives a perfectly neutral version (filtered with an 82A to convert this Type A film to Type B lighting).

If daylight-balanced film is used with these lamps, the image will have a distinct cast to it. One alternative is to use a bluish filter to bring the neutral colours in the picture back to normal – an 80A filter in Kodak's designation, or an equivalent from other filter manufacturers.

There is sufficient indoor photography carried out under tungsten lights, however, for a (limited) range of specifically balanced films to be available. These balanced for 3200 K are known as Type B films, while those designed for the slightly more blue 3400 K are Type A (the latter are now almost obsolete). Accurate colour balance is much more critical for transparency films than for colour negative emulsions; filtration of the latter when printing can take care of most discrepancies, and thus nearly all tungsten-balanced films are of the reversal (transparency) type. Even so, the choice of tungsten-balanced films is small. At present it comprises Ektachrome 50 (its sheet-film equivalent is Ektachrome 6118) and Ektachrome 160 from Kodak, and Fujichrome 64T. In addition to these 3200-K-balanced Type B films, there is Kodachrome 40, a 3400-K-balanced film that is not widely distributed outside the United States.

Kodachrome 64 + no filter

Kodachrome 64 + 80B filter

Kodachrome 40 + 82A filter

BLACK-AND-WHITE FILM

The essential simplicity of a black-and-white negative, with its image recorded in the modulation of black silver, makes it a very elegant medium. There are also some practical advantages to shooting in black-and-white. With only one emulsion layer, and no colour accuracy to worry about, processing is simple and adaptable. The developer forms the image in a single step, which then only needs to be fixed.

Most photographers who work in black-and-white process their own film; it is a straightforward matter But even more important from the photographer's point of view, is the marvellous control that the medium offers. From exposure to printing, black-and-white film allows you to manipulate the image in ways that are largely denied to those who use colour film. Coloured filters control the shades of grey that appear on the film; a green filter, for example, will lighten the appearance of grass, while darkening anything red. Different developing solutions make it possible to alter the graininess, contrast and sharpness, as does the strength, time and temperature at which they are applied. During printing, the density and contrast can be worked over in many ways, giving a variety of prints from one negative.

Fast films

Although it is difficult to make direct comparisons with colour film, it is still fair to say that the image quality from a fast (ISO 400) black-and-white film, when printed, is higher than that from a colour film of the same speed. The main reason is that there is only one emulsion layer in a black-and-white negative, but three in colour film. Also, the typical granularity of an ISO 400 black-and-white film is lower than that of a colour slide film of the same speed.

For this reason ISO 400 films are considered by many to be the standard black-and-white film type. For outdoor photography in daylight – reportage and similar types of shooting – high shutter speeds and relatively small apertures are normal with this film.

Slow and medium films

In the slow group of black-and-white films, speed ratings are either ISO 25 (Agfapan 25 and Kodak Technical Pan 2415) or ISO 32 (Ilford Pan F and Kodak Panatomic-X). These films share very high sharpness and slightly higher contrast than most other films. Contrast differences are usually cancelled by the changes that can be made in printing: paper grade in particular.

The medium-speed emulsions have speed ratings of ISO 100 or 125. Sharpness and graininess are not quite as outstanding, but still very good.

A classic use of slow and medium-speed film is in landscape photography, where the textural detail plays an important part in the image. The modest enlargement left from a rollfilm negative (Ilford FP4) shows no graininess at all.

Printing controls can make major changes to the image. The negative of the three versions right of a mountain stream on the Isle of Skye, Scotland, contained all the information, but the first version, a straightforward print on Grade 2 paper, exposed for the mid-tones, left the sky blank and uninteresting. In the second print, an extra $1\frac{1}{2}x$ the exposure time was given to the sky, and the lower two-thirds of the print was shaded by hand. The final version was printed for maximum drama on Grade 3 paper, with the sky given an extra $2\frac{1}{2}x$ exposure.

COLOURS INTO TONES

Black-and-white film converts colours into shades of grey, and the exact shade depends not only on how dark or light the colour is, but also on its wavelength. In other words, the colour sensitivity of the film plays an important part. So, changing the overall colour of the scene can alter the black-and-white image, and this is the principle of using coloured filters in black-and-white photography. Using a strongly coloured filter will make little difference to the appearance of any object in the scene which is that same colour, but other colours will look darker in the final print. As a result, a set of perhaps six filters of different strong colours gives you the means for exercising real control over the image.

Contrast control through filtration

The basic and most useful set of filters for black-and-white contrast control includes yellow, orange, red, blue and green; for most situations these will give you full control. No. 8 or 12 is a reasonable choice for yellow; 15, 16 or 21 for orange (the higher these numbers, the stronger the hue), 25 is the normal red filter, 47 blue and 58 green. These identifying numbers are from Kodak's Wratten series, but other filter manufacturers produce equivalents for most of them, usually in plastic or glass. Start with this basic set, and to get an idea of their potential effect, hold each up to your eye and view different scenes.

Tonal effects

After the few seconds it should take your eye to adjust to the overall colour cast, you will be able to see the tonal effects that they have. In fact, the strongest colours will drown the colours in the scene to such an extent that they give a monochromatic view.

FILTER	WRATTEN NUMBER	USE	EXPOSURE INCREASE IN DAYLIGHT	FILTER FACTOR
Yellow	8	Standard filter for darkening blue sky and slightly lightening foliage. Also reduces haze.	1 stop	×2
Yellowish-green	11	Corrects for tungsten lighting. Also lightens foliage more than yellow, and lightens Caucasian skin tones to a natural appearance.	2 stops	×4
Deep yellow	12	"Minus blue". A similar effect to Wratten 8, but more pronounced, strongly darkening blue sky.	1 stop	×2
Yellow-orange	16	Stronger effect on sky than yellow filters. Reduces skin blemishes and spots in portraiture.	1⅔ stops	×3
Orange	21	More pronounced contrast than Wratten 16, particularly at sunrise and sunset. Lightens brickwork, darkens foliage.	2¹²⁄₃ stops	×5
Red	25	Darkens blue sky dramatically, deepening shadows and exaggerating contrast. Underexposure gives a moonlight effect, especially combined with a polarizing filter.	3 stops	×8
Deep red	29	Same effect as Wratten 25, but even stronger. Useful with long-focus landscapes to darken sky close to a distant horizon.	4 stops	×16
Magenta	32	"Minus green". Darkens green	1⅔ stops	×3
Light blue-green	44	"Minus red". Darkens red	½ stop	×6
Blue	47	Accentuates haze for a sensation depth in landscapes.	2⅔ stops	×6
Green	58	Lightens green foliage	3 stops	×8

The chart left shows the functions of the most common filters for use with black-and-white film and the exposure increase they require.

Assemble a small group of objects with very pure, contrasting colours, as shown right. Include things in yellow, red, blue and green. Light them fairly evenly, with plenty of shadow fill, and use daylight or flash, not tungsten (the orange colour of tungsten lamps will itself affect the tones on the film). Set the camera on a tripod, and begin with a straightforward exposure on black-and-white film with no filter. Use an incident light reading to judge the exposure settings. Then repeat the shot through each of the filters, increasing the exposure according to the table opposite. Finally, take the same shot on colour transparency film as a record for comparison. Process the films.

When you print each negative from this series, take care to give each the same exposure and development, and use the first, unfiltered shot as the basis for the enlarger's aperture and time settings and choice of paper grade. The obvious lesson from this project is how extreme the results are. In addition, what you may find during printing is that the exposure is not necessarily a simple matter.

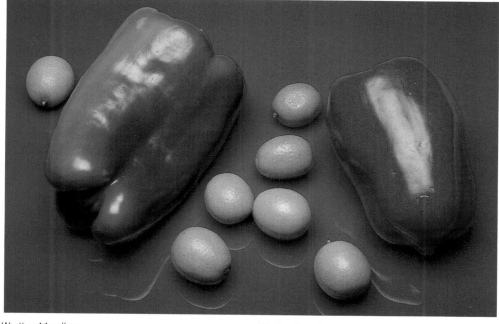

No filter

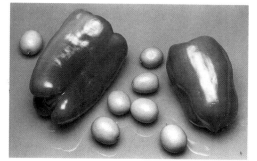

Wratten 11 yellow

Wratten 15 yellow–orange

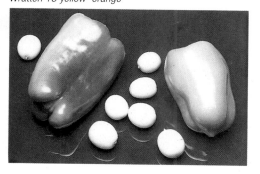

Wratten 25 red

Wratten 47 blue

Wratten 58 green

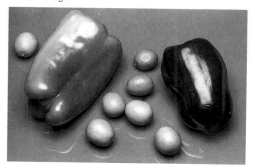

FILING AND EDITING

Original photographs – slides or negatives – deserve to be stored safely, and in a way that makes them easy to access and view. More than this, there are hidden benefits to a well-structured photo library – you can enjoy it and develop new ideas from it. At the very least, it encourages a fresh and analytical way of looking at pictures you have already taken. The second time around, you may feel differently about a particular image, and this is one of the most valuable ways of improving your photographic skills. A photo library, in other words, gives you feedback.

Retrieval

The acid test of efficient filing is retrieval. It should allow you to know exactly what images you have, and where they are, and to lay your hands on any particular one in a few minutes. The essentials of a well-planned system are: slide mounts, a storage system, light box, loupe and a method of cataloguing that allows you to cross-refer to any individual photograph.

It is worth devoting time to filing and editing your pictures properly. As well as preserving your work, you will come to appreciate the fact that the enjoyment of photography extends beyond the moment of shooting.

Slide mounts

Processing labs will return the slides to you either unmounted in sheets, or mounted individually – and usually the latter if you do not ask. Mounts for 35mm slides come in card, plastic, and occasionally metal. Plain white cards have a lot to recommend them – they are inexpensive, and you can write captions on them. Gummed card mounts sealed simply by pressing the two halves together are easily used, but the best are heat-sealed (with an iron or a small hand mounter). Plastic mounts, of which there are many makes, are usually in two halves, which either clip together simply or are sealed in some way. The precision with which the slide is located varies, and there is also a choice between those with and without glass. In theory, glass protects the slide's delicate surfaces, but it can also perform two less welcome functions: trap dirt and break. Either of these occurrences can scratch the emulsion.

Labels

There are two kinds of information that belong on a slide mount. One is your name – and copyright mark – and the other is a caption about the picture itself. Strictly speaking, your name is necessary only if the slides are likely to leave your hands – but it does no harm to identify that the picture is yours. You could also include your telephone number and/or address in case of loss, and you should definitely use a copyright mark – © – to protect your ownership of the image. Usually, the photographer's name goes on the upper part of the mount, with caption information below.

The easiest way is to write captions by hand on each slide, either directly onto the mount (if it is plain white card) or onto an adhesive label (1¾ x ½ inch/44 x 12mm) labels fit the "fat" sides of a 35mm mount). Many plastic mounts will not take ink, and so for these and metal mounts, adhesive labels are the only alternative. A desktop computer allows easier printing. More important, with a computer you can integrate your filing system with the captions and get the computer to print labels based on this information.

Storing slides

There may be a limited choice of location (and to start with, at least, you will not need much room), but wherever you keep your photographs should be reasonably dry and at a normal temperature. Heat and moisture damage film whether it is developed or not, and when they are combined the effects are worse. Ideally, the room where you store the slides should be no warmer than about 70°F (21°C), and the relative humidity between about 30 per cent and 50 per cent. Places not to use are near a radiator or in a damp basement.

Another good reason for taking care over these matters is that no image is completely permanent. Modern films are very good in this respect, and if the processing lab has done its job properly, the finished film should last for a few decades before you can notice any fading. However, the very gradual loss of image quality is an insidious process, and you tend to notice it only when it is too late.

Beware of contamination from paper materials not designed specifically for photographs: paper and card, however benign it may look, can at times be surprisingly harmful to film – some types contain acids that, over a long time, can affect the emulsion. The solution is to stick to containers that are made for storing photographs. Office cabinet files and trays, however, are perfectly safe because they are metal. If you are buying products from a photographic supplier, ask first. Some manufacturers make different versions of their display sheets: in ordinary PVC, for instance, but also in the more stable, and suitably archival, polypropylene.

Hanging files

Quite apart from the protection, filed slides should be viewable, and the fastest way to get an overview is by using standard-design hanging files. A single transparent sheet holds two dozen 35mm slides, and with the metal bar that slides into the strip at the top, it can be hung in a normal office filing cabinet, or an individual box file. In addition, consider a bulk storage system for slides that are left over from the editing process (see below). Boxes or a standard office file with trays that are 2 inches (5cm) deep save space – although they do not allow easy viewing.

Light boxes

Even if you regularly use a slide projector, a light box is infinitely more convenient for sorting and filing pictures – and the larger the better, as it allows you to sort slides into a number of groups. Building your own is not complicated. The essentials are a translucent plastic surface (Perspex/Plexiglas is usual) and one or two colour-corrected fluorescent striplights, with the interior of the box painted white. It is also worthwhile investing in the best loupe you can find. The difference between good

optics and poor is immediately obvious if you compare them side by side, and makes a real difference in the pleasure of looking closely at your slides. The loupe should be large enough, of course, to cover the whole of the transparency.

Storing negatives

35mm negatives are normally kept in strips (usually 6 frames) in acid-free sleeves that hold one roll – these are easier to handle for printing than individually cut frames. As negatives are an intermediate stage, protection is more important than viewing, but for

making a selection, keep a contact sheet of each roll, either with the negative sheet or in a separate file.

Digital storage

Now that digital scanning is quite inexpensive, a completely different possibility is to store slides and negatives electronically. Kodak's Photo CD is one widely used system in which the images are scanned and transferred to a compact disc, which can then be played and viewed either with a special player on a regular television monitor, or via a CD-ROM drive on a computer.

One of the most efficient ways of storing slides is to use the plastic files designed to hang in a filing cabinet. Be sure to choose acid-free files from a reputable manufacturer, however, as some makers use an acid in the production of the plastic which harms the emulsion.

This does not, of course, completely replace the traditional filing methods (you still have to keep your originals somewhere), but it allows easy viewing and you can use the CD as a kind of electronic negative – hand it back to the photo-finishing lab when you want more prints. There are other kinds of scanner, of course, and other storage media – floppy disks for low-resolution images, your computer's hard disk, or removable media such as SyQuest and Bernoulli cartridges, tape, and writable CD-ROM.

To be useful, the images need to be of a sufficiently high resolution for whatever you normally need them for. The regular Photo CD format is designed to produce good quality prints of around 8 × 10 inches. If all you want is to view them on screen, they can be much smaller (computer screen resolution is 72 pixels per inch), but if you want to make high-quality duplicate slides or large prints, you will need higher resolution (in the tens of megabytes).

Editing

Editing can add a surprising dimension to photography, and in some form or another is inextricable from filing. One of the most important guidelines is to show only the best. Although editing starts with the prosaic task of weeding out the mistakes and the less good, it is also the time for evaluating the pictures you have shot. Under no circumstances treat it as a chore. If instead you give it time and clear thinking, you may be surprised at what it can contribute to your picture-taking. It can even be a creative skill in its own right, and all professionals take it seriously.

The idea of editing is to select the best, and a second chance to think about the images when you have more time. No photographer expects every shoot to be equally good. With wildlife, for instance, it is perfectly normal to shoot many frames to be able to guarantee one good image. Imagine, for example, that you see a deer a couple of hundred yards ahead, and decide to stalk it with the camera. As you approach, you will probably want to take some shots early, just in case it bolts suddenly. If you end up getting reasonably close, then you are likely to have a sequence of pictures that improves from first to last, and it may not be worth keeping the early ones. The same can apply to all kinds of shooting, and some photographers treat editing as a part of the photography; it allows deferred decisions. Below the time-honoured process of three-stage editing is described.

Detailed examination

When you are ready to edit a roll, it can be easy to forget the small but important decisions that you were taking at the time of shooting – particularly because the 35mm frames will look very similar as you spread them out on the light box. The first impression from a slide, looked at like this, is a general one of colour and basic composition; it is important not to let this overwhelm your judgement. Take the loupe to every slide, and examine it in detail. Not just for focus, blemishes and so on, but for the vital details of composition, moment, expression. Henri Cartier-Bresson wrote, "The difference between a good picture and a mediocre one is a question of millimetres." Relive the time of shooting – if the differences between one image and the next were important enough to explore at the time, they remain important when you carry out the editing.

Three-stage editing

The aim of this process is to make two piles of slides from a trip or a shoot. One pile should have just the very best – pictures you are proud of. The second, which will probably be the larger when you have finished, should have images that are workmanlike, competent, but not particularly outstanding. There is a third group, but it is not a pile - it should be in the waste bin, and contains the images that are just not worth keeping – either because of technical mistakes or because they are poor pictures. First: Pick out the transparencies that look good at first sight. Don't stop to think too much at this stage; just follow your immediate reactions.

Second: Look through the remainder, taking your time. Learn from the experience of revisiting the images. Pay particular attention to those you wanted to be good when you took them, but didn't quite make it.

Third: Now cast a more critical eye over the pictures you first selected. Weed out any that are repetitive – images you may have made too many times already, such as silhouettes of boats on sunlit water (to take just one example). Try to pitch your standards higher all the time. Be ruthless.

During: As you go through the sequence, discard all frames that are technically faulty – that is, out of focus, wrongly exposed, scratched, blemished or whatever. (The only reason for keeping any of these is if you think you can repair the damage at some later point by digital retouching on a computer. This is not for everybody, but the results can be amazing).

Sorting pictures by subject or place

The basic procedure with any system is to sort out the pictures by subject, and within this to classify them in categories within categories. The first decision to take is what the most natural groupings are for the way you shoot. This last point is important: if you have some special interest, such as flowers or portraits, then it makes sense to file pictures by these subject categories. On the other hand, many photographers are travel-oriented, and this would make the place where the picture was taken a more relevant category. So, for instance, you would have a file for Scotland, another for the Swiss Alps, and so on.

You can add subjects as they occur, but start by listing all the broad groupings that you think will encompass your range of photography. For instance, it might contain: Animals, Climbing, Landscapes, People, Plants, Sailing, Seascapes. Don't rush this step – think about it for a day or two and you'll find that new categories will come to mind. The next step is to sub-divide each of these categories, and even split them further if it makes sense. The more slides you have in the library, the better this so-called nesting of groups works.

Cross-indexing

The secret of making your slide library work is to include each good image in several different selections. This process is known as cross-indexing, and essentially it means matching the filed slides to a number of lists. The slide library itself is ordered only in one way – usually by place or subject as mentioned above – and to make different groupings you will need some paperwork. A desktop computer makes this much easier – provided that you file the information for each slide, you can generate the lists as and when you need them, and they will automatically update – but for now we look at the simple manual method.

On separate sheets of paper, make headings for different groupings of pictures. Say you decide to file the slides by place; make the headings for other ways of ordering the shots. For example, you might have the following: Animals, Mountains, Sports, Sunrises & Sunsets, and so on. When you put a new batch of slides into your library, add each one to whatever lists it fits. You can make up a new grouping whenever you think of one, and then browse through the files to add to it – itself not a bad way of refreshing your memory of the slide collection. One practical reason for making lists is that, as you continue to shoot, your slide library will eventually grow beyond the size at which you can easily remember every picture.

Levels of picture quality

You can, to an extent, "peel" back the layers of a photographic image in the manner of an onion – not physically, of course, but as a way of judging how good the picture is. Check it against the following criteria:

1. Any serious mistakes? Scratches, other blemishes, loss of focus, exposure more than one *f*-stop out.
2. Technical competence. Exposure, sharpness, focus, contrast.
3. Graphics. Are the composition, colour, tonal balance, lighting, visual contrasts competent? Or original?
4. Subject interest. Is the focus of interest a compelling subject?
5. Subject treatment. Is it handled in an original and/or elegant way?
6. Idea. Is there a distinct or important idea behind the image? Is the idea interesting, worth pursuing? Do the above (treatment, choice of subject, graphics, etc) serve the idea as well as possible?
7. Apart from all of this, does the image create an emotion or any sense that is hard to pin down?
8. Is it, for whatever reason, memorable?

Computer databases

A computer is the perfect workhorse for managing a collection of slides, and while it would be extravagant to buy one just for that reason (unless you were setting up a professional picture library), any personal computer can be used for the job. Not only is it easier than keeping records on paper, it is much more efficient.

Essentially, there are two approaches to computerizing a collection of slides. One is to use the computer for keeping records of the pictures; the other is to store the images themselves electronically so that you can scan through them on the screen. In computer terminology, the choice is between an ordinary database and an image database. Database is the kind of word that makes computerphobes' eyes glaze over, and evokes images of millions of customer files in an insurance company's office. A database can certainly be highly complex, but it need not be. Basically, it is the electronic version of an ordinary card index.

When setting up a database, first make a list of the details you want to record for each picture. Remember that the more items you specify, the bigger your database will be (and that usually means that it will

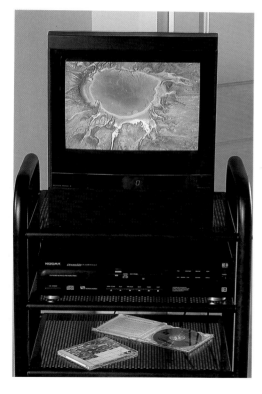

A computer-based filing system above *allows you to log and access with speed an extensive collection of pictures. The printer in the picture* top *produces captioned labels – a wonderfully efficient and timesaving device for the professional photographer.*

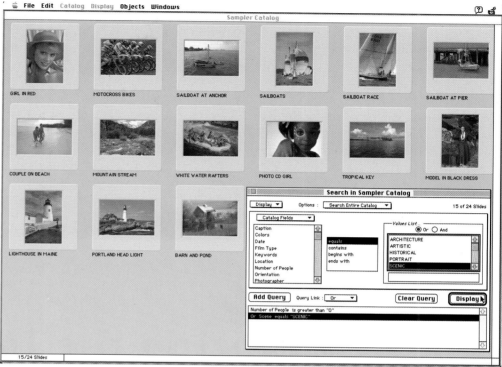

eventually work more slowly – and fill up the disk), and the more time you will spend filling in each record. Each block of information that you enter into a picture record goes into what is called a field, and it may be as short as a date, or as long as a several-line caption.

Some database programs make you choose which details you can search for. These are called key fields, and the more you want, the slower the program will run. If you have this kind of database, leave some of the information in non-key fields – descriptions and dates, for example. In other databases, you can choose to put the fields that you are most likely to use for searching into an index, which is a compact

The user of a computerized picture library can structure it according to his or her own precise requirements, creating (and revising) the categories, assigning images to them and setting up a cross-index.

file, hidden from view, that the computer can use to make a fast search.

Picture description

Finally, make sure that there is one unique description for each slide (if you have several all called "Beach at sunset", it will be difficult to distinguish between them). A number is a safe choice – unique to each picture, and usually quicker to search for than text.

Creating the Image

Most of the important decisions in photography take place in the viewfinder. That is to say, they are about the image itself: the reasons for making it, and the way it looks. Although improvements in camera and film technology continue to be valuable, they are not central to picture-taking. The best they can do is to help you realize your ideas, and provided that you have at least a basic minimum of equipment there should be few limits to the images you can make. In any case, simple changes of framing or viewpoint are usually more economical solutions than calling on a different piece of equipment.

The process of organizing the image in the viewfinder is design – or composition, if you prefer – and it is the most important single skill in photography. Oddly, it receives little attention when photography is written about or discussed – much less, for instance, than does the subject of design in painting or drawing. One reason for this is the common assumption that because a photograph is virtually instant there is no time to deliberate about design. Another reason is photography's preoccupation with hardware. Neither of these is a sound reason for neglecting the design of the image, and in this part of the book we examine, purely in terms of the image, how and why photographs work.

Like any other graphic medium, photography follows a number of design principles. It does so in its own way, but they are just as important as in, say, painting. The two most basic principles are contrast and balance, and they lie at the heart of everything to do with framing, selecting the subject, dividing the frame into areas, using lines and shapes, and so on. Contrast brings out the differences between elements in a photograph, such as tone or shape. Balance is the relationship between these elements, and how they offset each other in a single image. How you put contrast and balance to work depends on your own taste and ideas, but as principles they explain why certain pictures create the impression they do, and why a particular way of composing an image has a predictable effect.

One of the special features of photography is the speed at which it can work. However much time you put into thinking about a shot, executing it usually takes only a fraction of a second. This means that a picture can be taken casually, without thought. Unfortunately, because it can, it often is. The simplicity of pressing the shutter release too often provides an excuse for not bothering to think about giving a strong, effective design to the shot. The fact is, though, that experience in putting together a well-organized image is even more important if you have to shoot quickly. In reportage photography, for example, any design decisions have to be made instantly – virtually without thinking – and the best pictures of this type are taken by photographers whose eyes are so well trained that the design of the image comes naturally to them.

In looking at a view, most people assess what they see intuitively, liking or disliking it without stopping to consider exactly why. Most photographers also work intuitively, but to do it well time after time means having a sound idea of design already in mind. Some, but not many, have a natural eye for this; others reach the same point by training themselves. The more you can absorb of the principles of photographic design, the easier it becomes to compose a strong image unconsciously. In the following pages you can study at your leisure the ways in which images are put together. Inevitably there is something slightly unrealistic about this, since few photographs are taken so deliberately, and so you should read this part of the book as a preparation for taking photographs rather than as a working method.

Through a combination of design elements, this shot of Burmese novice monks is organized to be seen in just one way. The moment for taking the shot was very short – just the time taken for the gesture and glance of the boy on the right – but there was plenty of time to prepare and to anticipate most of the possibilities, including the fact that the statue may be taken as looking at the foreground. The coincidence of expression on the two boys' faces was, of course, unplanned, but anticipation of other details, such as the exposure, focus, and overall balance of the image, made it easy to recognize the potential and shoot in time. The result of this planning is a very structured image, as is demonstrated by the diagrams above, which analyse, from left to right, the picture's structure in terms of points, shapes, lines and eye-lines.

Design in photography has two roles. One is to improve the look of the image. If you exercise good judgement in contrast, balance and so on, the picture will be more satisfying. The second role is to direct the way in which other people look at the image. In the simplest sense, this means directing their attention to where you want it to be – ensuring, for example, that the viewer focuses on the intended point of interest. A more sophisticated possibility is to encourage the viewer's eye to move around the frame in a certain way. If you know why you are taking a photograph and understand what you hope to get out of it, then these design skills will help you to make the image more effective.

FRAMING THE SCENE

The frame *opposite* is the starting point for the making of every image in this book. There are other shapes, of course, and other cameras. But what really matters is that everything discussed here is about the changes that can be made within this frame – and not camera technique.

Using the frame

This frame is of much greater importance to a photograph than a canvas or paper is to a painting or illustration. The reason is the principal difference between photography and every other graphic art: the elements of a photograph are already in front of the camera. A painting or illustration is built up from nothing, out of perception and imagi-

nation. The process of photography, by contrast, is one of selection from real scenes and events. Potential photographs exist in their entirety inside the frame every time the photographer raises the camera and looks through the viewfinder. Indeed, in many types of highly active photography, such as street photography, making the image involves using the viewfinder, and so the frame, to watch the image as it evolves. The actual creation of the image – its commitment to film – is normally instantaneous.

Being instantaneous, however, calls into question the relative importance of the moment of shooting. If everything – more detail than the eye can possibly appreciate at the time – is converted into the finished photograph in a fraction of a second, then the essential part of the process must be in the period leading up to this. If the subject is static, like a landscape, it is easy to see that enough time can be spent studying and

evaluating the frame. With active subjects, however, there is not this period of grace. Design decisions, whatever they are, must often be taken in less time than it takes for them to be recognized as such. In other words, they must be intuitive.

Skills on demand

The only realistic way of improving how you design pictures is to first learn the principles of design, then put them on one

Whatever your lens's focal length, framing a view means selecting a small part of the scene. In the shot opposite *a 35mm frame crops into a Texan mountain landscape.*

The viewpoint of the photograph of robed aldermen above *was chosen to give a triangular composition, the apex being the feet nearest the camera.*

For the shot right *a viewpoint was chosen that makes the group of figures into a vertical shape. A vertical frame format has a natural feel to it.*

In the wide-angle shot of a classical frontage left, strong dynamic movement comes from the interplay of diagonal lines with the rectangular frame. Although the diagonals have an independent movement and direction, it is the reference standard of the frame edges that allows them to create tension in this picture. The dramatic effect of the photograph is heightened by the fact that the statue in the foreground is seen as a silhouette.

side and allow what you have absorbed to come up naturally at the precise moment that you need it.

Dynamics of the frame

The format of the frame is fixed at the time of shooting, although it is always possible later to adjust the shape of the frame to the picture you have taken. Nevertheless, whatever opportunities exist for later changes (see pages 102–5), do not underestimate the influence of the viewfinder on composition. With most cameras, your view of the world is a bright rectangle surrounded by blackness, and the presence of the frame is usually strongly felt. Although experience may

One simple device for creating an image that has prominent lines is to align one or two of them with the frame. In the case of the office block right, the alignment of two edges avoids the untidiness of two corner areas of sky. Alignment like this emphasizes the geometry of an image.

help you to ignore the dimensions of the viewfinder frame in order to shoot to a different format, intuition will encourage you to make a design that feels satisfying at the time of shooting.

The most common picture area is that of a horizontal 35mm frame. This is the most widely used format of camera, and holding it horizontally is the easiest method. As an empty frame it has certain dynamic influ-ences, as the diagram on this page shows, although these tend to be felt only in very minimal and delicately toned images. More often, however, the dynamics of lines, shapes and colours in the photograph take over completely.

Borders

Depending on the subject and on the treat-ment the photographer chooses, the edges of the frame can have a strong or weak influence on the image. The examples shown here are all ones in which the hori-zontal and vertical borders, and the corners, contribute strongly to the design of the photographs. They have been used as refer-ences for diagonal lines within the pictures, and the angles that have been created in this way are important features of the photographs as a whole.

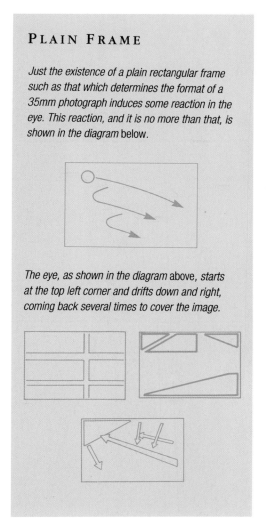

PLAIN FRAME

Just the existence of a plain rectangular frame such as that which determines the format of a 35mm photograph induces some reaction in the eye. This reaction, and it is no more than that, is shown in the diagram below.

The eye, as shown in the diagram above, starts at the top left corner and drifts down and right, coming back several times to cover the image.

In photographing an array of gold bars, a regular, orderly stack as in the diagram far left would have been dull. Angling three of the bars, as in the photograph above and as represented graphically in the diagram left, introduces a dynamic into the picture. This works entirely as a result of the angles that are created with the edges of the frame.

Frames within frames

The appeal of frames within frames is partly to do with composition, but at a deeper level it relates to perception. A frame enhances a photograph's dimensionality by emphasizing that the viewer is looking through from one plane to another; it is a kind of window.

Controlling the subject

Another part of the appeal is that, by drawing a boundary around the principal image, an internal frame is evidence of organization. A measure of control has been imposed on the scene. Limits have been set, and the image held back from flowing over the edges of the picture. Some feeling of stability and even of rigidity enters into this, and this type of photograph lacks the casual free-wheeling associations that you can see in, for example, classic journalistic or reportage photography. As a result, frames within frames appeal to a certain aspect of our personalities. It feels satisfying to see that the elements of a picture have been defined and placed under a kind of control.

On a purely graphic level, frames focus the attention of a viewer because they

Here, stepping back with a wide-angle shift lens into an archway resolves how to handle the sky area. Without the frame, the upper corners of the picture would simply be empty sky: by no means wrong, but certainly not lifting the shot out of the ordinary. The frame is relevant to the scene – because the archway is part of the architecture – and neatly matches the outline of the tower. In addition, notice how the attention is pulled down into the picture and the perspective is greatly enhanced. First, the black area between the picture frame and the arch pulls the eye down; then the distant archway establishes the perspective and directs the attention further down.

The simplest frame-within-frame treatment is this "window" shot, looking out from a dark interior. It is highly structured and precise, but these strengths are easily lost by cropping in at the sides, as in the sketch. The view is no longer contained, and the image runs off to left and right.

establish a diminishing direction from the outer picture frame. The internal frame draws the eye in by one step, particularly if it is similar in shape to the picture format. This momentum is then easily continued further into the picture.

Shape relationship

Another important design opportunity to note is the shape relationship between the two frames. The angles and shapes that are set up between the boundary of the picture and lines inside the image can be an important part of the composition. This is especially so with a continuous edge inside the picture. The graphic relationship between the two frames is strongest when the gap between them is narrow. When the internal frame is small and deeply inset, its edges hardly react to the edges of the photograph.

The opposite of the example above in both tone and direction, this shot of a Beijing vendor's window has less inward pull because the white surround is less forceful. However, its compactness and organization are strengthened by the fact that the window frame fits the uncropped 35mm film frame with unusual precision.

PLACING THE SUBJECT

In order to be able to talk about the different graphic elements in design, and to look at the way they interact, the first thing we must do is to isolate them, choosing the most basic situations for composing pictures. A little caution is needed here, because in practice you will normally be faced with a multitude of possibilities and design choices.

Single subject

The most basic of all photographic situations is one single, obvious subject in front of the camera. We have an immediate choice: to close right in so that it fills up the picture frame, or to pull back so that we can see something of its surroundings. What would influence the choice? One consideration is the information content of the pic-

The picture at the top of the page shows a conventional subject-in-its-setting approach. There is nothing unusual about this treatment, although the shot is enhanced by the crisp lighting. The picture above is a different kind of context shot. More informative than attractively designed, it shows us less of the ferry but more about where it is and what it does. Over-filling the frame, as in the shot left, takes us into the details of the subject. The lifebelts tell us that this is a boat, but the subject has altered: the shot is now concerned as much with the passengers as with the ferry.

ture. Obviously, the larger the subject is in the photograph, the more of its detail can be shown. If it is something interesting, this may be paramount; if very familiar, perhaps not. Another consideration is the relationship between the subject and its setting. Are the surroundings important, either to the content of the shot or to its design? In the studio, you can place an object on a plain roll of background paper so that it is on

The design appeal of this picture lies in the boat's almost exact fit in the 35mm frame. Shot with more water showing, it would have been more ordinary.

neutral territory; then the setting has nothing to tell the viewer, and its only value is for composition. Outside the studio, however, settings nearly always have some relevance. They can show scale (a climber on a rock-face) or something about the activity of the subject.

Presence

A third factor is the subjective relationship that you might want to create between the viewer and the subject. The most commonly used expression for this is presence. If you want the subject to be imposing, and if you want to take the viewer right up to it,

then filling the frame is a reasonable option. There are other things involved, such as the ultimate size of the picture when displayed (see pages 92–5), the focal length of lens, and the scale of the subject to begin with. Nevertheless, a big subject filling the frame of a big picture usually acquires force and impact.

The shape of the subject in relation to the format of the frame clearly has an effect. In the picture *below*, shot from this angle the boat just reaches the picture edges all round. In the majority of single-subject pictures, however, the focus of attention does not fill the frame. The shape may not

Although this silhouette is dominated by the tree's contrast with the sky and there is a massive vertical emphasis in the middle of the frame, the opposed positions of the birds create a strong diagonal.

coincide with the format of the picture (cropping a print to fit the subject is always possible, but not necessarily elegant). Another design disadvantage with running the edges of the subject right up to the borders of the picture is that the eye tends to feel uncomfortable concentrating on points at the edges of the picture. It often needs a little free area around a subject to be able to move without feeling constricted.

However, as soon as you allow free space around the subject, its position becomes an issue. It has to be placed, consciously, somewhere within the frame. Logically, it might seem that the natural position is right in the middle with equal space around, and often this holds true. If there are no other elements in the picture, why not?

One compelling reason why not is that it is very predictable – and, if repeated, boring. We are faced with a conflicting choice. On the one hand, there is a desire to do something interesting with the design, and so escape the bull's-eye method of framing a subject. On the other hand, placing the subject anywhere but in a natural position needs a reason. As an extreme example, if you place a subject right in the corner of an otherwise empty frame, you will need a

This straightforward arrangement of two objects on a featureless background is influenced by the two subjects' difference in size. It was for this reason that the ferry was positioned a little closer to the center than the yacht.

If the subject is to occupy most of the frame space, there is often no good reason for placing it anywhere else but in the middle. In the shot right the setting is more or less featureless, and off-centering the figure would just raise the question as to why, without giving an answer.

justification, or the design becomes simply perverse. Eccentric composition can work extremely well, but its success depends on there being some purpose.

Subject size

The importance of placement increases as the subject becomes smaller in the frame. In the photograph of the man standing against the Wailing Wall, we are not really conscious that the figure is actually in any position in the frame. It is, in fact, centered but with not so much space around it as to be obvious. At the same time, some off-centeredness is usually desirable simply in order to set up a relationship between the subject and its background. A dead-center position is so stable as to have no dynamic tension at all. If slightly away from the middle, the subject appears to be set against the background.

Often the foreground is uninteresting, distracting, or of little value to the picture. In this case a reasonable solution is to raise the camera and place the subject low in the frame. It may also, as in the shot below, help the composition by darkening the upper part of the sky (with a graduated filter) to give a little counterbalance.

DELAYED IMPACT

An interesting approach to controlling the reactions of the viewer to a photograph is to slow them down rather than to accelerate them. Whereas the most obvious requirement in directing the attention is to make sure that the viewer sees a particular point quickly and without confusion, there are occasions when the effect of a photograph will be all the stronger if the viewer notices the key point in the picture after a slight delay, only after having looked at some other part of the shot. This is particularly the case when there is humour deliberately hidden in the photograph.

Using the setting

Perhaps the most common situation in which a delayed reaction can be produced to good effect is when the idea behind the photograph is contained in the relationship between an object and its setting. In partic-ular, if the surroundings are felt in some way to dominate something, and if you want to communicate the impression that they are overwhelming, then there is a good case for wanting the surroundings to register first.

The means for achieving the effect described above are not necessarily compli-cated, and usually involve reversing the normal design techniques of placement and scale that are used to draw attention. However, there is a risk in that you may

The interest in this scene is not really the boat on a klong *in Bangkok but the fact that it is still there after a motorway has been built over the water. The concrete pillars make a landscape which one would not normally associate with a traditional way of life. Hence a close view of the boat, as in the smaller picture, does not serve the purpose. On the other hand, a simple long shot, with the boat very small, might just lose it from view. Instead, the viewpoint of the shot* right, *with the boat placed at the far right of the frame, helps to point it out through the convergence of the bridge pillars.*

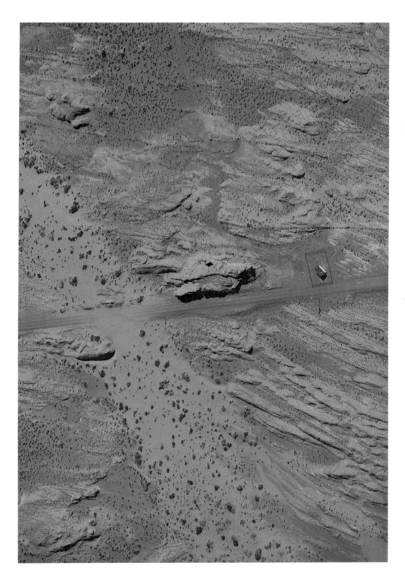

adjust the bias of composition to such a degree that the eye fails to notice the key point. The most common techniques, used in the photographs on these pages to varying degrees, are positioning the key point a little eccentrically, and choosing a viewpoint which keeps the point small.

The aerial view left gains its interest from the sense of isolation of the house and the road amid an empty stretch of rocky desert. The greater the area of the surroundings and the smaller the house, the stronger is this feeling. However, judgement is needed to discern at what point the house actually escapes notice altogether. Much of the effect of the picture depends on the scale at which it is reproduced.

The photograph right is a chance shot, for which there was very little warning. The framing is right for giving some humour to the situation: by making sure that the boy stealing the fish appears just at the bottom of the frame, there is a small delay before he is noticed. The viewer first sees the women in a conventional marketplace shot and then spots the pilfering going on behind their backs.

A BALANCED PICTURE

At the heart of design lies the concept of balance. Balance is the resolution of tension, opposing forces that are matched to give equilibrium and a sense of harmony. It is a fundamental principle of visual perception that the eye seeks to balance one force with another. Balance is harmony and symmetry: forces that are equally opposed.

If we consider two strong points in a picture, for example, the center of the frame becomes a reference against which we see their position. If one diagonal line in another image creates a strong sense of movement in one direction, the eye is aware of the need for an opposite sense of movement. In colour relationships, successive and simultaneous contrasts (see pages 270–7) demonstrate that the eye will seek to provide its own complementary hues.

Maintaining balance

When talking about the balance of forces in a picture, the usual analogies tend to be ones drawn from the physical world: gravity, levers, weights and fulcrums. These are quite reasonable to continue with, because the eye and mind have a real, objective response to balance that works in a very similar way to the laws of mechanics.

We can develop the physical analogies more literally by thinking of an image as a surface balanced at one point, rather like a weighing scale. If we add anything to one side of the image – that is, off-center – it

An unbalanced composition encourages the eye to produce its own equilibrium. Here, asymmetry is used to force the eye left into the slum in the background.

SYMMETRY AND PRECISION

Achieving symmetry in a photograph is not something that should be left to chance. A grid-etched focusing screen as in the diagram on the right below is an invaluable guide to positioning the subject within the frame in photographs like those on this page.

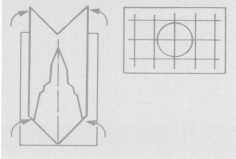

The line between symmetry and asymmetry is very fine. If you attempt a symmetrical composition like the picture above, then it must be precise to succeed, for the smallest misalignment will stand out immediately.

Some subjects, like those below right and in the left-hand diagram in the box, are symmetrical around one axis. Architecture is an obvious example, but head-on views of humans and animals reveal the same principle.

becomes unbalanced, and we feel the need to correct this. It does not matter whether we are talking about masses of tone, colour, an arrangement of points, or whatever.

Considered like this, there are two distinct kinds of balance. One is symmetrical or static; the other is dynamic. In symmetrical balance, the arrangement of forces is centered – everything falls equally away from the middle of the picture. We can create this by placing the subject of a photograph right in the middle of the frame. In our weighing scale analogy, it sits right over the fulcrum, the point of balance. Another way of achieving the same static balance is to place two equal weights on either side of the center, at equal distances. Adding a dimension to this, several graphic elements equally arranged around the center have the same effect.

The second kind of visual balance opposes weights and forces that are unequal, and in doing so enlivens the image. On the weighing scale, a large object can be balanced by a small one, as long as the latter is placed far enough away from the fulcrum. Similarly, a small graphic element can successfully oppose a dominant one, as long as it is placed out towards the edge of the frame. Mutual opposition is the mechanism

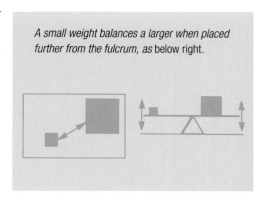

A small weight balances a larger when placed further from the fulcrum, as below right.

Two unequal subjects or areas can be balanced by placing them carefully in the frame, as in the picture below *and in the diagram* above left.

by which most balance is achieved; it is, of course, a type of contrast.

These are the ground rules of visual balance, but they need to be treated with some caution. All we have done so far is to describe the way the balance works in simple circumstances. In many pictures, a variety of elements interact, and the question of balance can only be resolved intuitively,

In this photograph, as in the one of a woman with an umbrella on page 76, an unbalanced composition was used to upgrade the visual importance of the surroundings.

according to what feels right. The weighing scale analogy is fine as far as it goes – to explain the fundamentals – but I would certainly not recommend actually using it as an aid to composition.

Apart from this, a more crucial consideration is whether or not balance is even desirable. Certainly, the eye and brain need equilibrium, but providing it is not the undisputed job of art or photography. If we accepted a definition of good photography as images that produced a calm, satisfying sensation, the results would be very dull indeed. An expressive picture is by no means always harmonious, as you can see

time and again throughout this book. This fact underlines many design decisions, not just in an obvious way – where to place the center of interest, for example – but in how much tension or harmony to create. The choice is ultimately a personal one.

Symmetry and eccentricity

In composing the image, the poles are symmetry and eccentricity. Symmetry is a special, perfect case of balance, not necessarily satisfying, and very rigid. In the natural run of views that a photographer is likely to come across, it is not particularly common. You would have to specialize in a group of

things that embody symmetrical principles, such as architecture or seashells, to make much use of it. For this reason, it can be appealing if used occasionally, but to succeed it must be absolutely precise. Few images look sloppier than a nearly symmetrical view that did not quite make it. Precise composition is by no means easy without some visual aid, and grid lines etched on the focusing screen are almost a necessity.

Unbalanced composition

We ought now to consider how tension actually works in an unbalanced composition. The mechanics are considerably more subtle than the balancing scale analogy can show. While the eye and brain search for balance, it would be wrong to assume that it is satisfying to have it handed on a plate. Interest in any image is in direct proportion

When a single subject is placed centrally, as below and in the two central diagrams, static balance is maintained.

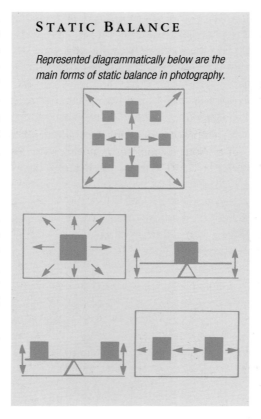

STATIC BALANCE

Represented diagrammatically below are the main forms of static balance in photography.

Maximum symmetry occurs when objects or lines are arranged radially around the frame's center, as above and in the top diagram.

Two equal elements equally placed around the frame's center are in symmetrical static balance, as below and in the bottom two diagrams.

to the amount of work the viewer has to do, and too perfect a balance leaves less for the eye to work at. Hence, dynamic balance tends to be more interesting than static balance. Not only this, but in the absence of equilibrium, the eye makes an attempt to produce it independently.

This can be seen in action in any eccentrically composed picture. To make the point as obviously as possible, the examples chosen are of extreme displacement – the photographs of the worker in the rice field on page 79 and of the woman with an umbrella on page 76. The rice field picture is graphically the simpler of the two. According to the weighing scale analogy, the equilibrium is completely upset, yet if you study the picture it is not, in fact, all that uncomfortable in appearance.

What happens is that the eye and brain want to find something closer to the center to balance the figure in the top right corner, and so keep coming back to the lower left center of the frame. Of course, the only thing there is the mass of rice, so that the

setting in fact gains extra attention. The green stalks of rice would be less dominant if the figure were centrally placed. As it is, you would be hard put to say whether the photograph is of a worker in a rice field or of a rice field with, incidentally, a figure working in it.

This process of trying to compensate for an obvious asymmetry in an image is what creates visual tension, and it can be very useful indeed in making a picture more dynamic. It can help draw attention to an area of a scene that would normally be too bland to be noticed. In the case of the second picture, of a woman with an umbrella, the photographer wanted tension because of the subject: a Manila slum built on a gigantic rubbish heap.

Asymmetry

A second factor involved in eccentrically composed images is that of logic. The more extreme the asymmetry, the more the viewer expects a reason for it. Theoretically, at least, someone looking at such an image

will be that bit more prepared to examine it carefully for the justification.

Finally, all considerations of balance must take into account the sheer graphic complexity of many images. In order to study the design of photographs, we are doing our best in this book to isolate each of the graphic elements we look at. Many of the examples, such as the rice field picture, are deliberately uncomplicated. In reality, most photographs contain several layers of graphic effect.

Implied movement

As an example of this, consider a picture of a car, very small in the frame, entering from the left, and placed close to the left edge of the picture. Although on one level a point, it also has implied movement, and its perceived position in the frame is actually closer to the middle because we see it as having potential movement into the frame. Were it in exactly the same position but facing in the opposite direction, the balance of the shot would seem quite different.

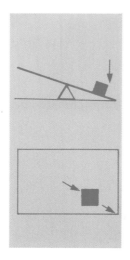

If one visual element or force is positioned away from the center of the photograph, even by a small amount, as in the example and diagrams right, the balance of the picture is upset.

DYNAMIC TENSION

Certain of the basic graphic elements have more energy than others: diagonals, for instance. Some design constructions are also more dynamic; rhythm creates momentum and activity, and eccentric placement of objects induces tension as the eye attempts to create its own balance.

Dynamic tension

However, rather than think of an image as balanced or unbalanced, we can consider it in terms of its dynamic tension. This is essentially making use of the energy inherent in various structures, and using it to keep the eye alert and moving outwards from the center of the picture. This approach produces the opposite of the static character of formal compositions.

Some caution is needed, simply because introducing dynamic tension into a picture seems such an easy and immediate way of attracting attention. Just as the use of rich, vibrant colours is instantly effective in an individual photograph but can become mannered if used constantly, so repeated reliance on dynamic tension can also become tiresome after a while.

Fleeting effect

As with any design technique that is strong and obvious when first seen, dynamic tension tends to lack staying power. Its effect is usually spent very quickly, and the eye moves on to the next image. As a result, it is better suited to, say, a magazine layout than to a coffee-table book; the magazine is likely to be consumed more rapidly. This is,

The wide-angle distortion and the position in the picture of the mansion bottom make it seem to move left, out of the frame, as in the diagram below.

The diagrams below show how the pictures opposite convey dynamic tension: one by a radial movement; the other by creating tension between two planes.

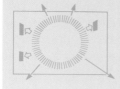

Diverging lines and movement are the key to dynamic tension. In the photograph of the mansion the branches of the tree and the trunk's strong curving shadow have powerful outward movement, which is exaggerated by the 20mm wide-angle lens.

of course, to some extent an opinion, but nevertheless these problems do arise and should be taken into consideration.

The techniques for achieving dynamic tension are, however, fairly straightforward, as the examples here show. While not trying to reduce it to a formula, the ideal combination is a variety of diagonals in different directions, opposed lines, and any structural device that leads the eye outwards, preferably in competing directions. Reviewing some of the previous projects, this argues against, for example, using circular enclosing structures, and suggests that good use can be made of a powerful standby, eye-lines.

Even though symmetrical, the lines here have considerable movement and tension, because the bright central glow pushes the attention out to the more conventionally exposed parts of the picture.

Eye-lines and the direction in which things face are responsible for diverging lines of view in this shot. The man faces left, and his stance reinforces this, while the hopper of molten metal faces forward and to the right. The two pull visually against each other.

Mud tiles laid out to dry in a village street suggested a photograph that exploited the strong linear arrangement. The most graphic treatment was a 20mm wide-angle shot, close to the ground but including the horizon. This approach produced the maximum linear perspective, emphasizing the dynamic tension set up by the curvature and convergence of the lines of tiles.

CONTROLLING THE EYE

In the photograph left the eye is first drawn to the foreground, and then, because of the converging curves, travels upwards and into the back of the picture, as in the first of the lower diagrams right. Finding the cyclist, it picks up his movement, and so travels back down to the foreground, as in second diagram.

The three upper diagrams right show how lines, shapes and points all contribute to the spiralling movement in the photograph of the men on the quayside below. The "points" in this case are the three men and the way they are arranged in the frame encourages the eye to move from one to the next.

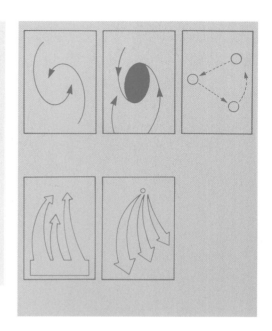

PROJECT: Producing dynamic tension

If you are used to framing shots in a balanced, regular way (which is normal and what comes natural to most people), you may have to make a deliberate effort to inject dynamic tension. Make this a project for the next time you see a suitable subject. As you can see from the photographs here, diagonals and sweeping curves lend themselves to this approach. You are likely to find these in an urban setting, and a wide-angle lens will exaggerate them. Experiment with the camera position and also with the angle – try tilting the camera or skewing the horizon. Movement towards the frame's edge also helps, so look out for a vehicle heading out of the frame, or a person looking out.

The structure of the picture right is essentially a spiral composed of three principal curved lines.

The raised head and extraordinary snout of the male gharial opposite cut across the image diagonally, setting up dynamic tension with the square frame.

DIVIDING THE IMAGE

Any image, of any kind, automatically creates a division of the picture frame. Something like a prominent horizon line does this very obviously, but even a small object against a bland background (a point, in other words) makes an implied division. Look at any of the pictures in this book which comprise a single small subject: shifting the position of the subject changes the areas into which the frame is divided.

Proportion

There are, naturally, an infinite number of possible divisions, but the most interesting ones are those that bear a definable relationship to each other. Division is essentially a matter of proportion, and different proportions evoke certain responses in the viewer, whether they were calculated exactly or not.

Before you even take a photograph, consider that the frame contains its own proportions – 2:3 in the case of the most commonly used 35mm cameras. This is a proportion based on two simple numbers, and the frame can also be sub-divided according to this ratio. There are many

Familiarity with the proportions of the Golden Section makes it easy to reproduce them in a composition without calculation. Needless to say, in this photograph no great thought went into the sub-division of the frame; it was done in an instant, by intuition. The lines overlaid on the lower picture show how the composition reflects this harmonious principle, which was already appreciated in classical Greece 2500 years ago.

other simple ratios that can be used to divide a frame, such as 1:1, 2:1, 4:5, 5:8.

However, these proportions produce an essentially static division. By contrast, a dynamic division can be made by constructing more interesting ratios. The Golden Section, which was known to the Greeks, is the best known "harmonious" division. It is based on pure geometry, and as a photographer you will never need to construct it. The importance of the division lies in the fact that all the areas are integrally related; the ratio of the small section to the large one is the same as that of the large section

An overlay of lines shows how the picture right was composed, and draws attention to the deliberate alignment of boat and castle on the left and two boats on the right.

INTEGRATED DIVISIONS

Coherent methods of dividing the same shape of frame as in the photograph above include those using a series of numbers and those based geometrically on the frame's own sides. Most of the useful sub-divisions are rectilinear, but diagonals can also be used to create harmonious triangular spaces, as in the diagrams right.

to the complete frame. They are tied together, hence the idea that they give a sense of harmony. The logic of this may not be clear at first, but it underlies more than just the sub-division of a picture frame. The argument is that objective physical principles underlie harmony. In this case, they are geometric, and while we may not be aware of them in operation, they still produce a predictable effect.

Slightly below the center, the horizon's position is conventional in the first shot below. *In the version below it the low horizon gives a more dynamic composition, making the sky dominate and lending a more spacious feeling. With the horizon just above the center, the first picture* below right *emphasizes the foreground water. In the final shot a slightly different camera position, and symmetry introduced through foreground detail, makes the horizon's position a little less important.*

35mm frame

In the sub-division of a standard 35mm frame according to the Golden Section, the proportions are, in fact, very close to those of the frame itself, 2:3 (and so the ratio of the shorter to the longer, 2:3, is fairly similar to that of the longer to the total, 3:5). We may be able to ignore the geometry, but we can not ignore the fact that these proportions are fundamentally satisfying. Notice also that, by dividing the frame in both directions, an intersection is produced, and this makes a generally satisfying location for a point, or any other focus of attention. Compare this with the off-center placement of a small subject on page 81.

The Golden Section is not the only way of making a harmonious division. Another basis is a sequence of numbers in which each is the sum of the previous two, hence

... 1, 2, 3, 5, 8, 13 ... In yet another method, the frame is sub-divided according to the ratio of its own sides. There is, indeed, a massive variety of sub-divisions that obey some internal principle, and they can all make interesting images that work. But how can the photographer make sensible use of these principles? Nobody is going to use a calculator to plan the division of a photograph. Intuitive composition is the only practical approach for the majority of pictures. The most useful approach to dividing a frame into areas is to prime your eye by becoming familiar with the nuances of harmony in different proportions.

The horizon

Probably the most common of all situations in photography where the frame must be divided cleanly and precisely is the one that

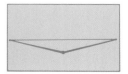

includes the horizon line. In landscapes of the type shown on these pages it becomes the dominant graphic element, the more so if there are no outstanding points of interest in the scene.

Plainly, if the line of the horizon is the only significant graphic element, placing it becomes a matter of some importance. There is a natural tendency to place the line lower in the frame than higher. This probably derives from the association of the bottom of the picture frame with a base; a low position for anything gives a greater sense of stability. This apart, the question of the exact position remains open. One method is to use the linear relationships just described on the preceding pages. Another is to balance the tones or colours (see pages 270-5).

Compositional priorities

Yet another method is to divide the frame according to what you see as the intrinsic importance of the ground and sky. For instance, the foreground may simply be uninteresting, distracting, or in some other way unwanted. In that case, you might

In the sequence left *the unattractive foreground is a problem. In the first photograph, where the foreground is both dull and visually untidy, the interest lies in a narrow band across the middle of the picture. Lowering the horizon solves the problem of the foreground in the second picture, but there are not enough clouds to justify a composition with such a large expanse of sky. In the final version, darkening the upper part of the sky with a graduated filter brings the eye down to the hills, which was the original intention of the picture.*

place the horizon low, by default. A more positive reason for the same proportions would be that the sky has some visual interest, notably clouds. If, on the other hand, there is some distinct feature of interest in the foreground, this will encourage a higher position for the horizon. Indeed, if the sky has no graphic value and the foreground has plenty of interest, it may make more sense to reverse whatever sub-division you choose, and place the horizon much closer to the top of the frame.

Another important division is often that between the foreground and the background. From our normal visual experience, we assume that in most scenes there is something that we look at (the subject), and there is a setting against which it stands or lies (the background). One stands forward, the other recedes. One is important, and the reason for taking a photograph, the other is just there because something has to occupy the rest of the frame.

In most picture situations this is essentially true. We select something as the purpose of the image, and it is more often than not a discrete object or group of objects. It may be a person, a still-life, a group of buildings, a part of something. What is behind the focus of interest is the background, and in many well-designed and satisfying images, it complements the subject. Typically, we already know what the sub-

ject is before the photography begins. The main point of interest has been decided on: a human figure, perhaps, or a horse or car. If it is possible to control the circumstances of the picture, the next decision may well be to choose the background: that is, to decide which of the locally available settings will show off the subject to its best advantage.

There are, however, circumstances when the photographer can choose which of two

components in a view is to be the figure and which is to be the ground against which the figure is seen. This opportunity occurs when there is some ambiguity in the image, and it helps to have a minimum of realistic detail. In this, photography is at an initial disadvantage to illustration, because it is hard to remove the inherent realism in a photograph. The viewer knows that the image is of something real, and so the eye searches for clues.

In this picture of a monk praying at a stupa, the subject is not immediately obvious because the figure is silhouetted against the golden wall of a large pagoda. The light and dark areas are equal in size, and the background is light. These contrasts provide alternation in the composition, making it more dynamic.

A similar graphic treatment – the use of a silhouette – to that seen in the photograph of the monk on the opposite page is exploited in this picture of a perching stork. However, although the alternation between and light areas is striking in the version below left, *the untidy branches and the strip of sky on the left diminish its impact by drawing the eye away from the main subject.*

Cropping in on the left of the picture, as in the version below right, *simplifies the distribution of the areas of tone, and so improves the alternation between the light and dark areas.*

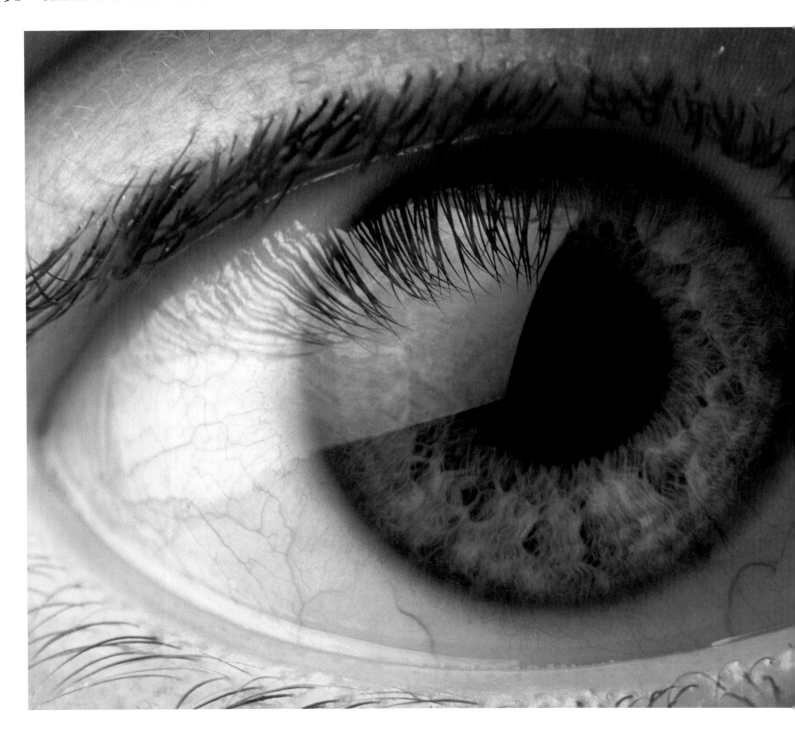

PICTURE SCALE

It is tempting to think that bigger is better. If you make a small, postcard-sized print from a photograph and then use the enlarger to produce an 8 x 10 inch (203 x 254mm) print you will almost certainly be impressed by the latter. If you then go up to 16 x 20 inches (406 x 508mm), that will seem more powerful still. This is true for each individual image, but consider how it will be for a succession of images. When everything is the same size, the effects of enlargement are, to an extent, dissipated. A more inter-

The graphic valuation of magnification is that it can give us unaccustomed views, as in the shot of an eye left.

Wide-angle views like the one below distort the image largely because we see it small. If this image were large enough and close enough to fill your field of view, it would not seem distorted at the edges.

esting approach is to display images at different scales, according to the particular needs of each, and according to how different photographs relate to each other when seen side by side.

If you have to choose between scales of reproduction, certain photographs need to be presented large, while others can survive being quite small. The images on the following pages demonstrate the difference. First, the photograph of the mass of pelicans in Kenya's Rift Valley. Seen large, this is an impressive picture, but small it is meaningless. Reproduced very large it is a very powerful image.

Demands of the subject

There are really two factors at work here; why the picture *needs* to be big and why it *deserves* to be big. The first is easy to see. The pelicans are packed so closely together, they are a jumble of form and colour. Only by being close can we distinguish one from another. We are not used to seeing this many animals at once, and so need some

help to appreciate the spectacle – such as the help of a big picture.

It is also a waste to be mean with the proportions of this shot, because the essential appeal is the staggering number of birds. The only way to do this is for the picture to be as big as possible, and for the viewer to stand close to it, so that the image fills the frame of view.

In the case of the portrait of the Chinese boy, there are no problems, of course, with reproducing this picture large, but if we shrink it to just 1¼ inches (30mm) across it still reads well. The essential elements in the picture remain easy to see; both the information (principally the expression on the child's face) and the design (the blocks of tone and colour, and their arrangement) are decipherable. This picture survives a reduction in size for two reasons: the design is simple, and its content is familiar. The photograph is composed of simple, flat

blocks, unmodulated by shadows because of the frontal lighting, and the principal subject is a face. Faces are one visual subject with which everyone is extremely familiar, and we can read an expression at a surprising distance. Hence, this photograph works even when small.

Over-enlargement

Both the boy and the pelicans are fairly straightforward examples. The solutions are logical and most designers would come up with them. However, there are sometimes opportunities for treating certain photographs in an unexpected way. Not a great deal can be done by reducing size – we then run into the problem of illegibility – but startling effects are possible by enlarging a picture well beyond what is reasonable. Again, the page size here limits the effect we can show, but the picture of the eye on page 92 gives some idea. Not only is it much larger, even here, than it needs to be; it is actually uncomfortable to look at. This is not just because the eye is magnified and we can see details of the iris that most of us are probably unfamiliar with. It is because we are looking at somebody from intimately close. Many pictures that contain intimacy, or aggression, have great impact when over-enlarged.

A separate consideration is the effect that the scale of reproduction has on the perspective effects of different focal lengths. We are used to compressed views from tele-

Pelicans, as in the photograph on the opposite page, are obvious enough as a subject, and yet their appearance becomes unusual when they are packed densely in a small space. When the picture is small, they become almost unrecognizable.

photos and stretched views from wide-angle lenses, but these effects are mainly attributable to the fact that the photographs are taken at one angle of view and seen at another.

Perspective

Imagine that you stand in front of a series of prints at a distance that gives you about a 40° view of each (40° is approximately what you would get by holding something about 18 inches – 450 mm – long at arm's length in front of you). As that is roughly the view you get with a standard lens, any photograph taken with one will look per-

fectly normal at that distance.

A view taken with a 400mm telephoto, however, has an angle of only 5° across the longer side; your view of the print is too close for a normal perspective effect. Equally, a 20mm photograph taken at an angle of 84° no longer wraps around your vision. If you stand right back from the telephoto photograph or much closer to the wide-angle view, they will lose their distortion. In practical terms, of course, the alteration of the perspective effect which is achieved by changing lenses is exactly what many photographers appreciate about employing different focal lengths.

Our natural interest in and familiarity with other people's faces makes them easy to read even when the image is small, as can be seen by comparing the large picture of the Chinese boy below with the much-reduced shot.

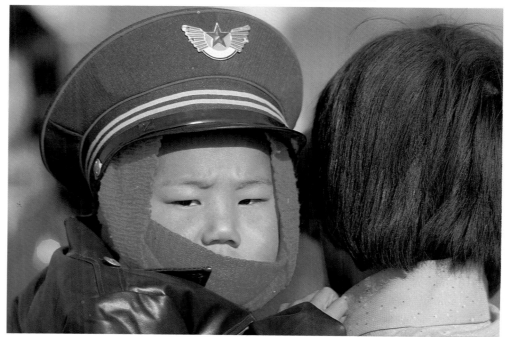

PICTURE SHAPE

We have already seen how the frame of a photograph can interact with the image. The shape of the picture clearly has a strong influence too, and here we look at the dynamics of the main camera formats.

In theory, there are no restrictions to the picture format; it can always be cropped. In practice, however, two things work against this. One is that most photographers stick to taking pictures and leave the production of the final prints to someone else, usually a photo-finishing laboratory. And if, like most professional photographers, you shoot colour reversal film, the end product is exactly the format that you saw through the viewfinder: a transparency.

The second reason why shooting unusual formats is not so easy is that, unless you place a specially cut frame mask in the viewfinder, the pressure is strong to compose intuitively right up to the edges of the viewfinder frame. This is why many pho-tographers do not care for square-format rollfilm cameras. The manufacturer's argu-ment has always been that a square format allows the photographer to compose freely vertically or horizontally. However, it takes long experience to ignore the parts of the image that are not being used.

2:3 format

Most photography, then, is built on a few rigidly-defined formats, unlike other graphic arts. By far the most common format is the horizontal 2:3 frame – that of the standard 35mm camera. The reason for these propor-tions is a matter of historical accident; there are no compelling aesthetic reasons why it should be so and more natural proportions would probably be less elongated. Most printing papers are, after all, in 4:5 propor-tions, and most rollfilm formats 6:7. Nevertheless, the popularity of the 35mm format demonstrates how easily our sense of intuitive composition adapts. This format is now the norm in photography.

There are two reasons why the 35mm format is mainly used horizontally. The first is pure ergonomics. It is difficult to design a camera that is to be used at eye-level so that it is just as easy to photograph vertical-ly as horizontally. Indeed, few manufactur-ers have even bothered. Normal 35mm SLRs and rangefinder cameras are made to be used for horizontal pictures. Turning them on their side is just not as comfortable, and most photographers tend to avoid it.

Horizontal vision

The second reason is more fundamental. Our binocular vision means that we see horizontally. There is no frame as such, as human vision involves paying attention to local detail and scanning a scene rapidly, rather than taking in a sharp overall view all at once. Our natural view of the world is in the form of a vaguely-edged, horizontal

The formats on the opposite page are the most common in photography. Their sizes as drawn here are approximately in proportion to their popularity.

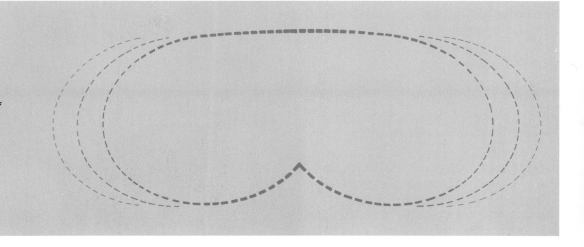

HUMAN VISION

Our natural view of the world is binocular and horizontal, so a horizontal picture format seems entirely normal. As the diagram right demonstrates, the edges of vision appear vague because our eyes focus sharply at only a small angle, and the surrounding image becomes more and more blurred the further away it is from this area of sharp focus.

The correspondence of the line of the horizon with the format makes a horizontal frame a natural and aesthetically satisfying choice for most long scenic views, as shown in the photograph right. In this shot, taken just before nightfall, the land's contrast with the sky is emphasized by its depiction as a silhouette.

3:4
4.5 × 6cm rollfilm cameras

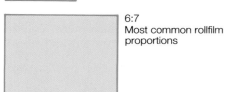

6:7
Most common rollfilm proportions

4:5, 8:10
Normal printing paper and sheet film proportions

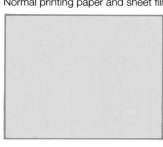

The horizontal format is not best suited to vertical subjects like figures and tall buildings. But one technique that can make it work is to off-center the subject as in the picture below and diagram left, since this persuades the eye to move horizontally across the frame.

2:3
Standard 35mm frame

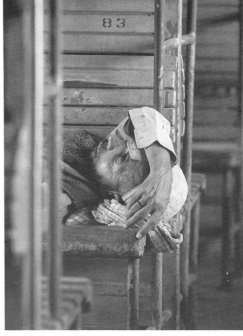

In the shot left the mass of people on a Disneyland paddle steamer is the main focus of attention. As the principal subject, they are placed below the center.

oval, and a normal horizontal film frame is a reasonable approximation.

The net result is that a horizontal frame is natural and unremarkable. It influences the composition of an image, but not in an insistent, outstanding way. It conforms to the horizon, and so to most overall land-scapes and general views. The horizontal component to the frame encourages a hori-zontal arrangement of elements, naturally enough. It is marginally more natural to place an image lower in the frame than higher – this tends to enhance the sensation of stability – but there are usually many other influences. Placing a subject or hori-zon high in the frame produces a slight downward-looking sensation, which can have mildly negative associations.

One of several classes of subject which suit a vertical format is the standing human figure left.

The sleeper's head above is best placed slightly low for a vertical shot and to one side for a horizontal shot.

Vertical

As explained, there is a slight natural resistance to photographing vertically, and if you make a rough count of how many of your shots are indeed vertical, you may be surprised at how few there are; certainly if you use a 35mm camera. Professional photographers usually make an effort to shoot vertically as well as horizontally because of the demands of their clients; most printed pages are vertical.

For naturally vertical subjects, this is the normal choice of format, and the human figure, standing, is the most commonly found vertical subject. The elongation of the normal 35mm frame is ideal; a fortunate coincidence, as in most other respects the 2:3 proportions are rarely completely satis-

Balancing two predominant but unequal areas, as with the altar and the window in the photograph above, reduces the significance of the frame.

factory. The usual tendency with a dominant single subject is to push the focus of attention sideways in the horizontal picture and downwards in the vertical image. This shows an inclination to avoid the upper part of a vertical frame. The naturalness of horizontal vision reinforces the eye's preference for scanning from side to side.

As with horizontal frames, there is a normal assumption that the bottom of the picture is a base; a level surface on which other things can rest. This is why it seems more natural than not to use the lower part

Radial and other symmetrical subjects suit the square format below left. Most subjects do not, although a definite axis – here vertical – works in the shot below.

of the frame. The 2:3 proportions of a 35mm frame are a little extreme, however, and this often leaves the picture's upper part underused.

Square

While all other photographic frames are rectangular, with varying proportions, one is fixed: the square. A few major current cameras have this unusual format, including the Hasselblad and Bronica, but a number of old twin lens reflex models also feature it. It is unusual in that very few images lend themselves well to square composition. It is the most difficult format to work with, and most design strategies for a square frame are concerned with escaping the tyranny of its equilibrium.

The reason why most subjects are ill-suited to a square arrangement has, in part, to do with the axis of the subject. Few shapes are so compact that they have no alignment. Most things are longer in one direction than in another, and it is natural to align the main axis of an image with the longer sides of a rectangular picture frame. Hence, most broad landscape views are generally handled as horizontal pictures, and most standing figures as verticals.

The square, however, has absolutely no bias. Its sides are in perfect 1:1 proportions, and its influence is a very precise and stable division of space. Here lies the second reason for the unsympathetic nature of square proportions; they impose a formal rigidity on the image. It is hard to escape the feeling of geometry when working with a square frame, and the symmetry of the sides and corners reminds the eye of the center.

Occasionally a precise symmetrical image is interesting; it makes a change from the normally imprecise design of most photographs. However, a few such images quickly become a surfeit. It is fairly normal for photographers who work consistently with a square format camera to imagine a vertical or horizontal direction to the picture, and to crop the resulting image later. Practically, this means composing fairly loosely in the viewfinder, to allow a certain amount of free space either at the sides or at the top and bottom. In either case, it is not ideal, and only the relatively large film size in a medium format camera like the Hasselblad makes it practical.

Panoramic

A panoramic frame has a special place in photography. Although its proportions sound extreme, it is for many images a more accommodating format than, for instance, a square. Through usage and familiarity, the 2:3 proportions of a 35mm frame are the reference standard for the rectangular format.

If elongated so that the horizontal is more than twice the vertical, however, the frame starts to behave differently, and no longer has the dynamics of an ordinary rectangle. This is because we see by scanning, not by

Much of the sky and the foreground are removed in this traditional use of a panoramic frame, leaving the eye free to follow the rhythm of the horizon line.

A panoramic frame can allow an interesting treatment of a subject, as in the picture above, *where the columns vertically divide the horizontal image into three sections.*

Breaking the normal rules, a panoramic frame is used in the photograph below *to exaggerate an abstract treatment of an adobe church. Compressing the image compels the eye to consider the geometry and texture.*

taking in a scene in a single, frozen instant. The eye's focus of attention roams around the view, usually very quickly, and builds up the information in the visual cortex. All of the normal photographic formats – and most painting formats, for that matter – are areas that can be absorbed in one rapid scanning sequence. The normal process of looking at the picture is to take in as much as possible in one prolonged glance, and then to return to interesting details.

We can do this with a 2:3 frame, but 1:3 and 1:4 proportions allow the eye to consider only a part of the image at a time. This replicates the way we look at any real scene. Apart from adding an element of realism to the picture, this slows down the viewing process and, in theory at least, prolongs the interest of exploring the image. All of this depends, however, on the photograph being reproduced fairly large and viewed from sufficiently close.

CROPPING

Think of cropping as a design option that is open to you after taking the picture, a way of deferring design decisions, and even of exploring new ways of organizing an image. Practically, it is tied to the enlargement of a print; small format transparencies do not lend themselves so easily to adjustments of the frame, because of their size.

Assuming you will produce a print, whether from a black-and-white negative, colour negative or a colour transparency, the final crop will be on the baseboard of the enlarger. You can use the enlarging easel as a cropping guide, but it is usually easier and more relaxing to experiment earlier, with the original film, on a contact print or a rough print. For this exercise, some kind of opaque adjustable mask is needed. There are one or two proprietary designs available, but you can make your own.

Framing

Why black frames? Most images have at least some tone at the borders, so a dark frame provides a stronger contrast. For transparencies viewed on a light box, the surrounding light can be very distracting, and also give a false impression that the image is darker than it really is, hiding shadow detail. When viewing transparencies, cover up as much as possible of the rest of the light box. If you take a significant number of black-background pictures, however, you will find white masks more valuable for prints. One idea is to cut the L-frames or window masks from card that is black on one side and white on the reverse.

It is important not to think of cropping as a design panacea or as an excuse for not being decisive at the time of shooting. It can lull you into imagining that you can perform a significant proportion of photography in the darkroom.

PROJECTS: Cropping

See what you can make of the two photographs shown on these four pages. It is best to undertake your own versions of cropping before looking at how they have been handled here. In the case of the misty Scottish landscape, simply see how many workable, distinct images you can make, without any limitations on format. Do not, however, crop in to less than half the area of the frame; even though the original was shot on 4 x 5 inch film and the resolution is good, over-enlargement lowers the picture quality.

With the deserted Thai temple in the middle of a rice field, the object is to limit yourself to one size and format of frame, as shown. In fact, what we have done here is to make 35mm frame size crops on a 4 x 5 inch transparency (see page 105).

Having undertaken your own cropping of these two pictures, select prints of your own and do similar exercises. In order to give yourself the maximum opportunity for selecting different images out

Even when a print does not need to be cropped, placing a black border round it opposite, left *when viewing helps to concentrate attention. In the case of a basically light-toned image, it also emphasizes the edges of the picture as a compositional check.*

Although a 35mm image is already small and leaves little space for major cropping and enlargement, there is often room for altering the proportions – cropping either vertically for a more panoramic view, or horizontally for a squarer picture opposite, right.

Use the full-frame print opposite *as a basic image within which to construct as many different framings as, to your eye, work effectively.*

L-frames below top left are used as cropping masks for prints up to 10 x 12 inches; adjustable masks below bottom left for transparencies from 35mm up to 6 x 7cm; and window frames below right for 4 x 5 inch and medium-format transparencies.

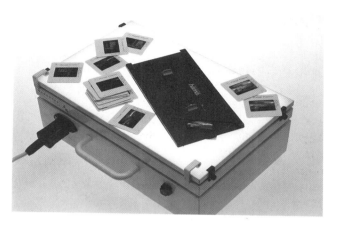

The photographs on this page illustrate three different ways of cropping the landscape on the previous page: panoramic, horizontal and vertical.

of one basic scene, you may find that a wide-angle landscape view is the easiest type of picture, as in these examples. It is almost like confronting the scene in real life, and choosing a shot with a longer focal length.

Let us look at the kind of decisions involved in both of these methods of cropping. In the Scottish landscape, the original framing has clearly been chosen to make something of the rippled clouds at the top of the frame, and the horizon has been placed correspondingly low. This in itself reduces our options a little.

Perhaps the first, obvious crop is to ignore the high clouds and concentrate instead on the mist-shrouded qualities of the rocky pillars. Now, once we have dispensed with the clouds, there are no limits to how far down we can crop the top of the frame. In this instance, I have chosen to reverse the proportions of land to sky, and to take the opportunity of making a panorama.

Next, what if we try to crop in and still retain moderate horizontal proportions? Unfortunately, it seems that if there is to be any significant area of sky it should go right to the existing top of the frame, simply in order to have some tone and weight in that part of the picture. Cropping in at the sides does very little to enhance the importance of the pillars. The only reasonable option will be to crop the bottom, and go for a horizon line that almost coincides with the base of the picture.

Is a vertical crop possible? Given that an upright

Use a proprietary brand of adjustable mask to experiment with different ways of cropping a 4 x 5 inch transparency of the rice field shown on this page.

The crops on the picture below *have all been made to one format of frame: 35mm, but yield a wide variety of different approaches to the subject.*

While the atmospheric landscape above *works well in the form in which it is seen here, cropping allows other, equally forceful images to be produced from it.*

image has even more need of the tonal weight of the clouds, the best that we can do is to crop in at the sides. The choices are to do with selecting the most interesting shapes on the horizon.

The Thai landscape requires a slightly different approach. We have used a transparency here, but on a print the best technique is to make a fixed window and slide it around the picture. The temple itself must remain the dominant element in the image – there is nothing else – and the choices are in the placement of the horizon line and in whether or not to include the clump of bamboo on the left. In this instance, placing the horizon low gives a more spacious, open feeling and emphasizes what is happening in the sky (sunrise and some threatening clouds). Raising the horizon line draws attention to the rice in the field.

THE IMPORTANCE OF LINE

Horizontal lines

Several arrangements of points, as seen opposite, produce the effect of being joined, which leads naturally on to a major group of elements in an image: lines. Whereas in illustration a line is often the first mark made, in photography it occurs less obviously and usually by implication. In this respect it is similar to the way we actually see the world, where most lines are in fact edges. Contrast plays the biggest role in defining lines visually. It takes many forms: contrast between light and shade, between areas of different colour, between textures, between shapes, and so on.

Direction and movement

As you might expect, the graphic qualities of lines are rather stronger than those of points. Like the latter, they establish location, a static feature, but they also contain the dynamic features of direction and movement along their length. And, because the frame of a photograph is itself constructed of lines, these invite a natural comparison of angle and length.

Expression

Lines also have some capacity for expression. It is perhaps best not to make too much of this, but different forms of line have distinct associations. Horizontal lines, for instance, have a more placid effect than diagonal lines; a zig-zag can be exciting. Strong, definite lines can express boldness; thin, curving lines, delicacy, and so on.

However, whereas in abstract art this can be used as the very basis for expression, it is not realistic to expect to make great use of it in photography.

Horizontal bias

These associations, which will be described in more detail on the following pages, are real enough, but in a photograph the subject often overwhelms them. Nevertheless, being sensitive to them pays dividends when the opportunity arises.

The horizontal is, in more senses that one, the baseline in composition. As already described on pages 96-8, there is a distinct horizontal component in the way we see. Our frame of vision is horizontal, and the eyes scan most easily from side to side. Not surprisingly, horizontal lines are visually the most comfortable. Moreover, the horizon is

Even irregular groupings resolve with distance into horizontal bands, then lines. In the shot left such bands exist only because of the acute angle of view.

The diagram below shows the tendency of groups of objects to appear as horizontal bands as distance increases.

A horizontal string of points implies that there is a line connecting them. If these points are sufficiently close together, as in the photograph left *of pelicans, they become a line.*

The photograph above *is a very precise example of how lines are formed by contrast. Here light and shade from a row of trees form bands of diminishing width along the drive of an English country estate.*

a fundamental reference line – the most familiar of any – and even gravity is a reminder that a horizontal surface is a base that supports.

For all these reasons, horizontal lines generally express stability, weight, calm and restfulness. Through their association with the horizon they can also suggest distance and breadth. Note, though, that generally speaking such expressive qualities only

It is hard in the shot of a Pathan hamlet right *to separate the content of the picture from the graphic effect of the strong horizontal line formed by the low buildings.*

become important when there is little real information to be derived from the content of the photograph.

Vertical lines

The vertical is the second primary component of the frame, and so is naturally seen in terms of alignment with the format and with the sides of the picture. A single vertical form understandably sits more comfortably in a vertical format than a horizontal. A series of verticals, however, acquires a horizontal structure, as can be seen from the photograph of the leg-rowers on this page. In this picture, the use of a horizontal frame actually allows more to be made of the series of vertical lines.

The horizontal line in the photograph of the American West above right is formed by the local horizon, and the vertical by a desert road rising up the slope. The static quality that these two lines create has been alleviated by slightly off-setting both within the frame.

Parallel verticals are often best suited to a horizontal frame, which gives them a greater spread, as in the telephoto shot of leg-rowers right.

The first diagram below shows how vertical and horizontal lines are combined in the shot opposite;and the second how the picture has been composed to include a car at the visually crucial point of intersection.

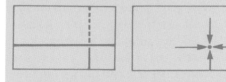

The diagram below illustrates how closely spaced vertical lines benefit from a horizontal frame.

Vertical subjects

A vertical line is the main component in the image of a human figure, and of a tree. Its direction is the force of gravity, or something escaping it. Without the inbuilt associations of a supporting base that give a horizontal line much of its character, a vertical line usually has more of a sense of speed and movement, either up or down. Seen as uprights from a level viewpoint, vertical forms can, under the right circumstances, confront the viewer. The dark tree-trunk on page 91 has some of this quality. Several vertical forms can have associations of a barrier, like posts, or a line of men facing the camera. To an extent, they can express strength and power.

On a practical level, exact alignment is very important, as it is for horizontal lines, also. In a photograph, both are immediately compared by the eye with the frame edges, and even the slightest discrepancy is immediately noticeable.

Equilibrium

Together, horizontal and vertical lines are complementary. They create an equilibrium in the sense that their energies are perpendicular to each other; each one acts as a stop to the other. They can also create a primary sensation of balance, because there is an underlying association of standing upright, supported on a level surface. If horizontal and vertical lines are used together strongly and simply in an image, they can produce a solid, satisfying feeling.

In the photograph left the vertical lines on a high-rise building provide unity and offer a counterpoint to the rounded forms of the church. The latter quality contrasts expressively with the associations of confrontation that all massed vertical lines possess.

Through its foreshortening effect, a powerful telephoto lens converts what would otherwise be diminishing perspective into a vertical design in the picture right. As in many shots with a dominant line, some discontinuity adds interest. Here it is the ragged line of the street's right side.

Diagonal lines

Freed from the need to be aligned exactly in the picture frame, diagonal lines have a variety of direction denied to horizontals and verticals. In practical terms, this means that in photographs that do not depend on a horizon or on some other absolute point of reference, there is an extra element of choice: the angle of the line.

Of all lines, diagonals introduce the most dynamism into a picture. They are highly active, with an even stronger expression of direction and speed than verticals. They bring life and activity precisely because they represent unresolved tension. If the relative stability and strength of horizontals and verticals is because of their symbolic associations with gravity, the tension in looking at a diagonal has the same source. It has an unresolved and unstable position; in the process of falling, if you like. Indeed, structurally most scenes and things are composed of horizontals and verticals, rather than diagonals, particularly in manmade environments.

For the shot of shrimps left a composition was chosen with all lines as diagonals. This arrangement sets up the greatest contrast of angles, adding interest.

For once, the diagonal in the photograph below is real rather than an optical effect. The shot is framed so that the steps exactly bisect half of the frame.

Controlling diagonals

When seen through the viewfinder, most diagonals appear as a result of viewpoint – oblique views of horizontal or vertical lines. This is very useful indeed, because they are,

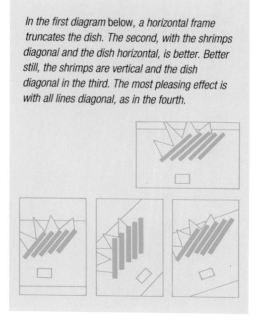

In the first diagram below, a horizontal frame truncates the dish. The second, with the shrimps diagonal and the dish horizontal, is better. Better still, the shrimps are vertical and the dish diagonal in the third. The most pleasing effect is with all lines diagonal, as in the fourth.

as a consequence, much more under the control of the photographer than are horizontals and verticals. This is discussed in more detail below .

In normal eye-level views, horizontal lines that run away from the eye converge in a photograph; this is the normal effect of perspective. By converging, they become diagonals, or at least most of them do. As this is entirely familiar, diagonals carry some associations of depth and distance, particularly if there is more than one and they converge. Considerable use can be made of this in trying to manipulate the sense of depth in an image. Including or strengthening diagonals in a landscape (often no more than a matter of aligning objects or edges) will tend to improve the impression of depth; even the arrangement of subjects in a still-life can produce, quite artificially, a

feeling of distance. These techniques are explored more fully later, on pages 160-3.

Long focal length

These perspective diagonals appear stronger through a wide-angle lens, the more so from a close viewpoint. Much of the usefulness of such lenses – 24mm, 20mm and less on a 35mm camera – derives from this simple fact (see pages 136-41 for more on this). However, telephoto lenses also have their uses in treating diagonals. By giving a selective view, a lens with a long focal length can emphasize one distinct part of a diagonal.

Repetition

Oblique views from some height typically produce the kind of diagonals seen in the photograph of the bathing tents on page

112. What strengthens these particular images is the repetition of diagonal lines; the compressing effect that a long lens has on perspective makes them appear parallel. A wide-angle lens used from a closer standpoint would cause the lines appear to converge in the image.

Dynamism

From the point of view of design, diagonals have two very important qualities. One, already mentioned, is that they activate an image, making it more dynamic and consequently eye-catching. This liveliness is greatest when other lines such as horizontals and verticals are present as contrast, but it still works without.

This is because the frame edges themselves give a certain amount of contrast, as you can see from the photograph of the

A wide-angle lens – 20mm on a 35mm camera – was used in the photograph right, taken in Italy, to exaggerate the dynamic effect of the building's lines.

Muslim women praying. This activating effect is in proportion to the angle that the diagonal forms with the edges of the frame. The maximum for a single diagonal, or parallel set, is 45°, but with two or three different diagonals combined, the strongest effect is when the relative angles are all great without being equal. There is never any point in trying to calculate these angles in advance, even in a still-life shot which would allow enough time. It is always better to make such calculations by eye. Look at the photograph and diagrams of the Japanese shrimps on page 110 as an example.

Movement

The other essential quality in a successful photograph of this kind is movement. A diagonal leads the eye along it, more than any other line. This makes it an extremely valuable device for encouraging the attention to move in certain directions in a photograph, something we will consider in some detail on pages 116-17.

Oblique views of right angles produce zig-zags, a chevron effect of multiple diagonals. The angles are joined, so the impression of movement along the diagonal is maintained. This dynamic effect can be seen in the pair of photographs of bathing tents below. *In the diagonal version of the beach scene* below left, *the graphic movement is single-minded (the directional bias is set by the walking figures). In the zig-zag version* below right, *the change of directional bias produces more internal activity in the shot.*

An oblique view with a telephoto lens, as in the picture of women praying at a Muslim festival above, *gives a diagonal result different from the expanding perspectives of a wide-angle lens. Here the raised viewpoint achieves a consistent and definite effect. A second design point is that the vertical figure of the child makes a strong contrast.*

PROJECT: Creating diagonals

Apart from changing focal length and viewpoint in order to manipulate the perspective effect on diagonals, tilting and rotating the camera can be used. If, however, the horizon or a similar reference is included, the effect may look contrived. It is obviously easier in strongly upward and downward-looking views, and probably easiest of all in close views; still-life images in particular lend themselves to this (they also usually allow rearrangement of the objects themselves in order to create diagonals). Apart from the examples here, you can see this in several other photographs in this book. A good example is the gold bars on page 67.

A wide-angle lens used close to a long wall produces a strong diagonal that radiates from the vanishing point. In the shot below of Hadrian's Wall, in the north of England, the 20mm lens and the composition were chosen to introduce visual drama.

In the photograph below, the diagonals were enhanced by the use of a neutral graduated filter, angled as shown so as to darken the sky in alignment with the diagonal line of the top of the wall.

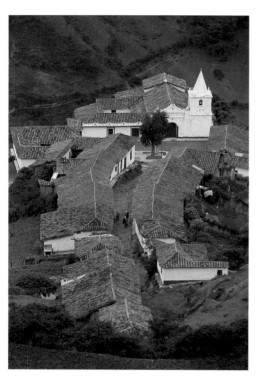

Rhythm

The progressive quality of a curve gives it a rhythm which straight lines lack (zig-zags are an obvious exception). The sense of movement along a curve is also greater. For example, if you were to animate the image of a vehicle by streaking its tail lights behind it, the greatest impression of speed would be if these were slightly curved.

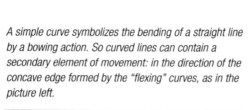

A simple curve symbolizes the bending of a straight line by a bowing action. So curved lines can contain a secondary element of movement: in the direction of the concave edge formed by the "flexing" curves, as in the picture left.

Curves

So far, we have been concerned only with straight lines. Curves have entirely different qualities, both graphically and expressively. As a line, the unique feature of a curve is that it contains a progressive change of direction, and so avoids, on the face of it, any direct comparison with the horizontal and vertical edges of the frame. Many curves are, however, aligned mainly in one direction or another, as can be seen from the examples shown here; in another way a curve can be thought of as a series of straight lines at progressively changing angles. For these reasons, curves do interact with straight lines in an image.

In a graceful act of intertwining, the curves of the two spiral staircases create a forceful effect in the photograph right.

In the picture left the curved pattern of oil globules in sea water forms a contrasting background for the diagonal line of baby shrimps.

Several concentric lines reinforce each other in the picture on the opposite page. A strong sense of movement is felt, even with these static subjects, because the rows approach the camera. A low viewpoint, giving an acute angle of view to the lines, strengthens the curvature.

This movement, however, is smooth, and many of the other associations of curved lines are in the areas of being gentle, flowing, graceful and elegant. Curves are inherently attractive to most people, particularly when they undulate. Just as diagonals have a specific character – active and dynamic – and a quality of movement, so curves have a character – smooth and flowing – and

also carry the eye along them. They are, therefore, a useful second device in controlling the way in which people will look at a photograph.

Fish-eye effect

Curves are, however, less easy than diagonals to introduce into a picture. While a diagonal is usually a straight line of any

direction that is altered by viewpoint, curves must usually begin as real curves. They can be exaggerated by being viewed at a more acute angle, but the only optical method of actually creating them that is open to photographers is to use a fish-eye lens (see pages 142-3), and this simply has the effect of bending all the lines into curves without discrimination.

LINES THAT MOVE THE EYE

The eye follows a line, or even the suggestion of one. This tendency is the most important single device available to a photographer in designing an image so that it will be looked at in a certain way.

Focus of attention

While, given enough time, a viewer will look at every part of the frame, lines can be used successfully to provide encouragement

In the photograph left, straightforward use is made of an eye-line to direct the eye from the Virgin to the cardinal on the stage.

The first diagram below shows how three lines converge in the picture left, making the seed the center of attention. The second diagram highlights the use of a diagonal line to point to the figure in the shot on the opposite page.

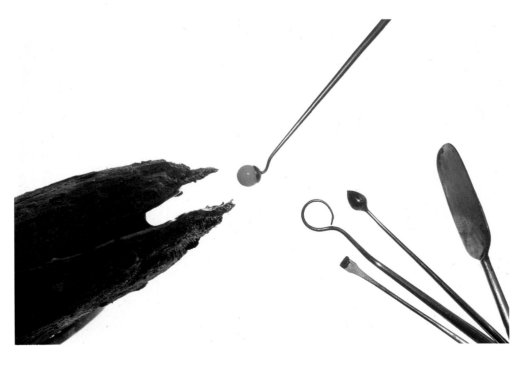

The seed used to seed a pearl oyster is the central, but also the smallest, element in the photograph left. Accordingly, the shot has been composed to focus on it.

to follow certain pathways. At the very least, a well-placed line will make sure that the focus of attention is not missed, even if it lacks outstanding graphic qualities. For example, it may be that what you want to point out may need to be small in the frame, and lacks the contrast necessary to stand out clearly. In such a case, a line that points to it can prevent it from becoming lost.

The strongest lines that you can use in this way are those with the most direction and movement. Diagonals, therefore, are particularly useful, and if there are two or more, and they converge, so much the better. Curves also have a feeling of movement, and on occasion even of speed and acceleration. However, the opportunities for using real lines are limited by the scene, naturally enough, and they are often not available when you want them. Implied lines, of the types we have just seen in the preceding pages, are not as definite and obvious, but can at least be created by the photographer, using viewpoint and lens to make alignments. These alignments may be of points, or of different short lines.

Movement

The image of a person walking contains a suggestion of direction, and this has momentum. The eye has a tendency to move a little ahead of such an image. The same thing happens with any object that we can see which is in movement. Because real movement in both photographs is frozen, even the direction in which an object is facing imparts a slight hint of movement.

This brings us to one of the most valuable implied lines that can be used in designing a photograph. So strong is our attraction to images of the human face that we pay instant attention to any face that appears clearly in a photograph. In particular, if the person in the photograph is looking at something, our eyes naturally follow that direction. It is normal curiosity to see where the eyes are looking, and it creates a strong direction in the image. Known as eye-lines, these are nearly always important elements in the structure of the image.

The aim in the picture below left was to show both stadium and runner, but the scale difference was a potential problem. The solution was to use a convenient, prominent diagonal line to emphasize him. The framing was chosen to give as much length as possible to the diagonal.

FINDING SHAPES IN A SCENE

As a row of points creates a line, so an enclosure of lines becomes a shape, and the eye is more than ready to conjure up a shape in an image. All discrete objects have a shape, but the shapes that have the most graphic interest in an image are those that occur a little less obviously, from the congruence of different elements. Subtly formed shapes that are implied and understated are some of the most useful of all; they help to order an image into a recognizable form and allow the eye the satisfaction of discovering them by making a little visual effort. The photograph of the old oak forest on page 123 is just such an example; the circular form is not what would normally be

As a result of using a frontal viewpoint, the balconies in the photograph right *exert a crushing effect on the single figure in the middle: an intended effect.*

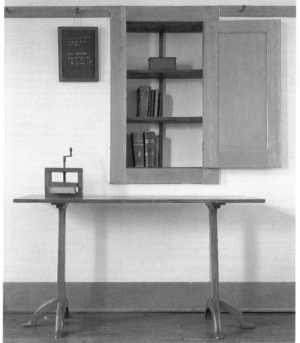

The predictable regularity of rectangles makes them especially adaptable to design that stresses balance and proportion, as in the photograph right.

expected in vegetation, and organizes the mass of leaves and branches without being immediately obvious.

Basic shapes

Although it might seem that there is an infinity of shapes, there are only three basic ones: the rectangle, triangle, and circle. All others, from trapezoids to ellipses, are variations on these, and as their importance in design relies on their fundamental recognizability, there is no need to go beyond these three basic planar figures. Each is intimately connected, both graphically and expressively, with the different lines that have just been considered. Rectangles are the prod-

A distant telephoto (and hence undistorted) view of a modern cityscape is the epitome of an assembly of rectangular shapes.

uct of horizontal and vertical lines, triangles are built from diagonals, and circles from curves.

As the principal design value of lines is to direct the eye, so that of shapes is to organize the elements of an image. At an order higher than that of lines, shapes have a more advanced function in composing a picture. Shapes also have expressive characters that can contribute to the mood of a photograph.

Rectangles

The shape that bears the closest correspondence to the frame of a photograph is a rectangle, and in many ways is the most natural. If you think about sub-dividing the frame, as discussed on pages 86-91, the most natural method will almost certainly be in a rectilinear fashion. A high degree of

precision is called for, as the most usual way of arranging rectangular shapes in a frame is to align them with the horizontals and verticals of the frame itself. Misalignments are then easy to spot.

Rectangles have associations of gravity, solidity, precision and sharp limitation, a result of their connotations with the two kinds of lines – vertical and horizontal – that compose them. They tend to be static, unyielding, and formal. As the perfect form of the rectangle, the square exhibits these qualities the most strongly.

At least one major reason for most of these expressive qualities is that completely natural rectangles are rare, and most are man-made (buildings in particular). Moreover, for a rectangular form to appear rectangular in the picture, it must be photographed square-on and level. Angled

The first diagram below shows how the rectangular blocks of the balconies bear down on the woman. An oblique view would have given a livelier image which, although more interesting, would not have reinforced the point of the picture in the same way. The second diagram illustrates the predominance of rectangles in the shot of Shaker furniture.

views and wide-angle lenses tend to distort rectangles into more triangular shapes. Hence, the manner of shooting that uses rectangular structures is itself usually formal and considered.

Triangles

In photographic design, triangles are considerably more useful shapes than rectangles, for a number of reasons. They are more common, partly because they are simpler to construct or imply (they need only three points for the apices, and these do

An upward-tilted view with a wide-angle lens causes the building's vertical lines in the picture below to converge dramatically into a triangle.

not need to be in any particular arrangement) and partly because of convergence – the natural graphic effects of perspective make convergent diagonals very common in photography, particularly with wide-angle lenses. They are also the most basic of all shapes, having the least number of sides. Moreover, they have the interesting combination of being both dynamic, because of the diagonals and corners, and stable – provided that one side is a level base. Triangles are thus a useful compositional device.

The triangle is such an inherently strong shape that it appears easily to the eye, not only through converging lines, but with three points alone. With lines, often two are sufficient; the third can be assumed or else

an appropriate frame edge can be taken as one side. As for points, any three prominent centers of interest will do, particularly if they are similar in content, tone, size or some other quality. Unlike rectangles and circles, both of which need to have their principal components in an exact order, triangles can be formed in almost any configuration. The only arrangement of three points that does not create a triangle is a straight row. For example, a portrait of three people usually contains a triangle, with each face an apex.

Vanishing point

The natural tendency of linear perspective is for lines to converge on a vanishing point in the distance, and form two sides of a tri-

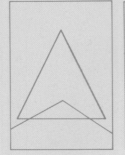

The first diagram below shows the triangular components of the picture left. The second diagram shows a triangular relationship in the heads and in the figures' outline in the shot right

Three-figure shots such as the photograph right usually contain the potential for creating interest with a triangular structure.

A standing view, looking down with a 20mm wide-angle lens, strengthens the triangular structure of the picture left *by downward convergence.*

angle. If the camera is level, the prime apex of the triangle will be pointing more or less horizontally. If the camera were pointing upwards instead, at a building, trees or any other group of vertical lines, the apex would be at the top of the picture, and the base level, at the bottom. This is also the most stable configuration of a triangle.

Stability

The sense of stability inherent in many triangles comes from structural associations; it is the shape of a pyramid, or of two buttresses leaning in towards each other. Therefore, arranging three objects so that two form a base and the third an apex above creates a stable form, and this association is carried into the image. It is the classic three-figure shot, and in photography that allows the subjects to be manipulated, it is a standard and usually successful technique to reposition things in this way. The two diagonals in such a triangle help it to escape the heaviness of a square or rectangular arrangement.

The reverse configuration, with the base at the top of the picture and the apex at the bottom, is an equally useful shape to introduce into a design. It has different associations: less stable, more aggressive, and con-

taining more movement. The apex points more obviously, probably because it appears to face the camera and viewer, and there is the kind of tension that you would expect from a shape that symbolizes extremely precarious balance.

A special use for inverted triangles in design occurs in still-life and other group pictures where objects are of different sizes yet need to be unified in one shot. Placing the smallest object near the camera, at the apex of the triangle, and the larger objects

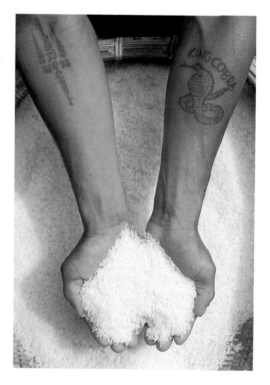

In the shot left *the upward convergence produced by a 20mm wide-angle lens is only partial, but it is enough for the eye to complete the sides of the triangle formed by ground and trees.*

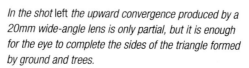

Another use of a triangular structure is to focus attention on the apex. In the picture above, *the arms are the converging sides of a triangle, bringing the eye down to the rice.*

behind, spreading out radially from the camera, is one solution. This same technique of arrangement can be used with one small and one large figure: for instance, a man standing in front of a large vehicle or a building. In these examples, a wide-angle lens will help to reduce the relative size of the objects behind the principal subject. A wide-angle lens, used from a raised position looking slightly down, will emphasize the proportions of an inverted triangle.

PROJECT: A variety of triangles
Make a series of three-person group portraits, using more than one triangular structure. Experiment with different positions for the three people (two sitting and one standing, two standing and one sitting, and so on) to produce a variety of triangles. Use the faces as apex points, and also use the lines of the figures. For a second project, take a group of household objects, such as tableware or kitchen utensils. Select different sizes. Make an inverted triangular composition so that the objects are tightly grouped and mainly visible (that is, avoid one object hiding important features of another behind).

Simplifying the image

Incidentally, emphasizing the triangular structure of an image like this is principally a matter of removing from view other distracting points, lines and implied lines. Simplification can be achieved by various means. Altering the viewpoint may be important (for instance, lowering the camera may hide some ground-level details from view; moving closer can tighten the composition), as may changing the lighting (or waiting for natural light to change) and rearrangement of the objects in view.

Under what circumstances is it useful to try to impose a triangular structure? It is

important to see implied triangles as one of a few devices for bringing order to an image, or of arranging the things being photographed. The occasions when such organization is needed are usually those when there is a need for clarity. This is common in still-life photography and in various forms of reportage when the most important thing is to make a clear representation of something, often in a visually untidy setting. As this is a common condition in professional photography, the idea of structuring an image in a simple graphic arrangement is principally professional.

The oak forest right *was lent interest by concentrating on the prominent curved branch and exaggerating the scene with a fish-eye lens.*

The curved branch gives a structure to the picture right, *as in the first diagram* below. *The second diagram indicates the circles apparent in the shot* below right.

The diagram below *shows how the circle of the plate in the picture on the opposite draws the eye down, away from the objects above.*

The basic dynamics of a circular structure are evident in the shot on the opposite page. The circle draws the eye inwards, away from the surrounding detail.

To imply circles in the shot right, *tight, cropped framing was used. Any further back and the illusion would have been lost.*

RHYTHM

Already, in looking at points, lines and shapes, we have seen something of rhythmical structure; a sequence of points in alignment, zig-zags and S-shaped curves. Repetition is a necessary ingredient, but alone does not guarantee a sense of rhythm in a picture. There is an obvious musical analogy, and it makes considerable sense. Like the beat in a piece of music, the optical beat in a picture can vary from being completely regular to "syncopated".

Rhythm in a picture needs time and the movement of the eye to be appreciated. The dimensions of the frame, therefore, set some limits, so that what can be seen is not much more than a rhythmical phrase.

However, the eye and mind are naturally adept at extending what they see, and in a photograph such as that of the row of soldiers, readily assume the continuation of the rhythm. In this way, a repeating flow of images is perceived as being longer than can actually be seen.

Left-to-right travel

Rhythm is a feature of the way the eye scans the picture as much as of the repetition. It is strongest when each cycle in the beat encourages the eye to move (see the examples shown here). The natural tendency of the eye to move from left to right (see page 67) is particularly evident here, as rhythm needs direction and flow in order to come alive. The rhythmical movement in a photograph is usually up and down, because vertical rhythm is much less easily perceived.

Momentum

Rhythm produces considerable strength in an image, as it does in music. It has momentum, and because of this, a sense of continuation. Once the eye has recognized the repetition, the viewer assumes that the repetition will continue beyond the frame.

When the rhythm of the subject is predictable, as in the picture below of a palace façade in Jaipur, India, the effect can be dull. In this case the answer was to make the image more dynamic by interrupting the rhythm. A man sweeping provides the required break. As the eye naturally follows a rhythmical structure from left to right, it works better to place the man on the right, so that the eye has time to establish the rhythm before noticing him.

In the shot above, *the eye travels in a wavelike motion, as in the first diagram* below. *The second diagram shows the rhythm of the elephants' outlines in the shot* above right.

Faces are always dominant in a photograph, and so in the shot of Thai soldiers above *a rhythm is set up by the eye's moving to each face and then down to the uniform as it travels from left to right.*

A more interesting beat is created by the elephants in the picture above. *The difference in size due to perspective sets up a progressive rhythm and the curved outlines produce a natural flow.*

The lower diagram shows the passage of the eye across the shot on the opposite page.

In the shot of wildebeest right, *slight abstraction and a strong horizontal emphasis help the rhythm produced by the animals' horns.*

PATTERN

Like rhythm, pattern is built on repetition, but unlike rhythm it is associated with area, not direction. A pattern does not encourage the eye to move in a particular way, but rather to roam across the surface of the picture. It has at least an element of homogeneity, and, as a result, something of a static nature.

Edge-to-edge pattern

The prime quality of a pattern is that it covers an area, thus the photographs that show the strongest pattern are those in which it extends right to the edges of the frame. Then, as with an edge-to-edge rhythm, the phenomenon of continuation occurs, and the eye assumes that the pattern extends beyond. The photograph of the bicycle saddles illustrates this. In other words, showing any border at all to the pattern establishes limits; if none can be seen, the image is taken to be a part of a larger area. At the

If they are irregular but still must appear as a pattern, objects must be grouped closely, as in the shot of bicycle saddles below.

Ordered rows and other geometric arrangements of large numbers of things produce regular patterns. However, the interest of the photograph right lies in the objects themselves— small religious plaques – as in their alignment.

The pattern of bicycle saddles left works because they fill the frame, as in the first diagram below, so that the eye assumes the pattern continues beyond it. An enlargement of the plaques above right, as in the second diagram, is no longer a pattern.

Natural patterns, like those formed by the stripes of the zebra opposite, develop in one or two directions, as in the third diagram below, and are most effective if they fill the frame.

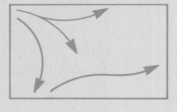

same time, the larger the number of elements that can be seen in the picture, the more there is a sense of pattern than of a group of individual objects. This operates up to a quantity at which the individual elements become difficult to distinguish and so become more of a texture (see pages 250-1). In terms of the number of elements, the effective limits lie between about ten and several hundred.

PROJECT: Pattern and scale
Take a large number of objects, at least a couple of hundred, which can be easily assembled: map pins, matchsticks, or something equally available. Arrange all of them in an evenly spaced pattern (it can be irregular). Photograph the entire group, making sure that they reach the frame edges. Take successive photographs, closing in, ending with just four or five of the objects (for which you will need a macro lens). Determine from the results at what scale the pattern effect is strongest.

One thing you should notice is that, unless the form of the pattern or the subjects themselves are interesting, the pattern alone will not make much of a picture. It will, however, make a very effective background. Place another, preferably related object against the grouping, in a way similar to the photograph of the jeans on this page.

Patterns can be directionless, as with the sea of jeans in the shot left. *A figure was added to emphasize the pattern by breaking it.*

TIMING

Timing is not only an essential quality in taking most photographs; it has a direct effect in many situations on the actual design of the image. Photographs of all except static subjects – and this means the majority of photographs – must be timed. One of the fundamental properties of photography is that it has to be performed according to what happens in front of the camera.

Action

To take a photograph is to make a picture of an event. The event may be rapid – a matter of milliseconds in catching the moment in a few instances – or it may be so slow, as in the change of daylight over a landscape, that the timing is chosen in terms of hours.

Whatever the action, whether it is a person walking through the scene or clouds gathering over a mountain, it will certainly have to move *across* the picture frame. The action, therefore, inevitably affects the design of the picture, because it alters the balance.

Visualizing photographs

This simple observation may well appear obvious in retrospect, but the natural reaction in any photographic situation is to follow movement and to make what seems intuitively to be the most satisfying composition at any moment.

If, however, a particular design of image is planned in advance, it is important to work this out by imagining the result when everything will be in place. To make a precise composition of this kind of situation, it is usually easier to frame the view as it will be, and wait for whatever movement is involved to pass into the frame, as in the photograph on this page.

A parked Land Rover gave a clear, and safe, view of a hippopotamus pool in Tanzania right. As there was no urgency, it was worth waiting for an out-of-the-ordinary moment – the arrival of an ox-pecker – before shooting.

In the sequence telling a short story of itinerant acrobats performing in a town in India left, only the second photograph really counts; the first and third pictures simply show the technique of the acrobatic act. In the second shot the photographer has taken the risk of following the movement but has still been able to achieve a good composition .

With more time available for the shot than there was for the acrobats, it was easy enough to plan in advance the photograph of rice planting above. It was felt that the best place for the planter would be at the far left, since there he would be occupying the brightest part of the rice terrace and thus be clearly visible. It was just a matter of waiting for him to reach that point.

Changing Lenses

The image in photography is formed optically, so the choice of lens is an essential part of the process of designing a picture. Lenses are interchangeable on SLR (single-lens-reflex) cameras, and for design reasons alone the variety of focal lengths and types is worth using. Instead of changing to a wide-angle lens just to broaden the coverage, or to a telephoto simply to magnify a distant subject, think of the lens as a means of altering the character of the image and of solving design problems. From this point of view, maximum apertures and lens quality are less interesting than those characteristics that actually change the geometry of the image. Principally, this involves different focal lengths, which are explained on the

following pages, although there some special optical constructions, fish-eyes and shift lenses, which will also change the shape of things in the photograph.

The reference standard for lenses used with 35mm cameras is 50mm (or 55mm), which is the focal length that gives approximately the same angle of view as we have. Only approximation is possible, because human vision and lens imaging are quite different: we see by scanning, and do not have an exactly delineated frame of view.

A lens can be a single piece of glass, but in a camera it consists of several pieces, called elements. Working together, these correct the natural faults that all lenses have, and determine characteristics such as

the angle of view and magnification. However, the main functions of a lens are focusing and determining the aperture.

Sharp focus depends on the distance of the subject from the camera, and to focus closer means moving the lens elements further away from the film. Most lenses do this by means of a helicoid gear, so that when you turn the focusing ring on the outside of the lens barrel, the elements inside move backwards or forwards, nearer or further away from the film plane.

The aperture diaphragm controls the amount of light passing through the lens to reach the film, and at the same time controls the depth of field: the distance between the nearest and farthest points in a

The most common use of a wide-angle lens is to include a large area of a scene from a close viewpoint. In the shot below the subject is bathers in an ancient pool near a Mayan temple in Mexico.

Telephoto lenses compress perspective and give a close-cropped view – both evident in the tightly framed image of a Vietnamese bronze lion right.

photograph that appear acceptably sharp. The mechanism is a set of curved metal blades arranged around the inside of a ring-shaped mount. Turning the aperture selection ring on the outside of the barrel causes the blades to open or close, processes referred to opening up and stopping down, respectively.

The size of the circle in the middle of the blades set in this way – the aperture – is indicated by an *f*-number (or *f*-stop). The smaller the number – which is actually the ratio of the diameter to the focal length of the lens – the larger the aperture. An aperture of, say, *f*1.8, is wider than one of, say, *f*11 and thus allows more light to pass through the lens and reach the film.

THE RANGE OF LENSES

Of all the features of a camera lens, none makes such an obvious difference to the image as focal length. Most of us think about focal length – if we do so at all – in terms of three types: wide-angle, standard and telephoto. This is the normal terminology, but strictly, wide-angle lenses are short-focus, and telephoto lenses long-focus. The differences lie in the angle of view, in magnification, and in the image's character (for instance, "compressed" or "expansive").

The focal length is the distance between the principal point of a lens and the focal point, at which light rays from a distance are in focus. For example, imagine a normal (also referred to as standard) 50mm lens focused on a tree; the size of the tree's image is, say, ½ inch (12mm) on the film frame. Now, if the lens were designed differently, so that it focused further back, that image would be larger because the light rays would still be spreading from the lens. If the focal length is double, 100mm, the image of the tree would be 1 inch (25mm) high, almost filling a 35mm frame.

Using a 50mm lens as the base line, anything longer magnifies. At the same time, of course, the view is restricted. Now, if we reduce the focal length with yet another design of lens, the film will be closer to the lens, the light rays will have less space in which to spread out, and the image of the tree will be smaller. The size of the picture frame, meanwhile, has not changed, so that the lens takes in more of the scene.

These are the two main effects of changing from a lens of one focal length to another: magnification and angle of view. But what about perspective? One important reason for using a different focal length is to give a particular visual style, and this is intimately connected with perspective. Yet perspective stays the same as long as the camera is not moved, regardless of what lens is used. Confusingly, the word "perspective" is often used loosely. It really means the impression of distance and relative positions, and this only changes if the viewpoint is changed.

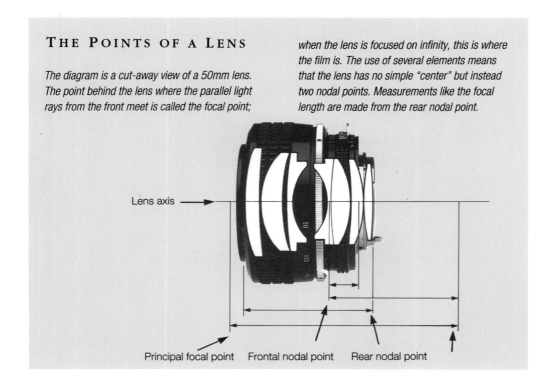

THE POINTS OF A LENS

The diagram is a cut-away view of a 50mm lens. The point behind the lens where the parallel light rays from the front meet is called the focal point;

when the lens is focused on infinity, this is where the film is. The use of several elements means that the lens has no simple "center" but instead two nodal points. Measurements like the focal length are made from the rear nodal point.

Lens axis →

Principal focal point   Frontal nodal point   Rear nodal point

400mm   600mm   x 1.4 teleconverter to give effective 800mm

105mm   55mm   35mm   24mm   20mm   180mm

20mm *Linear perspective and distortion in the foreground's corners reflect a wide angle of view.*

24mm *Predictably, this wide-angle shot was little different from the 20mm version.*

35mm *A moderate wide-angle lens produces a view approaching that of the human eye.*

55mm *This standard focal length gives an image that seems normal in magnification and angle of view.*

105mm *A moderate telephoto marks the point in this sequence where the view starts to appear magnified.*

180mm *The cartoon characters in the middle of the scene become the clear focus of attention.*

400mm *With a fairly long telephoto lens, the cartoon figures are now isolated from the scene.*

600mm *The strong magnification provided by this lens excludes information about the surroundings.*

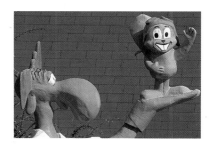

800mm *Extreme magnification, achieved with a x 1.4 teleconverter, gives a clear sense of compression.*

To illustrate the enormous difference focal length can make to an image, each of the photographs above was shot from exactly the same point on Hollywood's Sunset Boulevard. Nine focal lengths were used, ranging from 20mm to 800mm. To try this kind of project yourself, first preview a subject with your longest lens to find a worthwhile small central subject, such as the cartoon figures in the comparative sequence.

THE NORMAL LENS

There is, surprisingly, no good single reason why the "normal" or "standard" lens for 35mm cameras should be 50mm in focal length. Certainly it is the lens that is usually sold with the camera, but it owes its position as the normal lens only to historical accident : 50mm is a round figure. Yet it remains the most often used focal length for very sound reasons: above all, because it gives an apparent perspective that is roughly the same as the way we see. This is why it is the reference for other focal lengths.

Field of vision

It is best not to compare the angle of view too closely to that of the eye, however. It is in fact a fallacy that the 43-50° diagonal angle of view (that is, corner to corner of the picture) is the same as that of the eye. The comparison is almost meaningless; our eyes do not have a frame. Look straight ahead for a moment. What can you see? You can vaguely notice things out of the corner of your eye, while having a sharp, detailed view of just a small area in front of you. Your total field of vision is probably more than 220°, but you may be concentrating on only about 2°.

The focal length of the normal lens has acquired an unfair reputation for being dull. The existence of so many other focal lengths has led to the idea that extreme perspective, being quite exciting in a graphic way, is more "creative". It would be wrong to ignore all the possibilities of wide-angle and telephoto lenses, but there are obvious dangers in using their special effects as a creative crutch.

Most still-life photographs are taken with a normal lens. This is not to say that a 50mm lens on a 35mm camera is always used, but simply that the "standard" view in 35mm and other camera formats is a perfectly good choice for the subject-matter. In any case, there are many other elements involved in effective design, as the selection of still-life pictures shown here demonstrates. To test the versatility of the normal lens, shoot a selection of still-life subjects. Make the images interesting by the way you position the objects.

WIDE-ANGLE LENSES

Wide-angle lenses cover a range of focal lengths; in theory, anything shorter than standard. In practice, the most moderate wide-angle lens for a 35mm camera has a focal length of 35mm, but it has more of the character of a standard 50mm lens than the qualities normally associated with this group of lenses.

At the other end of the scale of focal lengths, the limit is around 13mm or 15mm: expensive, heavy lenses that give diagonal angles of view well over 100°. Wider coverage than this is possible with fish-eye lenses, which have focal lengths as short as 6mm. These are dealt with on pages 142-3.

Wide-angle characteristics

The essential qualities of wide-angle lenses are that they give expanded coverage of a scene, their great depth of field if used at small apertures, and the way they emphasize linear perspective. All of these effects

A prime function of a wide-angle lens is broad coverage, as in the shot of a cockpit below.

are illustrated on these pages with a 20mm lens to give a relatively strong impression.

Wide-angle lenses affect the structure of the image in three main ways. They change the apparent perspective and so the perception of depth; they have a tendency to produce diagonals (real and implied) and consequently dynamic tension; and they induce a subjective viewpoint, drawing the viewer into the scene. The perspective effect depends very much on the way the lens is used, specifically the viewpoint. Used from the edge of a cliff or the top of a tall building, with no foreground at all in the picture, there is virtually no effect on the perspec-

Because the actual sizes of the apertures in a wide-angle lens (not the f-stop) are smaller, the depth of field is greater than with longer focal lengths. The strongest impression of depth of field is when the smallest aperture is used and the focus is set so that the farthest limit is in the distance. In the photograph below a 20mm lens was used at its minimum aperture, f22. The point of focus was just over 2 feet (0.6m), so that everything from the far buildings to the foreground fence (a little more than 1 foot/0.3m away) is sharp.

The term "linear perspective" defines what many people think of as the "creative" use of wide-angle lenses, and used sensibly it can indeed produce a powerful graphic impression. One of several ways of emphasizing the depth relationship between parts of the scene, converging diagonal lines are given more prominence by a wide-angle lens. In the cemetery overlooking Jerusalem right *the important lines are the long edges of the gravestone. The camera, fitted with a 20mm lens, is far enough forward for these lines to go beyond the frame's edge, so that their flow is unbroken and they appear to be moving into the picture.*

tive; just a wider angle of view.

However, used with a full scale of distance, from close to the camera all the way to the horizon, a wide-angle lens will give an impressive sense of depth. As this contributes to realism in photography, wide-angle lenses used this way are a useful standby for the representative photography of landscapes.

The diagonalization of lines is linked to this effect on apparent perspective. The angle of view is great, so more of the lines

The bare simplicity of the Shaker meeting house in Maine below *is emphasized by the linear perspective of converging lines provided by a 20mm lens.*

that converge on the scene's vanishing points are visible, and these are usually diagonal. Moreover, the correction of barrel distortion in the construction of a normal wide-angle lens results in rectilinear distortion, a radial stretching that is strongest away from the center of the frame.

Wide-angle lenses tend to be involving for the viewer because they pull the viewer into the scene. The foreground in such pictures is close and the stretching towards the edges and corners has the effect of seemingly wrapping the image around the viewer. In other words, the viewpoint provided by the lens makes the viewer aware that the scene extends beyond the frame.

Distortion

Distortion is the side effect of the powerful linear perspective that makes wide-angle lenses exciting to use. In itself it is neither good nor bad, but it needs to be treated with care if it is to contribute to the image.

Outdoors, one of its most recurring forms is the convergence of lines when the camera is tilted upwards. For buildings this is difficult to avoid; the easiest viewpoint is usually at ground level from fairly close, leaving little alternative but to raise the camera.

Exploiting converging verticals

The first thing to establish is that there is nothing wrong with converging verticals. Perceived textbook wisdom is that they should be avoided, but if you like the effect, use it; the issue is only one of taste. Make sequences of shots from slightly different positions so that you can judge the importance of the visual differences.

In the picture opposite, the strong perspective of a 20mm lens exaggerates the size difference between a bronze Botero sculpture and the background figure.

PROJECT: Converging verticals
Distortion is the essence of wide-angle lenses, and is responsible for their most interesting graphic uses. The down side of this distortion, however, is that it can appear unintentionally and in the wrong parts of the image. Unwanted distortion tends to look peculiar rather than interesting. Despite the danger of laying down rules of acceptability, some exercises show the differences between workable and unworkable distortion.

One of the most common situations of converging verticals is the view looking up at a building. For this, use as short a focal length lens as possible and, most important, take a sequence of shots while trying to "develop" the image by changing the viewpoint. Analyze the results from the photographs rather than at the time of shooting.

The isolated building with space in front left is ideal for the project on converging verticals. The sequence shows some of the possibilities of this subject with a 20mm lens. In the first shot the viewpoint is from a standing position and with the lens at an upward angle that includes the entire courthouse. However, the background is intrusive and the branches cut into the building. The branches can be made to serve a better purpose, and in the second picture, to the right, they no longer overlap the image of the building. The camera is on the ground, with the prism head removed, so that little of the background can be seen, while showing all of the courthouse. The third shot is an attempt to simplify the image even more. Using the line on the façade just above the door as a base, the camera is tilted upward more strongly, and all of the background is lost. The final picture, which does not work satisfactorily, is an attempt to balance the weight of the building against the branches and surroundings by placing it off-center. Although this is a reasonable way of handling the balance of the picture, the distortion is overwhelming.

PROJECT: Stretch distortion

Barrel distortion is a natural, but now rarely seen, fault in short focal length lenses, showing up as a curvature near the edge of the picture. It survives deliberately in fish-eye lenses, but in others is normally corrected. However, rectilinear correction, as it is known, introduces a different kind of distortion. Dimensions are stretched radially: that is, on lines away from the center. It is most extreme in the corner of a wide-angle view, and most obvious with simple, familiar shapes, such as circles and human faces. For this project, take a clean, obvious shape and shoot it framed in the center, then framed near the edge; the distortion should be obvious.

The sequence of three photographs on this page demonstrates that the possibilities for combining two subjects in one image lie not just in good depth of field, but also in strong perspective. Here a 20mm lens's minimum aperture of f22 is sufficient to keep everything from a distance of 80 feet (25m) – the hotel – to just over 1 foot (0.3m) – the Rolls-Royce – sharply focused. Within this range of distance, there was a wide choice of viewpoint, and as can be seen from these three shots, relatively small changes in the camera position – forward/backward, raised/lowered, and the degree of tilt – produced big graphic changes. Standing back, and from about shoulder level, the view top is of the car in a setting – fairly conventional. In the second shot, moving closer at the same height, and tilting the camera down, introduces a strong linear perspective and alters the balance of visual weight in favour of the car. In the third picture, taken at the same distance but looking up from below the radiator grill, the car occupies a little less of the picture frame, but by looming over the camera seems to be even more prominent.

Lens accentuates perspective of diagonal lines leading out

Entire car in normal proportions faces out, matching outward direction of diagonal lines above

Hotel façade subordinates to car

View down onto car gives strong converging lines, makes bonnet appear long and introduces symmetry to the picture

Close viewpoint draws attention to the famous mascot and insignia

Mascot still prominent

Identity of car represented by its key features: radiator grill, mascot and headlights. Low viewpoint increases strength of this part of the image

The photographs on this page of Munich's Residenz Museum illustrate some of the choices and problems that influence composition in two formats. Distortion is, as always, a consideration; the solution with a non-shift lens of levelling the camera creates design difficulties because there is little of interest on the floor.

PROJECT: Juxtaposition

Drawing a relationship between two subjects, even though they may be very different in size, is a common requirement in photography for all kinds of reasons, commercial and otherwise. Wide-angle lenses are regularly used for certain types of juxtaposition, for two reasons. One is that their depth of field with a small aperture is usually good enough to bring everything into sharp focus. The other, more important for practice and experiment, is perspective. Used close to one of the objects, a wide-angle lens can make it dominate the image, even if it is relatively small. As we have seen, small changes in the camera angle with a wide-angle lens create major changes in the design, and the theme of this project is to take two subjects in one shot, trying different viewpoints to discover the range of graphic relationships.

PROJECT: Vertical/horizontal choice

Wide-angle lenses have an inherent design problem in 35mm photography. Because the proportions of the picture frame are 2:3, there is often too much "empty" foreground when you shoot a vertical picture. For this project, whenever the natural format for a wide-angle shot seems to be horizontal, in addition take as good a shot as you can with a vertical composition.

Camera levelled for a convergence-free shot, considered necessary for a faithful representation of traditional architecture

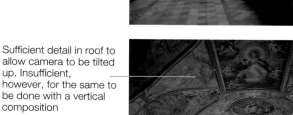

Floor area reduced in image by swinging camera right, drawing attention to foreground statuary

Sufficient detail in roof to allow camera to be tilted up. Insufficient, however, for the same to be done with a vertical composition

Converging distortion present, but suppressed by curved lines of roof

Uninteresting and largely empty floor eliminated by tilting camera up

Vertical composition fights to some extent against the horizontal visual bias of the hall, so the shot makes more of the detail of the arches and statues

Figure helps to overcome visual emptiness of the floor

FISH-EYE LENSES

The fish-eye lens is a mild oddity in the range of commercially available lenses. Its special design, originally intended for use in astro-photography and meteorology, restricts its value enormously. Thus it is a lens that you will rarely need, yet there may well be occasions when no other will do the job. Being so specialized, fish-eye lenses can usually be hired from photographic dealers who have a rental department. One thing above all others that you will probably find in doing the projects suggested

The interior of the capsule is partly curved, and in any case unfamiliar to most viewers. Consequently, even curved distortion here does not look out of place

Viewpoint chosen so that as many lines as possible appear radial, and so stay relatively straight

The image of a dummy head in the space suit's helmet would have been unacceptably distorted. The only solution was to keep it outside the picture frame

Corners occupied by nearest parts of scene and the center by the most distant

The strong perspective of a fish-eye gives very different images when the camera position is changed. The added feature of curvature heightens this effect. Even though the giant figure of the Buddha dominates each image below, the relative proportions of the interior are altered substantially. In a different way, though, the curved lines introduced by the fish-eye lens give a recognizable similarity.

Although there is the problem of curved distortion, the way to achieve the best coverage inside a normal rectangular picture frame is to use a full-frame fish-eye. The example above, a shot of the interior of John Glenn's Mercury capsule, shows some of the techniques

that can be used to minimize distortion and give as realistic and natural a view as possible. The criterion in this case was to give the fullest possible coverage of a cramped interior, but at the same time keep an acceptably straightforward treatment.

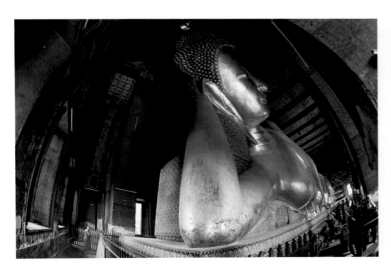

The principal characteristics of the fish-eye image can be seen in the photograph right. These are: 180° coverage, great depth of field, even at f8, strong barrel distortion of straight lines and a prominent perspective between the center foreground and the edge distance. The image circle is 23mm, almost the height of the horizontal film frame.

here is that a full roll of 36 exposures of fish-eye images looks very repetitive. This in itself is a useful encouragement to find different ways of structuring the images, but if you were to select only one lens to carry, this would probably be the last choice.

A true fish-eye gives a circular image that covers a full 180°; if you laid the camera flat on the ground outdoors, pointing upwards, the horizon would appear all around the edge of the picture. As you can see from the picture of the lens, the front element is strongly curved, and refracts light to such an extent that even from the side you can see the inside elements. This front element gathers 180° of image and refracts it into a 90° cone, which is then projected by the rear element onto the film.

PROJECT: Angle and distance

As small movements of the camera make significant changes in the image, the basic exercise with a fish-eye lens is to view potential subjects with the camera to your eye from as many different angles and distances as you can manage. If you walk while looking through the viewfinder, you may find the changing image very interesting.

Specifically, do two exercises. In one, take a subject and approach it in a direct line, taking a sequence of shots. In the second, photograph an outdoor scene with the camera level, and then with it tilted up or down; notice the effect this has on the horizon line.

At a distance of 3 feet (1m) the door frame bows out prominently. Depth of field is so great that the focus is fixed

Barrel distortion causes lines close to the circumference of the picture to be curved almost to the same degree as the circumference itself

The 180° coverage is obvious here: the entire length of this street is included

If the camera is hand-held, standing, the photographer's feet may appear. Here they are inches out of the shot

The following simple exercise illustrates the characteristic tendency of fish-eye lenses to produce a curvature in the horizon. Take any outdoor scene, and photograph it with the camera horizontal to the subject, as in the first picture below. Then photograph the same scene with the camera tilted upwards by the same amount as in the second shot; that is, so that the horizon line appears nearly at the bottom of the picture. Only radial lines (that is, leading from the center directly outwards) stay straight, so that the only condition that allows a straight horizon is when this passes exactly through the center of the photograph.

Camera level: horizon level and centered

Tilted camera brings tops of buildings behind into view

Radial pavement lines stay fairly straight

Empty foreground is a visual waste of space

Radial and near-radial lines, such as the verticals of these buildings, are the least affected by curvature distortion

Camera tilted up until horizon line almost at bottom of picture, becomes strongly curved

TELEPHOTO LENSES

Popularly, telephotos are synonymous with long focal length, although the word "telephoto" actually refers to a particular design of lens. The distinction is not normally important, but, for the record, the backfocus in a telephoto lens is shorter than that in a long lens of traditional design. In other words, the distance from the lens to the film is shorter, and so the physical dimensions of the lens can be smaller: a matter of convenience for hand-held shooting. For example, in a 400mm telephoto the distance from the lens elements to the camera may be considerably less than 400mm.

With view-camera lenses, the distinction is more practical. The longer focal lengths that are available in normal lenses are usually designed with greater covering power for larger formats. For instance, 150mm is the standard focal length for a 4 × 5 inch camera, but the most easily available longer focal length is 300mm or 360mm – the standard focal length for an 8 × 10 inch camera. These are not telephotos, and so the bellows length would have to be doubled: a considerable inconvenience outdoors. Large format telephotos are not very common, but they need less bellows extension.

Internal focusing
Two technical developments within the last few years account for the variety of telephoto lenses available. One is internal focusing, in which only the rear group of elements move to change focus. As these are considerably smaller than the front group in a telephoto lens, they can be moved without changing the length of the barrel. The advantages over the traditional helicoid system, in which the front part of the barrel moves forward for closer focusing, are that dust is not sucked into the lens in the same way, and the balance of the lens stays the same (try resting the front of a traditionally-designed telephoto on a support and then changing the focus).

Lens speed
The second development is faster telephotos; that is, bigger maximum apertures. It is the maximum aperture that sets the limit to the fastest shutter speed that can be used, and this can never be fast enough. Camera shake is a constant worry with a telephoto, so the advantages of a faster lens are obvious. However, this involves a lot of glass at the front, making such lenses heavy and expensive.

Focal lengths
First let us look at the strengths of telephoto lenses. The choice of actual focal length is even greater than for wide-angle lenses, ranging typically from 85mm to 800mm for a 35mm camera. As you might expect, all the effects that are characteristic of telephoto lenses increase in proportion to the focal length, and the big super-telephotos, which give the most extreme graphic results, also demand the most care in use. It is worth noting here that certain focal lengths are considered particularly useful for some specific types of photograph; for example, 85mm for head-and-shoulder portraits, 135mm, 150mm and 180mm for street photography, and 300mm, 400mm and 500mm for sports coverage. These, lenses, however, are not necessarily what you may need to complement your own style of work.

Magnification
The most objective quality of a telephoto lens is its magnification, and most of the reasons for using one probably depend on this. There are situations where a close approach is impossible (for example, keeping beyond the boundary line in sports matches, or the "threat" zone perceived by wild animals), and there are situations where the view of a subject is simply less satisfactory from nearby; it may be interrupted by foreground obstructions. The degree of magnification is easy enough to judge; when comparing the view between two focal lengths, just divide the larger by the smaller. In practice, you are likely to be interchanging a group of lenses, so there is a definite advantage in having some viewfinder indication of a longer lens when using a shorter focal length.

The more subjective qualities of a telephoto image are isolation, compression of perspective, and presence. This last is the least definite, and occurs only with single subjects that are framed quite tightly.

Image structure
Telephoto lenses have various effects on the structure of the image: they appear to reduce the impression of depth by compressing the planes of the image; they give a selective view, and so can be used to pick out precise graphic structures; they generally simplify the line structure of an image, with a tendency towards horizontals and verticals; they make it relatively easy to juxtapose two or more objects; and they create a more objective, cooler way of seeing things, which has the effect of distancing the viewer from the subject (as, of course, the photographer is distanced).

The longer the focal length, the more the image is magnified. This fact is particularly relevant to wildlife photography, where there is nearly always a limit to how close the subject can be approached. To reach out beyond this requires magnification. In the example right, showing flamingos in Ngorongoro Crater, a 600mm lens gives 12 times the magnification of a standard lens (divide the longer focal length by the shorter) and 30 times that of the 20mm used in the comparison shot below. Whatever other graphic effects a telephoto lens is able to achieve – for example, compressing the perspective and giving presence to the subject – it does one simple task particularly well : it brings the subject nearer by enlarging the image.

The compression effect is valuable because it is a different way of seeing things (the unusual can be attractive for its own sake), and also because it makes it possible to compose in a two-dimensional way, with a set of planes rather than a completely realistic sense of depth. A specific practical use is to give some height to an oblique view of level ground. With a standard 50mm lens, the acute angle of view tends to interfere; a telephoto lens used at some distance from the subject gives the impression of tilting the surface upwards.

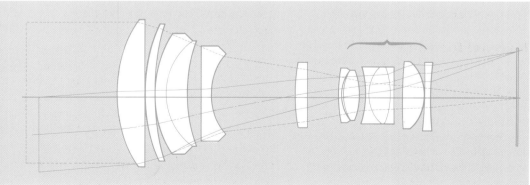

Tele-extenders, illustrated right, are small auxiliary lenses that fit between the telephoto lens and the camera. They increase the magnification of the prime lens by bending the light rays which are approaching the film less sharply, and have an overall concave construction. The most commonly used types of tele-extender are a 1.4 x pattern (a side-effect is that 1 f-stop of lens speed) is lost and a 2 x pattern (which sacrifices 2 f-stops of lens speed).

Controlling picture elements

The selectivity that the narrow angle of view gives makes it possible to eliminate distracting or unbalancing elements. Precise balance is also often easier, needing only a slight change in the camera angle; the arrangement of areas of tone or colour can be altered without changing the perspective. For the same reason, the direction of lines tends to be more consistent. Whereas a wide-angle lens used close to the subject pulls lines into a variety of diagonals, a telephoto lens leaves parallel lines and right angles as they are. This often gives a more static, less dynamic shot.

Juxtaposition

A major use of telephoto lens is juxtaposition. To make a particular point, it is often necessary to show one thing in relationship to another. This can be done with any lens simply by changing the viewpoint or by moving one of the objects. However, only a telephoto lens allows it to be done without major changes to the rest of the image. Moreover, when the two points of interest are some distance apart, the compression

By narrowing the angle of view (which reduces the elements in the scene) and by compressing the perspective (which makes it possible to select a "clean" background), a telephoto lens can isolate an image. To do this effectively, first select the subject, move back far enough to give a suitable framing with a long focal length, and find a viewpoint that puts a fairly simple background behind the subject. This last factor is the key to success, as illustrated in the pictures on this page. The church steeple and cross have been precisely centered against the corner of a modern building. The camera position had to be accurate to within a few inches, even at this distance.

Isolating effect much stronger in the lower, 400m shot than in the upper, 180mm version.

Practice certainly makes it easier to pre-visualize the frame – that is, to judge what focal length you need to change to for any particular composition. However, the view you obtain through whatever lens you normally leave on the camera can also be a good guide. Even if the focusing screen has no markings other than the central focusing circle, that on its own can serve to indicate the framing that would occur with a lens of greater focal length. It is more practical, however, to use a grid screen, as shown in the third diagram below left.

Achieving wider maximum apertures can only be done by increasing the light-gathering power of the front group of lens elements. This, in turn, calls for bigger front elements and produces a bulkier lens overall, as shown by the cross-sectional diagrams below.

300mm 200mm 100mm 85mm   50mm

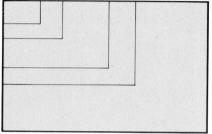

These are the relative frames for four common telephotos as seen through the viewfinder with a standard 50mm lens. Note that the 100m frame is exactly half the size, the 200mm frame a quarter and so on.

50mm

The central focusing circle on a normal SLR focusing screen can give an approximate idea of telephoto framing.

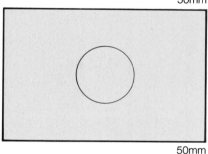

50mm

The grid lines etched on some focusing screens give a clear indication of framing, even though you may need to use them off-center.

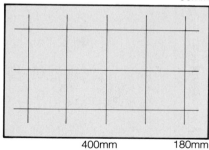

400mm   180mm

Also familiarize yourself with the framing of long focal lengths as seen through medium telephotos. As with all these examples, adapt to the range of lenses you normally use.

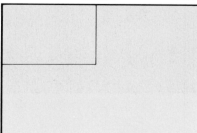

300mm *f*2.8 5lbs 10oz
(2551g)

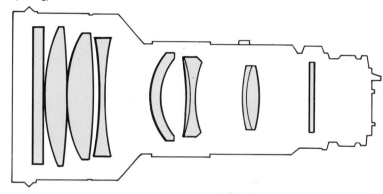

300mm *f*4 2lbs 1oz
(936g)

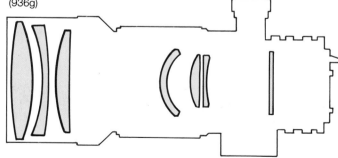

300mm *f*5.6 1lb 6oz
(624g)

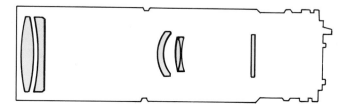

effect of a telephoto helps to bring them together.

Finally, the way that a telephoto lens is normally used – from a distance – communicates itself to the viewer and leaves an objective, less involved impression. There is a major difference in visual character between shooting within a situation with a wide-angle lens, and across-the-street views away from the subject.

What we might call "presence" derives in large part from the compression of perspective, and is enhanced by reproducing the picture large. In the example below the effect of a 600mm lens is to project the viewer forwards and to give more of a sense of bulk to the object.

PROJECT: Compression
First choose a row of same-sized objects and photograph them from a fairly acute angle. The photographs of a street of tenements on page 149 shows typical results. Also, photograph isolated subjects against a slightly elevated backdrop; for instance, a farmhouse against a hillside, or yachts in a harbour against waterfront buildings. Look at the way in which the background appears flattened and larger.

PROJECT: Slowest safe shutter speed
A telephoto lens also magnifies camera shake. Shoot a series of identical shots, varying the shutter speed (and adjusting the aperture to compensate). Start at the reciprocal of the focal length, that is, $\frac{1}{500}$ of a second if you are using a 500mm lens, and move to slower speeds. From this, done several times, find the slowest speed at which you can be sure of a sharp picture. The next slowest speed is still usable, but only if you take several exposures for safety.

The prime effect of a telephoto lens on perspective is to reduce the apparent differences in size due to distance. So, if objects of the same size are at different distances from the camera, a telephoto will make them seem more nearly identical. This is what happened in the picture right of a row of tenement houses and balconies. The longer the focal length, the stronger this effect.

PROJECT: Isolation

This characteristic is not simply a function of the narrow angle of view, and needs practice to achieve whenever you want it. Choose subjects that will occupy a substantial part of the picture frame at a convenient working distance with your longest lens. Concentrate on selecting a background (by moving the camera position) which is least distracting. Vary the aperture to change the depth of field; although selective focus (see page 33) helps to isolate an object from its surroundings, it is not always necessary.

Medium telephoto – people at a distance

One of the special uses of the middle range of telephoto lenses is in reportage photography. A focal length of between, say,

In the two photographs below the compression of perspective is seen in different degrees. The first was shot with a 180mm lens, the second with a 400mm lens, and both from the same camera position.

Theoretically the perspective is the same (because the viewpoint is the same), but the overall visual impression is different: notably that the 400mm shot contains less information about how the pillars recede from view.

135mm and 200mm on a 35mm camera, puts you at a sufficient distance from other people to shoot without being noticed – or at least, without being intrusive. For instance, with a 135mm lens, if you hold the camera normally so that the frame shape is horizontal, a standing or walking figure will fill the height of the picture at about 30 feet (10m). If you turn the camera to shoot a vertical frame, the same figure would fill it at around 20 feet (7m). The advantages of this are immediately obvious, for instead of needing to be within arms' length of someone you want to photograph, you can work at the sort of distance at which they may not even see you.

Street photography

For this reason, a medium telephoto lens is an important tool for street photography. One of the archetypal uses of a 35mm camera, this is a kind of social documentary photography that involves covering an urban area on foot. Its main feature is that the photography is unplanned: you respond to whatever picture possibilities occur, and shoot either quietly and unnoticed, or at least without posing people or trying to improve the image by interfering. Its success mainly depends on how well you observe, and behave – blending into the background yet being able to shoot quickly and decisively are the keys – but at the same time, the kind of camera equipment you have makes a considerable difference.

Two Italian ladies taking a stroll through Lucca's Piazza del Salvatore. Because the photographer and the subjects were walking towards each other, there was time for only one shot, calling for quick, accurate focusing (a perfect situation for autofocus).

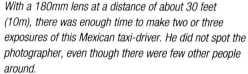

With a 180mm lens at a distance of about 30 feet (10m), there was enough time to make two or three exposures of this Mexican taxi-driver. He did not spot the photographer, even though there were few other people around.

Tight framing and a clean, unobtrusive background are the hallmarks of a telephoto shot, here evident in a 180mm photograph of a girl sitting on a railing in Siena.

Certainly, the masters of reportage photography, like Henri Cartier-Bresson, have generally preferred to use a standard 50mm lens, relying entirely on their skill to be able to work close, from a few feet if necessary. Nevertheless, this takes time to develop, and not every photographer has the ability, or the self-confidence to do this. Many people simply feel uncomfortable at poking their cameras into other people's faces, and this is entirely natural. Much depends on temperament. Some photographers are naturally retiring, others outgoing, and these natural differences become reflected in the way they use a camera. Robert Capa, one of the first great wartime photo-journalists, believed: "If your pictures aren't good enough you're not close enough."

Fortunately, you can get closer by using a lens with a longer focal length.

Clear view

Naturally, a medium telephoto works best when there is clear shooting space between you and the subject. In practice, this is one of the technical problems of telephoto reportage – there is always the risk of something cross in front of you, such as a car or a passer-by. In some situations, such as a market or a crowded event, it is not even a risk, but a continuous condition. It helps to keep *both* eyes open, so that you can be prepared for something crossing your field of view.

Reportage photographs taken with telephoto lenses have an identifiable character.

They encourage the photographer to stand back, and this tends to give a cooler, more objective look to photographs of people taken with these lenses. Photographers who prefer the close approach with a standard or wide-angle lens complain that telephoto images communicate a lack of involvement, ad it is true that more often than not this kind of reportage shot makes the viewer an observer rather than a participant. They compress perspective, which can give strong graphic effects under the right circumstances. This also make it easier to isolate figures graphically – the background is a tightly cropped area rather than the entire surroundings including sky, and is usually a little out of focus because of the telephoto lens's shallow depth of field.

EXTREME TELEPHOTO LENSES

Mirror lenses can be used as alternatives to some of the long telephoto focal lengths, yet they have a very different construction and some different picture qualities. Also known as reflex and catadioptric lenses, their design is similar to that of some telescopes: a combination of lenses and mirrors, in two groups. The diagram on the opposite page shows a typical section and light path of a mirror lens. The purpose of the two mirrors is to bounce the light rays back and forth within the lens, so effectively doubling the distance they travel. Optically, this is a convenient way of making a lens that is half the length of its equivalent telephoto. And, as much of the weight of a lens is in the barrel and the glass, a mirror lens is light for its focal length.

The most common focal lengths for mirror lenses are between 300mm and 1000mm, and their main physical characteristic is their ease of handling. A typical 500mm mirror lens weighs in at around 25 oz (700 g); much less than a telephoto lens of the equivalent focal length.

In this backlit shot left, taken with a 500mm mirror lens, the ripples in the water produce pinpoint reflections of the late afternoon sun. However, as they out of focus they record as bright rings, reflecting the construction of the lens.

The visual effect of the 500mm mirror lens is more subtle in the image below left. In out-of-focus areas a slight fringing is seen, particularly beside definite straight lines.

In the angled shot of a car after rain below, the water droplets reflect the sun. As the mirror lens cannot be stopped down to less than its f8 maximum aperture, only a narrow band of droplets appear sharply focused.

PROJECT: The mirror lens "signature"

A telltale picture characteristic of mirror lenses is the ring shape of bright highlights, such as reflections of the sun on water. These small rings, by no means always unpleasant in appearance, are in fact miniature reflections of the rear mirror, the center of which is open to allow the light through to the film. Experiment with this by shooting backlit scenes against reflective surfaces – water, glass or chrome metal, for instance – and with night views that include small lights. A more subtle but consistent effect of this mirror construction is the mildly fringed, diffused treatment of areas in the image that are out of focus.

Potential problems are the fixed aperture, aberrations and, paradoxically, the light weight. The reflex mirror design does not incorporate a variable aperture, so that altering the shutter speed is the usual way of varying exposure (by the equivalent full *f*-stops rather than half *f*-stops). With more effort, neutral density filters can be used in the internal drop-in mount.

Spherical aberration and astigmatism are typical faults in this optical system, making most of these lenses unsuitable when maximum sharpness and contrast are needed. The light weight of the lens coupled with its relatively thick dimensions, make it unusual to hold, and the balance is not to everyone's liking.

Rotating collar mount

Internal filter mount fits behind lens element

The 500mm mirror lens above, is half the length of an equivalent non-mirror telephoto and weighs about the same as a 200mm telephoto.

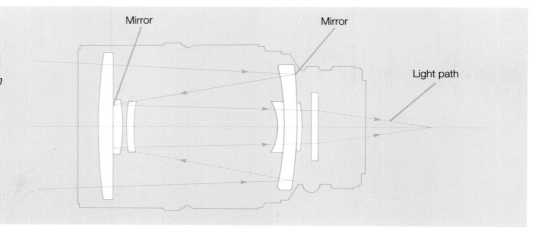

The long telephoto lenses based on the mirror principle have a construction that allows an extremely long focal length to be accommodated within a relatively short, thick barrel. The diagram right shows how, in mirror lenses, the light rays travel through the front of the lens, and are reflected off two internal mirrors to effectively double the distance they travel.

Mirror

Mirror

Light path

ZOOM LENSES

Zoom lenses are an alternative to regular, fixed focal length lenses rather than a supplement. Their principal advantage is that a single zoom lens can encompass a range of focal lengths that would otherwise require two, three or four lenses of fixed focal length. The extent of this "replacement value" depends on how comprehensive a set of lenses you would normally carry, and what importance you attach to being able to select an exact composition.

Precise framing
As the focal length can be altered continuously over the range, there is rather more to a zoom lens than just being able to change from, say, 35mm to 50mm to 70mm. The intermediate transitions allow a precision in the framing that is not normally available. However, although this is obviously useful, you should consider what little difficulty most photographers have in working with a set of fixed focal lengths. The choices in designing photographs are so varied, even with one fixed focal length, that the additional option of a zoom is by no means necessary.

Weight
Zoom lenses are optically complex, in most cases containing between 10 and 20 elements, and the need for this many elements makes them heavier than the equivalent regular lenses, and slower. While one or more zoom lenses will be lighter in the camera bag than the equivalent set of regular lenses, they are heavier in the hand when shooting. Maximum apertures are small by ordinary standards.

A number of zoom lenses at the telephoto end of the range incorporate a "macro" mode in which focusing as close as 18 inches (0.46m) is possible with the lens set at its shortest focal length.

> **PROJECT: A range of composition**
> Choose a fairly static subject, such as a landscape, stay in the same position and make as many different images as possible within the range of focal lengths.

On occasions when there is sufficient time, it is good practice to set the focus at the maximum focal length before zooming back to the length chosen for shooting. As zoom lenses tend to have relatively small maximum apertures, viewing is a little darker than with most regular lenses, and precise focusing is therefore marginally more difficult.

A zoom lens encourages a greater number of composition decisions than does a set of regular fixed focal length lenses. The jump from one focal length to another is replaced with a continuous transition, and the framing choices can be fairly subtle. The best use of a zoom lens is not normally a matter of aiming at one central point and zooming in and out. As you move the zoom control, it is important to reassess the composition. For instance, the best framing may move off-center up to a certain focal length, as show in the example right. There may also be different centers of interest at the longer end of the focal length scale.

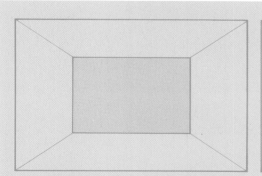

Zoom ratio 2

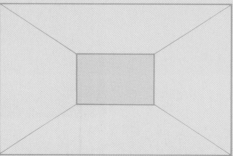

Zoom ratio 3

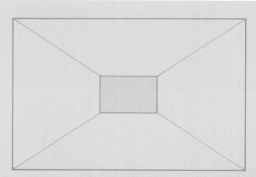

Zoom ratio 4

Expressed here in diagrams, the zoom ratio is the difference in magnification between the minimum and maximum focal lengths of a zoom lens; that is, the longer focal length divided by the shorter. The most common ratios are between 2:1 and 3:1. Lenses with longer ratios are more useful and consequently more desirable, since they replace a wider range of fixed focal length lenses. However, although some zoom lenses are only slightly larger than a standard 50mm lens, most are much heavier than fixed focal length lenses, because of the large number of elements they incorporate. Moreover, their versatility is reflected in a higher price.

CHANGING VIEWPOINT

At least as important as the choice of lens is the camera position – the viewpoint. In many situations, indeed, it is an alternative to solving design problems. Among the basic repertoire of techniques, it should be one of the first considerations.

Altering perspective

Changing the viewpoint is the one action that alters the real perspective in a photograph. That is, it alters the actual relationship between the different parts of a scene. Its effectiveness, therefore, depends on how much of the scene you can see as you move, and this naturally favours wide-angle lenses. It is perhaps fair to say that only a small change of viewpoint is needed with a wide-angle lens for a substantial change to the image. The juxtaposition effects that make telephotos so valuable (see pages 144-51) are controlled by viewpoint, but with a long lens you need to move further to see the relationship change.

In a series of pictures exploring changes of viewpoint with a wide-angle lens, the first shot below left is a medium-distance view. The windmill's symmetry encouraged a central placement in the frame, but the windmill does not balance the two areas of cloud very well. Also, placing it low, to avoid seeing the surroundings, gives too much sky.

Proportion

With a single object, viewpoint determines its shape and its appearance. Moving closer alters the proportions of its different parts, as the sequence of the windmill demonstrates. Its circular base is hardly noticeable in the distant pictures, but in the closest shot it makes up a good third of the building and is an important contrasting shape to the diagonal sails. Moving around a subject gives even greater variety: the front, sides, back and top.

Position and size

The viewpoint controls the relationship between an object and background, or two or more objects, in two ways: position and size. Simply the action of bringing two

Vertical format exaggerates the excess of empty sky

Windmill centered laterally for symmetry

Surroundings cropped at bottom to simplify colours and shapes

Frame kept high to limit appearance of trees and vegetation

Image of windmill shifted left for more balanced composition

Shot timed and positioned so that clouds clear sails of windmill

The second shot above is better organized. The viewpoint is closer, so that the windmill fills more of the frame and is off-centered to give a better balance. Also, the windmill has been moved to the right, to occupy the space between the clouds.

things together in one frame suggests that there is a relationship between them; this is a major design tool. Relationships depend on who chooses to see them, and what one photographer may see as significant, another may ignore or not even notice.

Isolating the subject

The sequence of the Acropolis on page 159 is a case in point. Isolating it with a telephoto lens at sunrise places it deliberately out of context; all relationships have been deliberately avoided to give as timeless a view as possible: the historical version. The last view, by contrast, makes a point of juxtaposition; a decidedly unromantic relationship between the Acropolis and the modern face of Athens.

Changing viewpoint with a wide-angle lens

To explore the effect of changing viewpoint when using a wide-angle lens, as in the sequence of photographs on this and the facing page, find one prominent subject and a reasonably open setting. Both should be fairly large, so that you can alter the perspective substantially and move around to take advantage of a number of viewpoints. The example chosen here is a windmill in an open rural setting, and the lens is 20mm, one of the shortest focal lengths available, with a pronounced wide-angle effect.

Subjective decision

During the course of the exercise, the viewpoint varies from medium-distance to close-up to long-distance. Each version has something to commend it – and perhaps this is a good reason for treating a subject like this in a series of photographs – so that to a large extent the choice of viewpoint is a matter of personal preference.

Views from above

Walking around a subject and changing the distance are the usual ways of altering viewpoint. Less often explored are downward views from overhead. While they are limited by availability, high viewpoints are usually worth trying out. Choose a building with a high balcony, preferably over a busy street or wherever there is plenty of activity. The location for the photograph of the man performing yoga was the Centre Pompidou

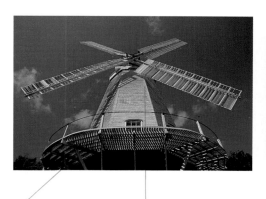

Exaggeration of perspective makes curve dominant

Viewpoint and frame accurate for symmetry

For the third shot above, the viewpoint is directly facing the windmill, to make the most of its symmetry. The exaggerated curve contrasts pleasantly with the triangular features.

Low viewpoint close to foreground vegetation

Horizon high to give prominence to surroundings

Windmill as small as possible while remaining recognizable

The classic depth-enhancing use of a wide-angle lens is seen in the shot above.

Windmill slightly larger and clearer

Structure of vegetation a little clearer

Maximum depth of field gives front-to-back sharpness

The last shot above is similar to the fourth, but a new viewpoint shows more distinctive detail in the foreground, making this part of the picture more prominent.

in Paris, on a Saturday afternoon, when crowds gather and it can be difficult to get an uninterrupted view of the subject from ground level. Using a telephoto lens in this project for its selectivity; you can expect, as here, a simplification of the image; as well as overcoming the problem of intrusive elements, it is also likely, as it has done in this example, to make the background plainer.

PROJECT: Altering viewpoint and lens together

Use whatever focal length seems appropriate for this project, so that you can take all the opportunities offered by different viewpoints. In fact, go further than this, and from different viewpoints make a point of trying out all the lenses you have. Not all of the available focal lengths will be worth using from every camera position, but by changing position you will usually find at least one wide-angle and one telephoto possibility.

In order to be able to make full use of the extremes of focal length, it is important to find a subject that is visible from a distance. The version of this project shown here is a sequence of photographs of the Acropolis in Athens, and specifically the Parthenon, the central building.

The first two shots use a wide-angle lens (20mm) from close to, and make deliberately pronounced graphic arrangements; in the first picture these are triangular, in the second radiating diagonals from the horizontal line. Both pictures use the exaggeration of converging verticals that a wide-angle lens creates.

The third photograph, also from fairly close to the building, uses a telephoto lens to isolate a pattern of verticals from the row of columns, choosing an oblique viewpoint to close the gaps between them. The triangular shadows at the top of two of the columns are deliberately included to relieve the regularity of the vertical lines.

Then, from a distance. Whereas the close views experimented with shape and line, the fourth phot-

ograph deliberately sets out to give a romantic, atmospheric impression of the Acropolis, isolated from its modern surroundings. To this end, a telephoto lens gives a selective view, and the dawn lighting conceals unnecessary modern details in a silhouette. With a longer focal length from the same viewpoint, the graphic possibilities are explored: these are chiefly ones of blocks of tones and horizontal and vertical lines.

At the same time of day, the Acropolis was hardly distinguishable on the skyline with a wide-angle lens; instead, this view was made during the afternoon, when the whiteness of the stone helped it to stand out. With a nearby hill as foreground, and plenty of sky, the setting diminishes the visual importance of the city.

Finally, to make a distinct contrast with modern Athens, a viewpoint was chosen to show the very ordinary, drab streets that surround the Acropolis, and the composition gives them prominence. A standard lens was used to give a view, such as a passer-by might glimpse while walking along.

Taken from ground level, a shot of the man in a yogic position left *would have had a fairly ordinary visual effect, even though the subject is unusual. From directly overhead with a telephoto lens, however, it is graphically strong, simple and unexpected.*

Wide-angle: close

Wide-angle: close

Telephoto: close

Wide-angle: close

Telephoto: distant

Wide-angle: distant

Telephoto: distant

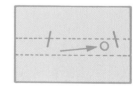

Standard: distant

The sequence of photographs on this page explores just a few of the permutations of viewpoint and focal length used in response to a particularly challenging subject. The Acropolis offers a challenge because, apart from the dramatic shifts in lighting that daily dramatize its form, the frequency with which it is photographed risks making further shots of it look clichéd unless some thought is given to how it is to be treated.

DEPTH AND PERSPECTIVE

Photography's constant relationship with real scenes makes the sense of depth in a picture always important. This is, after all, the way in which three-dimensionality is conveyed and this, naturally, influences the realism of the photograph.

In virtually every photograph, a certain sense of depth is carried across to the viewer, even without the photographer's intervention. How strong or weak this is depends on a considerable number of variables. Knowing what these are is a step towards using them. The sense of depth can be controlled, and it is an important skill.

Using perspective

Perspective is the appearance of objects in space, and their relationships to each other and the viewer. This is its broadest sense. More usually, in photography it is used to describe the intensity of the impression of depth.

The various types of perspective and other depth controls are described in a moment, but before this we ought to consider how to use them, and why. Given the ability to make a difference to the perspective, under what conditions will it help the photograph to enhance, or to diminish, the sense of depth.

Realism

A heightened sense of depth through strong perspective tends to improve the realism of the photograph. It makes more of the representational qualities of the subject, and less of the graphic structure. What Edward Weston, the American photographer, called "straight" photography is better served by use of perspective effects than by techniques that emphasize the purely graphic elements.

Form and content

However, these graphic elements may themselves by sufficiently interesting to merit being the subject of the picture. In photographs such as that of the Thai soldiers in their bright turquoise uniforms on page 125 or the dockside bathed in red light on page 261, the form of the image is at least as important as the content. These are both cases where any available methods

The combination of a 20mm wide-angle lens and a viewpoint that shows the parallel lines of Hadrian's Wall receding directly from the camera proves ideal in the picture right for exploring strong linear perspective.

of reducing perspective are likely to be worthwhile, provided that they do not conflict with the original purpose of the shot.

The following types of perspective contain the main variables that affect our sense of depth in a photograph. Which of these dominate depends on the situation, as does the influence that you can exercise over them.

Linear perspective

In two-dimensional imagery, linear perspective is, overall, the most prominent type of perspective effect. This kind of perspective is characterized by converging lines. These are, in most scenes, actually parallel, like the edges of a road and the top and bottom of a wall, but if they recede from the camera, they appear to converge, towards one

The angle of view to the surface that carries the converging lines determines the strength of the perspective effect. As the diagrams below demonstrate, if this angle is too low, the scene fails to read clearly; if it is too high, little convergence is visible.

Low

Medium   High

or more vanishing points. If they continue in the image for a sufficient distance, they do actually meet at a real point. If the camera is level, and the view is a landscape, the horizontal lines will converge on the horizon. If the camera is pointed upwards, the vertical lines – the sides of a building are the classic example – will converge towards some unspecified part of the sky. Visually, this is more difficult for most people to accept as a normal image.

Diagonal lines

In the process of convergence, all or most of the lines become diagonal, and this, as we have already seen (pages 110-11) induces visual tension and a sense of movement. The movement itself adds to the perception of depth, appearing to happen into and out of the scene.

By association, diagonal lines of all kinds contain a suggestion of depth. This includes shadows: if seen obliquely, they can appear as lines. A direct sun, particularly if low, will enhance perspective if the shadows it casts fall diagonally. Viewpoint determines the degree of convergence. The more acute the angle of view to the surface, the greater the convergence. A minimum angle is, however, necessary: for ground lines to converge, the camera must be at a reasonable height, as the diagrams here show.

Focal length

The focal length of the lens in use is another important factor in influencing linear perspective. Of two lenses aimed directly towards the vanishing point of a scene, the wide-angle lens will show more of the diagonals in the foreground, and these will tend to dominate the structure of the image to a

greater degree. Hence, wide-angle lenses have a propensity to enhance linear perspective, while telephoto lenses tend to flatten it.

Diminishing perspective

This is related to linear perspective, and is in fact a form of it. Imagine a row of identical trees lining a road. A view along the road would produce the familiar convergence in the line of trees, but individually they will appear to be successively smaller. This is diminishing perspective, and works most effectively with identical or similar objects at different distances.

For similar reasons, anything of recognizable size will give a standard of scale; in the appropriate place in the scene, it helps to establish perspective. Also associated with diminishing perspective are placement (things in the lower part of the picture are, through familiarity, assumed to be in the foreground) and overlap (if the outline of one object overlaps another, it is assumed to be the one in front).

Aerial perspective

Atmospheric haze acts as a filter, reducing the contrast in distant parts of a scene and lightening their tone. Our familiarity with this effect (pale horizons, for example), enables our eyes to use it as a clue to depth. Hazy, misty scenes appear deeper than they are because of their strong aerial perspective. It can be enhanced by using backlighting, as in the example here, and by not using filters (such as those designed to cut ultraviolet radiation) which reduce haze. Telephoto lenses tend to show more aerial perspective than do wide-angle lenses if used on different subjects, because they

The diminishing size of the jars above establishes a strong sense of depth. Overlap is also present, and some linear perspective.

Warm hues advance, while cool ones recede, thereby enhancing depth, as in the photograph of an orchid left. That the colour contrast is responsible for this effect, known as colour perspective, is demonstrated by the accompanying monochrome version.

show less of nearby things that have little haze between them and the camera.

Tonal perspective

Apart from the lightening effect that haze has on distant things, light tones appear to

Selective focus, as in the photograph of the boy above, not only isolates a subject and makes it stand out more clearly from its setting; it also establishes a sense of depth.

advance and dark tones recede. So, a light object against a dark background will normally stand forward, with a strong sense of depth. This can be controlled by placing subjects carefully, or by lighting.

Colour perspective

It is universally agreed that warm colours advance and cool colours recede. Other factors apart, therefore, a red or orange subject against a green or blue background will have a sense of depth for purely optical reasons. Again, appropriate positioning can be used as a control. The more intense the colours, the stronger the effect, but if there is a difference in intensity, it should be in favour of the foreground.

Sharpness

Good definition in a photograph suggests closeness, and anything that creates a difference in sharpness in favour of the foreground will enhance the impression of depth. Atmospheric haze has something of this effect. The most powerful control, however, is focus. If there is a difference in sharpness across the image, the eye tends to assume that the foreground is where the area of sharpest focus is to be found.

3   2   1

Progressively lighter shadow tones (1, 2 and 3) indicate the effect of an increasing level of atmospheric haze, *and so establish depth in the street scene above The effect appears strongly in backlighting similar to this.*

Frontal lighting and clear weather are the two conditions that reduce aerial perspective, as in the early morning dockside photograph right. The tones and local contrast in the background and foreground, as marked, are very similar, and give little sense of depth.

Close-up and Macro Lenses

Macro lenses have a number of features which are designed to give better image quality at close distances and more convenient focusing. While any lens can be used for close-up photography (in conjunction with either extension tubes or bellows), the optical characteristics of a non-macro lens do not give the best performance at these scales. Simply extending the focusing range, is not the same as designing a lens specifically for the task.

Resolution

A characteristic feature of macro lenses, by contrast with lenses not specifically designed for this area of photograph, is that the maximum resolution of a macro lens is in the close focusing range rather than at infinity (although for practical purposes image quality is good at conventional distances). The construction is designed for high contrast and for maximum correction of astigmatism. (This, a common problem in close-up photography, is a lens aberration in which a point off the lens axis is focused at the image plane not as a point but as two short lines, at right angles to one another). A further function of the design is suppressing the aberration fluctuation caused by the big range of shooting distances.

Extension tubes and bellows

Most macro lenses can focus down to a distance that gives ½ x (0.5) magnification, and some down to 1 x. For greater magnifications, use either extension tubes or a bellows extension. The former are available in different widths, and a set of three (typically around 35mm, 10mm, and 5mm) can cover most requirements. Bellows extensions allow greater magnification, and over a continuous range. They are best used for controlled indoor work.

For purposes of definition, there are three ranges of photography at shorter-than-conventional distances. The limits of each are practical ones of camera operation. Using magnification of the subject as the standard, close-up photography covers the range from about ⅐ x (0.14) to 1 x. The lower limit is the point at which exposure begins to be affected by the lens extension.

From 1 x up to about 20 x the range is known as photomacrography (not, incidentally, macro-photography, despite the accepted abbreviation "macro"). The lower limit is set by the fact that the lens is now nearer to the subject than it is to the film; at this point an ordinary lens should be reversed so that it faces the camera. Magnification beyond 20 x is the province of photomicrography, for which the special optical and lighting systems of a microscope are more suitable. The main application of this particular area of photography is naturally in scientific work.

To correct the exposure in close-up or macro work, read off the lens-to-film distance against the lens's focal length. Then open up the lens by the number of f-stops indicated. For example, with a lens-to-film distance of 150mm and a focal length of 60mm, increase exposure by 2⅔ f-stops.

LENS FOCAL LENGTH	LENS-TO-FILM DISTANCE (mm)																	
	50	60	70	80	90	100	110	120	130	140	150	160	170	180	190	200	210	220
35mm	1⅓	1½	2	2⅓	2⅔	3	3⅓	3½	3⅔	4	4⅓	4½	4⅔	4⅔	5	5	5⅓	5⅓
50mm	—	½	1	1⅓	1⅔	2	2	2½	2⅔	3	3⅓	3⅓	3½	3⅔	4	4	4	4⅓
55mm	—	⅓	⅔	1	1⅓	1⅔	2	2⅓	2½	2⅔	3	3	3⅓	3½	3⅔	3⅔	4	4
60mm	—	—	½	⅔	1⅓	1½	1⅔	2	2⅓	2½	2⅔	3	3	3⅓	3⅓	3½	3⅔	4
80mm	—	—	—	—	⅓	½	⅔	1⅓	1½	1⅔	1⅔	2	2⅓	2⅓	2½	2⅔	3	3
90mm	—	—	—	—	—	⅓	⅓	⅔	1⅓	1⅓	1½	1⅔	1⅔	2	2	2⅓	2½	2½
105mm	—	—	—	—	—	—	—	⅓	½	⅔	1	1⅓	1⅓	1½	1⅔	2	2	2
120mm	—	—	—	—	—	—	—	—	⅓	⅓	½	⅔	1	1⅓	1⅓	1½	1½	1⅔
135mm	—	—	—	—	—	—	—	—	—	—	⅓	⅓	½	⅔	1	1	1⅓	1⅓
150mm	—	—	—	—	—	—	—	—	—	—	—	—	⅓	½	½	⅔	⅔	1
180mm	—	—	—	—	—	—	—	—	—	—	—	—	—	—	—	⅓	⅓	½
200mm	—	—	—	—	—	—	—	—	—	—	—	—	—	—	—	—	—	⅓

Magnification

Macro and close-up photography are performed at extremely short distances, so there are a few special technical aspects to consider. Regular camera systems are designed for use at normal distances – generally between about 3 feet (1m) and infinity – so that apart from some special equipment, macro and close-up work needs some special optical precautions. The principal ones are:

• Exposure. Magnification involves light loss, so that either the film needs more exposure, or the illumination must be stronger, or both.

• Depth of field. This diminishes as the magnification is increased. The traditional answer of stopping down the aperture does not work very well at these scales, because diffraction increases strongly.

• Optical quality. Regular lenses are optimized for normal distances. Either special macro lenses are needed for best image quality, or a regular lens should be reversed. Diffraction is an additional problem.

Supplementary close-up lenses

In terms of optical performance, supplementary lenses for close-up work do not have quite the same quality as a prime lens used at an extension, but for modest magnifications they are quick and convenient to use. Also, no allowance needs to be made for exposure. The magnification varies with the point of focus of the prime lens.

R	M	E	F	X
1:10	0.1×	1.2	⅓	1.1
1:5	0.2×	1.4	½	1.2
1:3.3	0.3×	1.7	⅔	1.3
1:2.5	0.4×	2	1	1.4
1:2	0.5×	2.3	1⅓	1.5
1:1.7	0.6×	2.6	1⅓	1.6
1:1.4	0.7×	2.9	1½	1.7
1:1.2	0.8×	3.2	1½	1.8
1:1.1	0.9×	3.6	1⅔	1.9
1:1	1×	4	2	2
1.2:1	1.2×	4.8	2⅓	2.2
1.4:1	1.4×	5.8	2½	2.5
1.6:1	1.6×	6.8	2⅔	2.7
1.8:1	1.8×	7.8	3	2.8
2:1	2×	9	3⅓	3
2.2:1	2.2×	10.2	3⅓	3.2
2.4:1	2.4×	11.6	3½	3.5
2.6:1	2.6×	13	3½	3.7
2.8:1	2.8×	14.4	3⅔	3.8
3:1	3×	16	4	4

If you have worked out the reproduction ratio or magnification, increase exposure using the table above. R = reproduction, M = magnification, E = exposure, F = exposure increase in f-stops. X (an alternative to F) = decrease in flash-to-subject distance.

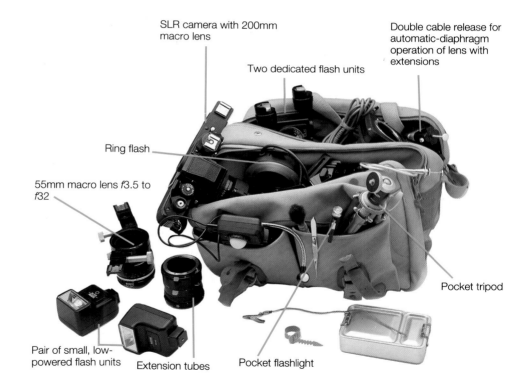

SLR camera with 200mm macro lens

Double cable release for automatic-diaphragm operation of lens with extensions

Two dedicated flash units

Ring flash

55mm macro lens f3.5 to f32

Pocket tripod

Pair of small, low-powered flash units

Extension tubes

Pocket flashlight

The equipment above has been selected for a close-up field trip. Although only one or two focal lengths are needed, the extra equipment needed to extend the lens and to provide additional illumination makes for a heavier bag than in most normal photography.

The chart right *shows the reproduction ratios and magnification produced by using lens extensions ranging from 5mm to 150mm on a 50mm, 100m and 200mm lens, respectively.*

LENS EXTENSION: REPRODUCTION RATIOS AND MAGNIFICATION						
	50mm lens		100mm lens		200mm lens	
Extension (mm)	Reproduction ratio	Magnification	Reproduction ratio	Magnification	Reproduction ratio	Magnification
5	1:10	0.1×	1:20	0.05×	1:40	0.025×
10	1:5	0.2×	1:10	0.1×	1:20	0.05×
15	1:3.3	0.3×	1:7	0.15×	1:13	0.075×
20	1:2.5	0.4×	1:5	0.2×	1:10	0.1×
25	1:2	0.5×	1:4	0.25×	1:8	0.125×
30	1:1.7	0.6×	1:3.3	0.3×	1:7	0.15×
35	1:1.4	0.7×	1:2.8	0.35×	1:6	0.175×
40	1:1.2	0.8×	1:2.5	0.4×	1:5	0.2×
45	1:1.1	0.9×	1:2.2	0.45×	1:4.4	0.225×
50	1:1	1×	1:2	0.5×	1:4	0.25×
55	1.1:1	1.1×	1:1.8	0.55×	1:3.6	0.275×
60	1.2:1	1.2×	1:1.7	0.6×	1:3.3	0.3×
70	1.4:1	1.4×	1:1.4	0.7×	1:2.8	0.35×
80	1.6:1	1.6×	1:1.2	0.8×	1:2.5	0.4×
90	1.8:1	1.8×	1:1.1	0.9×	1:2.2	0.45×
100	2:1	2×	1:1	1×	1:2	0.5×
110	2.2:1	2.2×	1.2:1	1.1×	1:1.8	0.55×
120	2.4:1	2.4×	1.2:1	1.2×	1:1.7	0.6×
130	2.6:1	2.6×	1.3:1	1.3×	1:1.5	0.65×
140	2.8:1	2.8×	1.4:1	1.4×	1:1.4	0.7×
150	3.1	3×	1.5:1	1.5×	1:1.3	0.75×

The chart right *compares the reproduction ratios and magnification obtained with a standard 50mm lens on a 35mm camera and focused on infinity with the same lens focused at 3 feet (1m).*

	50mm lens on 35mm camera, focus ∞			
Add supplementary lens	+½ diopter	+1 diopter	+2 diopters	+3 diopters
Reproduction ratio	1:40	1:20	1:10	1:6
Magnification	0.025×	0.05×	0.1×	0.17×
	50mm lens on 35mm camera, focus 3 feet (1 m)			
Reproduction ratio	1:20	1:10	1:6	1:5
Magnification	0.05×	0.1×	0.17×	0.2×

Width of butterfly is equal
to width of the frame:
50mm

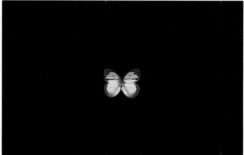

Magnification 0.1x

Magnification 0.5x

To demonstrate the range of normal performance of extension tubes and bellows, select a subject that has plenty of structural detail, a relatively flat surface (to avoid depth-of-field problems) and which is not much larger than, for example, a 35mm mount. Note that the magnifications given here are for the images as they appear on each 35mm slide. For the purposes of clarity, the three photographs shown here have been enlarged on the page.

Magnification 5x

CREATIVE FOCUS

Sharp focus is such an accepted standard in photography that it is rarely treated as anything other than a way of producing a "correct" image, on the lines of loading the film properly and other essentials. Only occasionally does it occur to most people to vary the focus for the effect it has on the design. Yet, under the right circumstances, this can be effective.

Spontaneous focusing

The question of where to focus seldom arises because the normal practice of making a photograph is first to decide what the subject is and then to aim the camera. Natural enough, certainly, and the usual focus problems are those of accuracy rather than of selection. Under normal circumstances, the point to be focused on – the eyes in a face, or a figure standing in front of a background – presents itself without an alternative, and if there is any variation in the way the focus appears in the final photograph, it is in the form of a mistake. The popularity and success of autofocus lenses is testimony to how predictable are most people's focusing decisions.

Certain situations, however, do offer a choice, and this lies mainly in how you define the image. When photographing a

In wildlife photography there is often no alternative to shooting through foliage with a telephoto lens. Nevertheless, it is no bad thing to have out-of-focus elements in the foreground. They reinforce the sense of a hidden glimpse, and emphasize the sharp focus more clearly.

group of objects, should they all appear in sharp focus? Would it be more effective if just one or a few were sharp and the rest progressively soft? If so, which ones should be in focus and which not? Moreover, there might not necessarily be such a choice of deep or shallow focus. If the light level is low for the combination of film and lens, it may only be possible to have one zone of the image in focus, and in this case you will be forced into a selective decision.

Experimenting with focus

Whatever the reasons, never underestimate the visual power of focus. The fact that sharpness is the virtually unquestioned standard is enough to show that whatever is focused on becomes, a priori, the point of attention. Deliberate misuse, or rather, unexpected use, often works well.

If you are using focus in an expected way, it is important to appreciate its different uses with different focal lengths. Even without any knowledge of or interest in the techniques of photography, most people looking at a photograph are familiar with the way the focus is normally distributed. With a telephoto lens, the depth of field is shallow, and there is typically a range of focus that can be seen in one photograph, from soft to sharp. As the sharp area is expected to coincide with the main point of interest – where the eye is expected finally to rest – the range of focus contains a sense of direction from unsharp to sharp. This is not nearly such a strong inducement to the eye as the lines of view that we have just looked at, but it works nevertheless. What is important is that it works through the familiarity of the viewer with the way his or her own eyes will focus on an object.

Shorter focal lengths give images with better depth of field, and we are accustomed to seeing wide-angle views that are sharp throughout. As a result, focus is not normally a quality that is noticed. However, a fast wide-angle lens used at maximum aperture with a deep subject will show unsharpness somewhere in the frame, and this needs to be handled carefully.

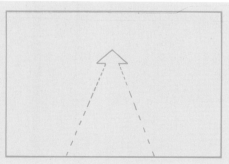

In the shot above a 600mm lens focused on the distance gives a very shallow depth of field. From the slightly elevated viewpoint of a vehicle's roof, the focus is progressive.

The diagram left shows how the eye is led rapidly upwards to the point of focus. Placing the main subject high in the frame makes the most of this effect.

MAKING GOOD USE OF FILTERS

The range of filters is considerable, but comprises these six groups:

- Filters which enhance contrast by absorbing ultraviolet rays
- Filters which alter tonal values in black-

1 Oversize plastic holder that screws onto the front of a lens, using an interchangeable set of screw mounts. It accepts its own range of plastic rectangular filters in two sets of grooves. These can be rotated or shifted. 2 Screw-fitting glass filter for shooting with daylight-balanced film in fluorescent light. 3 Smaller, regular version of the most widely used patented system, in design identical to 1. Shown here with a graduated filter, one of the most useful for altering the balance of light from one part of the picture to another. 4 Semi-transparent tape for mounting gelatin filters behind lenses, inside the camera body. 5 Gelatin filter. Normally available as squares — this is the common 3 x 3 inch (75 x 75mm) size — they come in a wide range of colours. 6 Internal lens mount. This model fits inside a 600mm telephoto behind the rear lens group. The small glass filters are interchangeable. 7 Bellows lens shade that has a slit which accepts 3 x 3 inch (75 x 75mm) gelatin filters. Adaptor rings allow it to fit the majority of 35mm and rollfilm camera lenses. 8 Metal sleeve holder for gelatin filters to fit in the bellows lens shade. 9 Screw-on glass light-balancing filter. 10 Light-balancing square plastic filter for use in the patented holder 1. 11 Optical flat. This example, a polarizing filter, is made of relatively thick glass that is free of optical distortion, bound in a metal frame. Expensive. 12 Glass correction filter for photomicrography: a plain disc that fits in the microscope converter. 13 Polarizing filter in rotating mount, with small handle. The polarizing effect depends on the angle of the view to the light source, so that rotation is an essential control.

and-white photography
- Filters which reduce the quantity of light
- Filters which alter the colour temperature of light
- Filters which alter colour.
- Effects filters.

In these pages we concentrate on the forms in which filters are available and the types of mount. Filters are most commonly available as thin gelatin (a wide range but damageable), glass that screws directly on to the lens, and plastic that fits in a special holder.

Effects filters

Whereas the prime function of most filters is to make corrective adjustments to the light transmitted by the lens, the purpose of effects filters is to alter the picture substantially. They are valuable only if used sparingly and intelligently but are not, under

any circumstances, responsible for producing "creative" images, manufacturers' claims notwithstanding.

There is some overlap between effects filters and basic filters. This is in areas where there is a consensus on what are considered acceptable alternatives to an image, and include the use of a polarizing filter and a neutral graduating filter. Many filter effects are very specific – for instance, the use of shaped masks. Although they can be fun to use occasionally, I feel that most photographers are probably better off without them.

Colour correction filters

These filters are, for the most part, designed to improve the accuracy of colours recorded on film. They are particularly important for colour transparency film, as most people

can easily detect a colour shift of as little as 5 or 10 per cent. Colour negative film can be filtered quite strongly later, during printing, and does not need the same degree of precision.

Filter terminology can be confusing, with different descriptions commonly used for the same group of filters, but there are basically two types: one alters the colour temperature, and the other covers primary and secondary colours. Filters on the colour temperature scale are either bluish or amber, in a variety of strengths, and are designed to match light source to film.

There are two kinds of colour-balanced film – daylight and tungsten – and each is intended to give a neutral rendering of colours when used with its respective lighting. For convenience, strong amber and blue filters allow film balanced for one kind of light to be used in another. These filters – 80A for using daylight-balanced film in photographic tungsten light and 85B for using tungsten-balanced film in daylight or with flash – are the extremes of this range of filters. They are sometimes known as colour conversion filters, but also as colour balancing or light balancing filters.

Tinted effects

In between these two points on the colour temperature scale are filters in milder tints of the same colours. On the Kodak scale,

For making small adjustments to the colour temperature in daylight shots, the mildest colour correction filters are 81A, for warming, left and 82A, for cooling, right. In practice, 81A and the slightly stronger 81B and 81C are the most often used when overcast weather raises the colour temperature.

The same scene photographed with and without a filter, top and above, respectively, shows the effect of a graduated filter very clearly. The typical use in a landscape is to bring the brightness of the sky colour to that of the ground (or, in this case, water). Note that it also concentrates the attention more towards the center of the frame.

the "80" series and "85" series are for major conversions between film types, but the "81" series and "82" series are for making small adjustments. In daylight, the colour temperature varies from the standard of a bright midday sun in a clear sky. In cloudy weather the colour temperature is slightly higher, and the effect a little more blue, or "colder", and in open shade under a blue sky, the blue cast is even stronger.

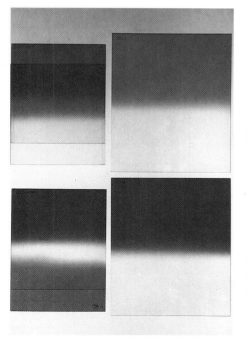

Two different sizes and strengths of plastic neutral graduated filter are shown left *in different combinations. The two larger filters are of normal strength,* above *and double strength,* below. *For a greater degree of shading, filters can be laid on top of one another, as shown* top left. *To emphasize a horizon only, filters can be opposed to each other, as seen* far left. *The upper shot of the pair* above *was taken with a single normal-strength filter.*

Both of these conditions can be made to appear neutral with one or more of the straw-tinted 81 series of filters. Towards sunset and sunrise, the colour temperature on a clear day falls as the sun appears more orange, and in theory at least, this could be brought back to "normal" by using a bluish filter from the 82 series. In practice, hardly anyone ever bothers to do this, as people are used to seeing light from a low sun that *is* rich and warm. The 82 "cooling" range of filters is more often used in tungsten lighting to make non-photographic lamps appear less orange.

Colour compensating filters

Colour compensating filters are available in the six colours used in film dyes – the colours of the photographic process, in other words. These are red, green and blue, and their complementary opposites cyan, magenta and yellow. One major use of these filters is to correct the greenish and bluish casts from fluorescent and vapour discharge lighting.

Pale filters

There are also, however, less extreme shifts of colour that may need attention, and the range of colour that may need attention, and the range of colour compensating filters includes very faint tints, from CC05 (a density of 0.05) to CC50 (0.5 density). The range can be added together to produce any density and colour combination. One reason for using compensating filters is if the colour accuracy of a particular batch of film is not perfect (manufacturing tolerances and ageing effects may throw the balance out of neutral). Another is when duplicating slides: in this case, a mismatch of dyes between the original transparency and the film with which it is being photographed is a fairly common occurrence.

Graduated filters

If you hold a coloured or neutral density gelatin filter so that it covers only a part of the camera's lens, its edge will appear blurred in the viewfinder – precisely how blurred will depend on the distance at

The surface of the rock carrying these prehistoric rock carvings, or petroglyphs, left *and* below, *was sufficiently shiny to respond well to the use of a polarizing filter. From this angle to the sunlight, the effect of adding a polarizer was dramatic: the glare was cut out and the petroglyphs rendered clearly visible.*

which the lens is focused and on the depth of field. In turn, the depth of field depends on the aperture setting and on the focal length. At one extreme, a fully stopped-down wide-angle lens focused close will make the filter's edge almost sharp, at the other, a telephoto focused at infinity and at full aperture will hardly even show that the filter is there. If you could control the exact amount of blurring of the filter's edge, it would be possible to cover just a selected part of the image without an obvious line across the picture.

This is the principle of the graduated filter, long a standard item in cinematography, where none of the tonal controls used in printing still images are possible.

On a wide-angle lens the edge will be less soft, as it will if the lens is stopped down. In practice, the range of settings that can be tolerated visually is wide, but a graduated filter has little use with a telephoto lens. The distinction between the two halves is too soft to be noticeable, and the thickness of the filter (most are plastic) can cause a significant deterioration in image quality.

Critical shading

A graduated filter has an even tint covering half of the area; the remainder is clear. The border between the two is critical, for to be unnoticeable in a photograph, it must shade smoothly between the two halves. Even so, it depends for successful use on the psychology of perception. The neutrally tinted

One of the most frequent uses of a polarizing filter is to reduce troublesome reflections when shooting through a window, as in the photograph opposite.

version is extremely useful in adjusting the light selectively. Its most common use is to darken the sky without affecting the remainder of the scene. Although a graduated filter has the same effect on any film, it is needed less with colour or black-and-white negative emulsions, as these are always used for printing and it is a relatively simple matter to darken a broad area during enlargement by the equivalent of a few stops. Colour transparencies, unless used only for printing, offer no opportunity for post-correction, and any alterations to the density of the image must be made while the film is in the camera.

One occasional problem with colour transparency film is that the toned part of the filter may not appear neutral with certain emulsions. This is another version of the familiar problem of using one set of dyes (in the film) to photograph another (in the filter). A mismatch sometimes occurs; in addition, the dyes in a filter are also prone to fading and discoloration with time.

Polarizing filters

Polarizing filters, medium-grey in appearance, are made of specially stressed plastic sandwiched in glass, and will cut certain kinds of reflected and scattered light. What makes them particularly useful for photography is that they have three main practical effects: they can darken blue skies, cut down reflections from non-metallic surfaces, and increase the colour saturation in colour images. They are visually neutral, and so they add no colour cast to the picture. For photographers who value intense colour images in outdoor photography, they are among the most useful accessories, and for more specialized applications, such as

copying paintings under glass, they can solve problems in a unique way by cutting reflections.

How polarization works

Light, although it travels in straight lines, vibrates from side to side – that is, at right angles to its directions of travel. Under normal conditions, the light vibrates in all possible directions (i.e. right, left, front, back, etc). Under certain conditions, however, the light can be made to vibrate in one direction only (e.g. left to right) – still at right angles to its path. Any non-metallic surface has the ability to make this happen when light bounces off it. So, light reflected from water or glass, as two common examples, is partially polarized, although this is still not a visible effect.

A polarizing filter is made in such a way that it allows to pass through it only light that is vibrating in one plane. An analogy would be trying to drop a series of thin straight rods through a slatted screen: only those that fell parallel to the slats would fall through the screen.

Intensification of colour

Sunlight is rarely completely polarized, so that even if the filter is rotated for its maximum blocking effect, some light still passes through. Reflections from water and glass, where the light has been partially polarized, can often be virtually removed. The effect on a blue sky occurs because the atmosphere scatters light by reflection. Colours in general appear more intense because the amount of light reflected from a coloured surface and striking the film is reduced, so reducing the brightness of the surface as seen through the viewfinder.

Light

Light is the essential commodity in photography. It creates the image, and at the same time is responsible for much of the style and feel of a picture. Film records light, and making sure that just the right quantity passes through the lens and the shutter is the job of the camera's exposure system. How you use the light, though, is a matter for your eye as a photographer. The way in which it strikes a landscape or a surface has an important bearing on the detail and texture that your photograph will show, while the quality of the light can often determine whether the image is attractive, striking, gentle or dramatic.

The film is one variable in dealing with the amount of light. The other two are both in the camera – the shutter and the aperture, each regulating the amount of light reaching the film. At the same time they have other functions, and in many picture situations you can choose which has the higher priority – a higher shutter speed to freeze movement or a smaller aperture to give better depth of field. Unless you decide to override the controls, most cameras now adjust shutter and aperture automatically, so that you can usually assume that the exposure will be acceptable.

A further major consideration is the colour of light – not normally something you would think of when just looking at a scene. Unlike the eye, which can accommodate to many variations in colour without our noticing, film reacts selectively. Human vision is sophisticated enough to make its own compensations. For example, tungsten light never seems quite as orange to the eye as it really is; nor does skylight on a clear day appear its full blue. Film responds more literally, and if you want the results to be completely realistic, the light – or the film – needs to be balanced for colour. Filters are the usual method, and are used either over the lens or over the light source. The alternative is to use a film that is specially designed for a certain colour of light.

Finally, if the light source you are using is flash, it must be synchronized with the camera's shutter. All the other kinds of light that you are likely to use in normal photography

Carefully chosen lighting brings out textural quality. In the close-up of a large Oriental bronze urn above, the warm colours of a low sun emphasize both the relief and the patina of the metal.

Natural lighting at its most unusual – the underground lake left refracts and reflects a single shaft of midday sunlight that pierces a small hole in the limestone roof.

are continuous – even fluorescent tubes, which flicker, work as if they are continuous as long as you use a shutter speed slower than about $\frac{1}{30}$ second. Flash, however, is an important kind of photographic lighting, and has special needs.

Modern electronic cameras take care of most of these technical requirements, which is all to the good because it is in the quality of light that the really important decisions lie. This means appreciating what kind of lighting works most effectively for different subjects and scenes; how to make the best use of the lighting conditions that you are faced with when you cannot change them; and being sensitive to the varieties of mood that lighting can create.

SUNLIGHT

Sunlight's direction is a major variable in photography. The sun moves across the sky, reaching different heights according to the time of day, the season and the latitude. The camera angle can be altered in any direction, and many subjects can be moved to face towards or away from the sun. The result is a variety of possible angles between the sun on the one hand and both the camera and the subject on the other.

Atmospheric effects

Before it reaches any subject, sunlight first has to pass through the atmosphere and is modified. It is slightly softened, the more so if it passes through a greater depth of atmosphere, as it does when the sun is low. It is also scattered selectively, so that the sky appears blue, and the sunlight can be any colour between white and red. Added to this, weather conditions filter and reflect the light even more strongly. Clouds take an infinite variety of forms, combinations and coverage, while haze, fog, mist, dust, rain, snow and pollution have their own distinctive filtering effects.

Finally, the surroundings themselves alter the illumination by the way they block off some of the light and reflect other parts of it. The net result of all this is that four things happen to sunlight. It is diffused, absorbed selectively (which changes the colour according to which wavelengths are removed from the spectrum), reflected and selectively reflected (with a colouring effect).

The blue of the sky is caused by scattering of the short wavelengths, and is sometimes referred to as skylight. In shade, the eye expects skylight to be neutral – that is, white. Occasionally it is, but usually it is blue, and then the problem is to work out exactly how blue. Using the colour temperature table below as a guide, find a shade situation under an intense blue sky, as opposite, and shoot several frames with progressively stronger amber conversion filters. Avoid shaded areas that receive reflected light from buildings and other surroundings – the idea is to work with a strong blue skylight.

The pair of photographs of a wallaby, on the opposite page, taken within minutes of each other, shows the typical difference in light level and colour temperature between sun and shade on a bright day. To the eye, the colour of the animal when it had moved into the shade seemed neutral; in the film, we can see the distinct blue cast from the skylight.

K	MIREDS	NATURAL SOURCE	ARTIFICIAL SOURCE
10,000	56	Blue sky	
7500	128	Shade under blue sky	
7000	135	Shade under partly cloudy sky	
6500	147	Daylight, deep shade	
6000	167	Overcast sky	Electronic flash
5500	184	Average noon daylight	Flash bulb
5000	200		
4500	222	Afternoon sunlight	Fluorescent "daylight"
4000	286		Fluorescent "warm white"
3500		Early morning/evening sunlight	Photofloods (3400K)
3000	333	Sunset	Photolamps/studio tungsten (3200K)
2500	400		Domestic tungsten
1930	518		Candlelight

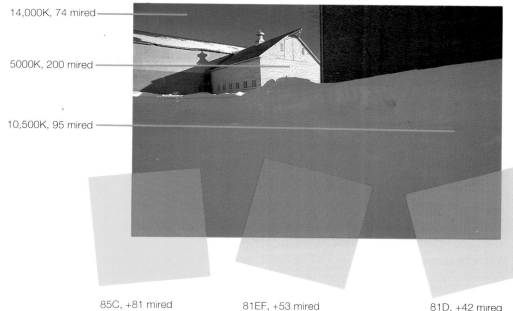

14,000K, 74 mired

5000K, 200 mired

10,500K, 95 mired

85C, +81 mired   81EF, +53 mired   81D, +42 mired

Colour temperature

In photography, colour temperature is the usual way of describing the main colour differences in light. Light can be any colour, but the most important form, sunlight, varies along one scale, from reddish-orange to blue. A rich sunset is red, a clear sky, blue, while the sun in the middle of the day appears white. The scale is referred to as colour temperature because this range of colour change is what happens when a substance is heated. As heat increases, the first sign of colour is a dull red glow, and then the colour becomes more orange and then yellow, until it reaches white heat. Beyond white-hot, the colour changes to blue, and some stars burn this intensely.

You can define a colour on this scale precisely by referring to its temperature. The reason for doing this is that there are many occasions when neutral (that is, white) lighting is needed. The eye tends to adjust to changes in colour: if you sit under tungsten lighting at night, before long it appears more or less white. By contrast, film reproduces colour exactly as it is. Tungsten lighting, being created by heat, is on the colour temperature scale, and light from a 100-watt lamp appears quite orange on film. Its colour temperature is 2860 K. (K = kelvin, the standard unit of thermo-dynamic temperature.) In photography, white is 5500 K, the colour temperature of sunlight at midday in summer. To make what you see by the light of the lamp look like the image on film, the light passing through the lens must be more blue. Hence the use of colour conversion filters and colour film that is balanced for tungsten light (Types A and B film).

DIRECT SUN

The least complicated form of natural light is the sun in a clear sky. Without clouds or other weather effects, the lighting conditions are predictable during most of the day. The sun's arc through the sky varies with the season and the latitude, but it is consistent. As the sun rises in the sky its intensity increases, but as the diagrams *opposite* show, the light levels are not in proportion to the sun's height. They rise quickly in the morning and fall quickly in the late afternoon, but during the middle of the day they change very little. Once the sun is at about 40° above the horizon, it is almost at its brightest. How long it spends above this height depends on the season and the latitude. In the tropics this can be as much as 7 hours, in a mid-latitude summer 8 hours, and in a mid-latitude winter, no time at all. On a winter's day in the northern USA or Europe, light levels change steadily but slowly from sunrise to sunset. In the summer, the levels change more quickly at either end of the day, but very little for the hours around noon.

Light absorption

The thickness of the atmosphere affects the light's intensity. At higher altitudes, the light levels are higher because the more particles that are in the air, the more light is absorbed. The atmosphere also scatters different wavelengths selectively. White light from the sun reaches the earth only after passing through the molecules that make up the atmosphere, and these are small enough to have a scattering effect on the shortest wavelengths. As these are at the blue end of the spectrum, there are two visible effects. One is that, away from a direct view of the sun, you can see the scattered wavelengths in the form of a clear blue sky. Looking directly at the sun, the colour of the light depends on how much of the blue wavelengths have been scattered and lost; when the sun is high, very little, but close to sunrise and sunset, when the light has to pass obliquely through a much greater thickness of atmosphere, the light is shifted towards the red end of the spectrum. The lower levels of the atmosphere have the greatest effect on sunrise and sunset, and as these vary locally quite a lot, the colours can differ from place to place and from day to day, between yellow and red. The scattering effect performs a kind of large-scale division of the spectrum. The light source remains white, but it reaches us in a split form. In the middle of the day, this is predictable, but at either end, less so.

The effect of the blue sky, also known as skylight, is so much weaker than direct sunlight that it is felt only in the shade. It acts as a reflector, with little measurable influence close to the angle of the sun, but acting so as to tint shadows when opposite. The third lighting element on a clear day is the surroundings. These also act as reflectors, and so affect the shadows.

The atmosphere scatters sunlight, and its effect is at its greatest when the sun is low in the sky. Because the shortest wavelengths, which occur at the blue end of the spectrum, scatter the most easily, what remains visible when we look at a low sun is the red or orange wavelengths from the other end of the spectrum. The soft shadows on these airport buildings are lit by the scattered, bluish light.

In order to illustrate the daily variation in lighting provided by the sun as it travels across the sky, a series of shots was taken of a sea arch on the coast of Mallorca. The effects of the changing angle of lighting on modelling, colour, contrast and the balance of the image are very clear in a side-by-side comparison like this.

Sunrise

Anticipating the sun's path

The angle at which the sun rises and sets varies considerably according to the time of year (and also to the latitude). In both instances, the arc of the sun's passage becomes higher or lower. In the summer the angle is steeper, and the position of sunrise and sunset further apart.

When planning a photograph for the best light, particularly when the sun is low, it is important to know what path the sun will trace. In an unfamiliar place, where the sunrise and sunset times are different than at home, first find out when they are (the times are usually given in a local newspaper) and where on the horizon they occur (this you must check by seeing it).

The most difficult prediction to make is the exact alignment of sun and subject. With a large subject, such as a mountain on the horizon, even small changes in the alignment will need movement over some distance between camera positions. As the apparent movement of the sun is greatest close to the horizon, last-minute changes may not be possible. Sunset is easier to anticipate than sunrise, because the path can be seen. If you are waiting for sunrise, remember that the pre-dawn glow is *not* where the sun will appear; the glow will move south if you are in the northern hemisphere and north if you are in the southern.

Early morning

Mid morning

Noon

Mid afternoon

Late afternoon

Sunset

A High, Bright Sun

Quality of illumination is primarily responsible for the atmosphere of an image. The sun's angle to the subject is mainly important for those subjects that "face" in a particular direction, and in revealing plastic qualities such as shape, form, and texture.

Predictable effects

Suitability and aesthetics apart, the fairly high angle of the sun of the hours around the middle of the day has a reputation for being standard. However, there are problems with a high sun, the most obvious of which is that it is over-familiar, and certainly not inherently exciting.

People living in the tropics usually shelter from the sun, and this can be used as a visual symbol. The worker in Manila above is heavily masked, despite the heat.

In flat subjects like this beach landscape off Borneo left there is nothing to cast a shadow under the vertical lighting, and the contrast range is remarkably low.

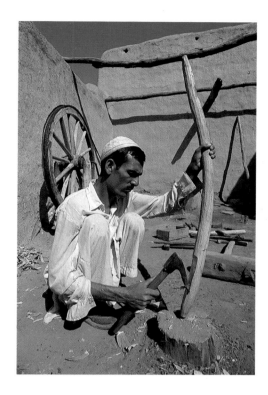

The contrast range in the shot of a Pathan craftsman above was high at about 6 stops: the highlight reading, taken from his shoulder, was f32, and the shadow reading, taken from his neck, was f4. The average tone, and incident light reading, was f4. However, his white clothes are such an important part of the image that they control the exposure setting; over-exposure would be unacceptable. This exposure gives deep shadows, but the viewpoint was chosen to keep these small.

Bright, clear weather adds to the complexity of the street corner in Jaipur, India right by throwing extremely dense shadows. The stark, graphic effect produced is in itself visually interesting, however, and made the photograph worth taking.

For an audience, there is an undeniable visual premium on interesting and unusual lighting. However, it is important not to go overboard with the idea of spectacle. Dramatic lighting effects are only powerful in comparison with a variety of other conditions, and it would be wrong to think that a midday sun is good for nothing. The positive qualities are a crispness and detail that are bright and definite. As long as the shadows contain nothing important, these are good opportunities for making highly representative photographs. Subjects with a strong intrinsic form – i.e. shape or colour – do well in this light. If the air is clear, the precision of the image is heightened.

One of the principal difficulties is in the way the shadows fall. The higher the sun, the more they fall underneath. In a facial portrait, this lighting is unsuitable as the shadows tend to conceal the eyes. It is also unflattering, which becomes a problem if the photograph is intended to be a pleasing portrait, rather than a piece of reportage. With many other subjects it simply reduces the modelling effect that might have been useful for showing form and volume (hence the success of strong shapes and colours which can make this unnecessary). Flat, horizontal subjects, like level landscapes, suffer as much as any: shadows are minimal, showing little texture.

Tropical sunlight

In the tropics, the sun is noticeably high for about two or three hours a day, and there is no sense of front, back or side to the sunlight. Shadows lie directly underneath things. Roofs and awnings cast deep shadows, but under many subjects, such as people or cars, the shadows are very small. Anything more or less level, like most landscapes, appears without any significant shadows at all. It is easy to regard this overhead light as harsh and unattractive, and by conventional standards it probably is for many subjects, but it would be dogmatic to dismiss it as being generally unsuitable.

Look for scenes that convey the impression of tropical heat, and light and shade.

MORNING AND AFTERNOON LIGHT

For effective lighting, the morning and the afternoon are probably the best times of day. The lower angle of the sun is more flattering to most subjects than that around midday. In addition, while the sun – well clear of the horizon but not really high – may lack the potential drama that it has around dawn and dusk, it still gives attractive and more reliable lighting. The colour is nearer a neutral white, and for those who find a long run of orange- and red-hued images exaggerated, it is more straightforward. If a true colour rendering is important, shoot with the sun at least an hour or two away from the horizon.

Make full use of the sun's lower angle by choosing its angle to the camera: behind, in front, or to one side. The visual effects are quite different, and are more accentuated when the sun is closer to the horizon. Silhouettes made by shooting into the sun are covered on pages 186–7, but in mid-morning and mid-afternoon you need tallish subjects.

Side lighting

The most characteristic lighting effect at these times is side lighting. In fact, of all the types of direct sunlight, side lighting is probably the most useful when modelling and texture are important characteristics in the subject. Shadows are the most important feature of side lighting, and it is these that show the relief of surfaces and objects. As the diagrams *below* show, shadows appear longest to the camera and most distinct under side lighting. The other condition under which the sunlight is at right angles to the camera's view is when the sun is overhead, but in this case, the ground limits the extent of the shadows, and also tends to act as a reflector to fill them in.

The shadows from side lighting have three effects. The first is that the shadow edge traces the shape of the front of the subject, and so has a modelling effect. You can see this in the photograph of the two women on the opposite page. The second effect is on surface texture. Shadows are longest under side lighting, and so the small ridges, wrinkles and other fine details of a surface show up in the strongest relief, as in the photograph of the paper lantern opposite.

Contrast

The third effect of side lighting is on contrast. If the sky is clear, and there is nothing nearby to reflect the light, such as buildings, the contrast between light and shade will be high. Moreover, as the diagrams *below* show, it needs very little to change a lit background into a shaded one, and a dark setting will help a side-lit subject to stand out very clearly. The photograph of the two women illustrates both points.

There is an alternative camera position: overhead. In this case, the contrast is usual-

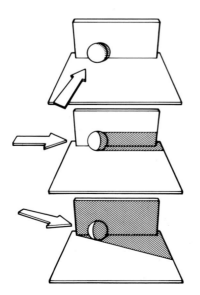

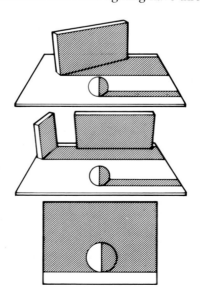

Side lighting far left *produces the most distinct shadows. This sequence shows what happens as the direction of sunlight moves from frontal to back. The shadows are smallest from the camera's viewpoint in frontal lighting, and in back lighting shadows dominate to the extent that there are few sunlit parts to give local contrast. The maximum light/dark contrast within the subject is when the sun is at right angles to the camera.*

High contrast left is typical of many side-lit scenes. The lighting is at right angles to the view, and thus the shadows are too. As the diagrams show, a surface needs to be angled only slightly away from the sun, or be shaded by quite a narrow obstruction, to give high light/dark contrast.

ly much less, because of the ground, or whatever surface the subject is resting on, but the texture remains strong.

Subject shape and exposure

Light measurement and exposure depend on the shape of the subject. If a major part of it faces the sunlight, this will be the most important tone to expose for. Take a direct reading of this, or an incident reading with the meter's dome receptor facing the sun. If, on the other hand, there is no prominent surface facing the sun, or if what you can see of the subject is virtually flat and facing the camera the most appropriate reading will probably be of this mixture of light and shade. For incident light reading, aim the dome directly at the camera, and so that it is partly shaded. The variations in light levels shown are typical, but depend on the amount of shadow fill opposite the light.

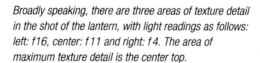

The angle of this Japanese lantern's paper surface changes gradually from left to right, and this affects the amount and distribution of shadow. The strongest impression of textural detail is when the sunlight grazes the surface at a very acute angle.

Broadly speaking, there are three areas of texture detail in the shot of the lantern, with light readings as follows: left: f16, center: f11 and right: f4. The area of maximum texture detail is the center top.

One of the most effective uses of side lighting to outline a subject depends almost entirely on the camera viewpoint. Ideally, as in the Montreal park left, the sun is at right angles to the view, and the background is in shadow; this is the equivalent of the second diagram on page 184.

In the shot right side lighting establishes the texture, an essential quality in food photography, where any tactile sensation helps to stimulate taste. A white card on the side of the dish opposite the late afternoon sunlight opened up the otherwise strong shadows.

Silhouette exposure

It is normal practice to bracket exposures for silhouettes, shooting several frames. The usual criteria for judging exposure do not apply here. In a high-contrast silhouette shot there is no mid-tone area that needs legible exposure. The absence of a midtone actually gives a certain freedom of choice in the exposure, which is why you should bracket very widely, over at least 5 stops, possibly more. You will probably find that more than one exposure looks acceptable.

The upper limit on exposure is usually when the density of the silhouette weakens noticeably into grey and the edges of the outline begin to lose definition due to flare. The lower limit is when the background becomes dim, obscuring the silhouette's outline. These are the conventions, but you

Flare caused by an unshaded lens leads to a loss of contrast and image quality. It is a constant problem in back-lit shots such as the telephoto view above *from Zabriskie Point overlooking California's Death Valley.*

At a very low angle, almost into the picture frame, the sun can produce the rim lighting effect left. *How brightly the edges appear depends on the texture of the subject – here the uniform of Javanese ceremonial guards.*

might find that, for instance, overexposure gives an attractive effect in some situations.

Backlighting and rim lighting

Shooting into the sun gives some of the best opportunities for atmospheric and abstract images. The hallmark of direct shots is the silhouette, in various forms; this can be powerful if you take care to show a clear shape and expose appropriately. Off-axis shots, with the sun only just out of

SHOOTING INTO THE SUN

There are four basic kinds of effect when shooting towards the sun, depending on the height of the sun and the camera position. Shooting directly into sun produces a hard silhouette against a concentrated area of brightness. A higher angle into a reflective surface, such as water, also gives a silhouette, but the bright background will be larger. When the sun is higher and out of frame, some shadow detail can be retained. With rim lighting the background is dark enough to show the brightly lit edge of the subject.

frame, can give a more interesting and unusual range of images, which draw very much on the texture of surfaces to produce their effects. As a class of pictures, back-lit photographs are intrinsically dramatic and exciting, although as with any other distinctive technique, their strength also lies in being used sparingly. If, for example, you are making up a portfolio of your best pictures, in a sheet of twenty transparencies one or two such images will probably be the limit.

Lighting conditions

First, the lighting conditions. There are essentially four. One is a direct shot into the sun, another a direct shot into a reflection of the sun. The other two are off-axis shots, one normal, usually with the horizon visible, the other a slightly special condition, with a dark background that throws up the lit edges of the subject in sharp contrast. It is possible to use enough fill lighting or reflection to give reasonable shadow detail

in such a case, but as this is only practical in close-up, we deal with it under Portable Flash on pages 230–3.

With a direct shot into the sun, the contrast will almost certainly be very high indeed. Even accepting that any subjects in the foreground or middle distance will be very dark, you will usually have to lose legibility at both ends of the brightness scale.

The photograph of the beached fishing boat *below* is fairly typical of a wide-angle shot that includes both the sun and a main subject. Here you can see what is being lost in the distant light tones and in the foreground shadows. The brightness of the sun causes a loss of richness in the colour; the boat lacks full detail. These are technical points and not necessarily damaging to the overall effect of the picture; in fact, the atmosphere generated by the back lighting is very successful.

There is also one ameliorating condition: the light clouds on the horizon, which have weakened the intensity of the sun.

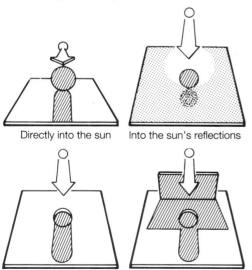

Directly into the sun | Into the sun's reflections

Slightly off-axis | Rim lighting

Clouds weaken sunlight | Shot timed for low sun position

SUNRISE AND SUNSET

The most concentrated period for working with the changing angle of the sun is the beginning and end of the day, within an hour either side of the sun crossing the horizon. Every quality of the light changes: direction, diffusion, colour, intensity. A fur-ther quality of these periods is that they are usually unpredictable because of atmospheric effects and the possibility of clouds, which reflect the light.

All the remaining directions of sunlight are those of a relatively low sun. In a mid-latitude summer, this is before 6 o'clock in the morning and after 6 o'clock in the evening. All four types of lighting can be found at the same time, with the same position of sun. The special value of a low sun

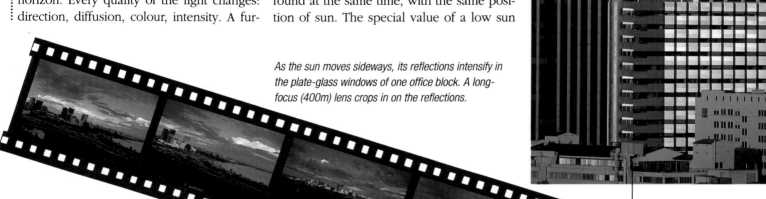

As the sun moves sideways, its reflections intensify in the plate-glass windows of one office block. A long-focus (400m) lens crops in on the reflections.

For the frontal lighting project described on the opposite page, a series of photographs of downtown Perth were taken in the 45 minutes preceding sunset. The most important lesson to be drawn from this sequence of shots is that the sunlight must be strong and direct if the full effect of this type of illumination is to be exploited. Unfortunately, clouds drifted across the sun at the end of the shoot, and the last photograph shows how much was lost in the image.

is a choice of three or four major varieties of lighting quality at once – frontal, side, back and rim.

Frontal lighting is when the sun is directly behind the camera. If you use it well, this can be very powerful, particularly with colour film, but it needs certain minimum conditions. In fact, the difference between success and an unremarkable image is more delicate and less predictable than with the other varieties of low sunlight. Being frontal, the sun in this position throws shadows away from the camera, and if the viewpoint is exactly along the lighting axis, they will be invisible. As shadows are responsible for modelling and texture, and help with perspective, the character of frontally sunlit shots tends to be flat and two-dimen-

sional. This is nearly a prescription for a dull effect, but what can make the difference is the colour and tone of the subject, and the intensity of the sunlight.

Strong colour

Where the lighting is fairly high, but behind the camera, the most immediate quality of the picture is the strength of the colours. With real frontal lighting, this effect is even stronger, with the addition that the colour temperature is lower, and the light more yellow-orange. Hence, the contrast of both colour and tone is high, and if these are already inherently powerful in the subject, as in the picture of the Japanese girl shown below, the combined effect is very strong.

When the sun is almost on the horizon,

and provided that it remains bright, shadows begin to appear, and can very quickly cover everything. A practical point here is that your own shadow will appear. In most circumstances, this will not contribute usefully to the photograph, and there are just two solutions. One is to alter the shape of the shadow you cast, so that it appears natural and indistinguishable (for example, withdraw your arms, duck your head, or cover over tripod legs). The other is to move so that the lighting in the picture is not exactly frontal. This is what happened in the case of the photograph of the cemetery *below*. Slightly off-axis lighting can, as in this example, produce graphically strong shadows that edge the lit shapes and can be used in the design of the image.

Narrow but hard shadows from a setting sun almost behind the camera play an important part in a view of a Shaker cemetery near Albany, New York. It was necessary to position the camera carefully to prevent its shadow appearing in the photograph.

The contrast between the black silk and gold embroidery is already strong. Frontal lighting enhances this by illuminating the embroidery as strongly as possible.

Shooting a tropical sunrise

The river mouth seen here, on the Malay Peninsula, had a convenient camera position: a bridge. The view was checked out one afternoon, but shooting took place the following dawn. Sunrise in the tropics is close to 6 am, and the sun moves very rapidly, so that the period of photography was relatively short, from about 45 minutes before sunrise to about 20 minutes after.

Camera position

The aim was to respond to the changing conditions by altering the framing, focal length, format – even the viewpoint to a limited extent. The essential requirement is to find a good basic camera position that gives a comprehensive view of a potentially attractive scene. The only way to do this is to research the location during the day. I say "potentially attractive" because one of the lessons to be learned here is just how different the scene will look between a visit at midday, and when actually shooting.

Lighting variety

Whether you shoot at sunrise or sunset will probably depend on the location. You can expect the greatest variety when you shoot into the sun, and few scenic locations offer a 180° choice of direction. Ignoring the actual direction of shooting, which is obviously vital in making the photographs, the differences in lighting quality between sunrise and sunset are indistinguishable to a viewer of the shots. If the viewer does not recognize the location, he or she will not be able to tell whether they were taken at the beginning or end of the day. During shooting, however, the times feel quite different. Fewer people are familiar with sunrise,

which is a good reason for doing at least one project then.

For dawn photography you will need to be in position at first light. Also, because of the increasing light, the possibilities of the view tend to reveal themselves slowly, but

because the eye is already well adapted, you will find that the light levels look much higher than they are. If there is any movement in the scene that needs a reasonable shutter speed, you may have to wait longer than you expect to be able to shoot.

The range of colours in the sky, from deep blue to orange, is at its greatest in the wide-angle shot below, taken more than half an hour before sunrise.

A selection of lenses is advisable for a project like this one, including a wide-angle such as the 20mm lens which gave a broad view of the sky.

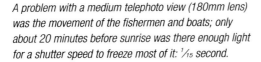

A problem with a medium telephoto view (180mm lens) was the movement of the fishermen and boats; only about 20 minutes before sunrise was there enough light for a shutter speed to freeze most of it: $\frac{1}{15}$ second.

About 15 minutes after sunrise, the sun broke through the low line of clouds. Immediately, the contrast rose rapidly. It was not possible to take any more worthwhile photographs after this shot. Already the sun and its reflections are showing signs of over-exposure. Although the whole session had lasted no more than an hour, it had embraced a wide variety of lighting effects.

Anticipating the shot

There are many occasions, particularly in landscape photography, when the shot can be anticipated, the camera set up in advance, and what remains is to judge the best time to shoot. The timing almost always depends on the lighting. If, as here, we restrict the project to clear weather, the question of the timing becomes simpler, although by no means predictable, as the examples show.

Angle of the sun

Find a landscape location with a reasonably definite subject. First select the viewpoint, and then decide what the preferred angle of the sun should be. In this example, the subject is Delicate Arch in Utah, the view one that shows the arch clearly with illumination that varies during the afternoon from side lighting to lighting that is nearly frontal. The potential for a rich colour to the rock is an important factor in deciding to shoot late in the afternoon, just before sunset, as is the possibility of interesting shadows. As first seen, an overall view of the arch looked as the first, horizontal photograph **1**. This was about two hours before sunset.

What was expected was that the intensity of colour would increase until shortly before the sun touched the horizon; around this point atmospheric effects would dim the light. It was not known how the shadows would fall across the scene. In principle, it was clear that they would creep forward, but the precise extent of the shadows could not be predicted.

In this kind of situation, it may be necessary to shoot at different times, in case the best moment passes without the photographer realizing in time. In this case, the principal two shots (described in captions **3** and **5** below) were taken on 4 x 5 inch film, the others, which needed to be taken quickly, on 35mm film.

1 *This is the first view from the trail of the dramatic arch of rock and its setting. Using a wide-angle lens (20mm on a 35mm camera), I took the photograph about two hours before sunset. It works well like this, but in preparation for what I confidently expected to be a rich sunset, I decided to change the camera position. The reason for doing this was that the arch is situated on the edge of a rock bowl, and with the late afternoon sun setting over my right shoulder, the foreground shadow which can be seen here would later creep forward. As a result, just before sunset, when the colour would be at its best, the bowl would be completely shadowed, thus becoming a large irrelevance in the composition. Therefore I moved the camera closer to the arch, near the top left of this view.*

2 *In the new position, an hour before sunset, I used the 20mm lens again. The camera is set back a little from the bowl's lip, so that a small band of foreground shadow lends weight to the lower part of the shot. This shadow is now moving more quickly towards the arch. With the sun now lower, the texture of the rock is more interesting. This shot is timed so that the small circular depression is just distinct on the edge of the main shadow. Any later, the shadow would dominate.*

3 *I still wanted the richer colours close to sunset, so I moved forward again. The middle distance and beyond are under control, and the variable is still the foreground shadow. Since the rocks behind might break the shadow's pattern as the sun sinks, I set the camera up in this position for my first principal shot. The shadow has reached the ledge just in front of the camera and briefly there is a double shadow line. Nothing more will happen until the shadow crosses the bowl.*

4 *With the bowl now rapidly being filled with intense shadow, I changed to a 50mm lens, concentrating solely on the arch. The aim is that the intensifying colour will carry the shot, but with the view framed like this I realize that the image design is not particularly interesting.*

5 *I move the camera a little further back, to keep some of the bowl's sweep. This, my second principal shot, is timed, like the others, for the exact position of the shadow line. The lower shadow, balancing the dark hills beyond, makes it possible to frame the arch off-center.*

6 *The sun begins to lose its intensity and colour near the horizon (out of my view in this position) before the shadow reaches the base of the arch, depriving me of my final principal shot. Even clear desert light is unpredictable, and the richest colour has already gone.*

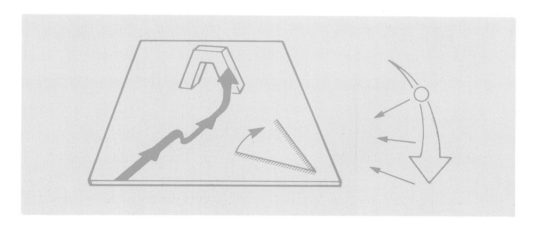

SHADOW PATH

In the last hour or so of the afternoon, the sun's path across and down caused the shadows in the picture area to move as shown in the diagram. These shadows were cast by rocks behind and to the right of the camera, and for the timing of the photographs there were two important breaks in the shadows' direction. The first was caused by the ledge in front of the camera making a break in the shadows. The second was the point at which they began to rise up the arch.

7 *Within seconds, the loss of direct sunlight becomes obvious below the arch. The moment has passed.*

TWILIGHT

Like normal daytime skylight, twilight is a reflected light source, but rather more complex in its effects. It is the light that remains once the sun has set, and in the opposite direction before sunrise. In a clear sky, the intensity shades smoothly upwards from the horizon, where it is brightest, and outwards from the direction of the sun. (The studio equivalent is a light placed on the floor, aimed up towards a white wall, and used as back lighting.) The sky in the direction of the light acts partly as a diffuser, partly as a

In many twilight shots, following the meter reading exactly gives an exposure resembling a daylit rather than a twilit scene. In the second shot, under-exposure by 1 stop produces a better impression of evening light.

reflector. The actual light levels vary considerably, reaching their maximum when the sky is completely clear immediately after sunset or before sunrise. An incident light reading is what you would need if you were taking such a photograph by twilight, facing more or less away from the light.

Exposure choice

A much shorter exposure can be used if the photograph is being taken *into* the twilight, making a silhouette of the horizon and subjects. In this kind of back-lit shot (the photograph *below* is a good example), the shading of the sky from bright to dark gives some choice of exposure, particularly with a wide-angle lens. Less exposure intensifies the colour and concentrates the view close to the horizon. More exposure dilutes the colour in the lower part of the sky, but shows more of the higher, bluer parts. In

When the sky is not red or orange at sunset or sunrise, an overall blue cast is typical, as in this winter scene.

other words, increasing the exposure extends the area of the subject within the frame. A range of exposures is acceptable, depending on what you want to achieve with the picture.

It is not only the intensity which shades from the horizon upwards, but the colour does also. The exact colours depend on local atmospheric conditions, and the different light scattering effects that we looked at on pages 180-1 are combined in a twilight sky. At a distance from the brightest area – opposite and above – the colour temperature is high, as it would be during the day. Close to the horizon in the direction of the light, however, the scattering creates the warmer colours at the lower end of the colour temperature range: yellow, orange, and red. These all merge in a graded scale of colour.

Effects of clouds
Added to this basic lighting condition, clouds are fairly unpredictable in their effect. If continuous, they usually destroy any sense of twilight, but if broken, they reflect light dramatically: high orange and red clouds create the classic "postcard" sunset. The tropical sunrise sequence on pages 190-1 includes twilight, and one of the things that becomes clear after a number of occasions is that clouds at this time of day often produce surprises. The upward angle of the sunlight from below the horizon is acute to the layers of clouds, so that small movements have obvious effects. On some occasions, the colour of clouds after sunset simply fades; on others, it can suddenly spring to life again for a few moments.

Shading
The gradual shading of light and colour can be extremely valuable for some shots. At a particular angle, it produces a broad reflection of light in water or other shiny surfaces, but one that has no distinct edge. This can be a very simple and attractive illumination for reflected things, and has its equivalent in studio lighting, as you can see on pages 234-41.

Twilight shooting
Equip yourself with both wide-angle and telephoto lenses. The wide-angle view, by including more of the height of the sky, will contain a wide range of colour, from approximately orange to blue. The telephoto shots, with a narrower angle of view, can only take in a small part of this; perhaps only a single colour. You can see something of this difference in the tropical sunrise sequence referred to above.

Smooth reflected light
To demonstrate the effect of smoothly-graded light on a reflected surface, photograph a car at twilight, facing the brightest part of the horizon and under a sky that is reasonably free of clouds. For the clearest lighting effect, shoot from a slight elevation; enough so that the image of the roof remains a little below the horizon.

A clear sky at dusk or dawn acts like a smooth reflective surface for the sun as it lies below the horizon. The light shades smoothly upwards from the horizon, and this effect is most obvious with a wide-angle lens, which takes in a greater span of sky. For example, while a 180mm telephoto gives a limited angle of view of only 11°, a 20mm wide-angle gives an angle of view of 84°.

MOONLIGHT

Photographing by moonlight needs very long exposures, even with fast film, as the intensity is in the region of 20 stops less than daylight. The readings are beyond the range of ordinary meters; the exposures, which may need to be many minutes, or even an hour or two, will cause reciprocity failure in the film.

Exposure problems

A bright full moon is about four hundred thousand times less bright than the sun, but many films perform unpredictably at long exposures. Use settings between four minutes and fifteen minutes at *f*2.8 with ISO 100 film (or equivalent) as a start, and bracket widely. Such long exposures make it tempting to use fast film, but if you are shooting a landscape or building, the grainy appearance will not be ideal. Reciprocity failure information supplied by film manufacturers does not usually cover time exposures of more than a few minutes, so use the direction of the colour shift in the published figures as a guide.

Photographing the moon itself is easier, but it may be a problem to measure its brightness except with a hand-held spot meter or a spot reading facility in the camera's TTL metering system. Again, the brightness depends on atmospheric conditions and on the phase. A bright, full moon needs an exposure on ISO 100 film in the region of $\frac{1}{250}$ second at *f*8, but bracket exposures with this as the shortest.

Unless the photographer uses photographic lamps (if permitted) for a shot such as the temple at night, opposite, the only answer is to work with available light – in this case tungsten lamps and hazy moonlight.

Shutter speed

For the moon to be a reasonable size in the frame, a powerful telephoto is needed, and as the maximum aperture of the lens is likely to be small, bracketing usually has to be done by altering the shutter speed. The limit to the slowest shutter speed is the movement of the moon's image in its orbit around the earth. The moon seems to move its own diameter in two minutes. For a 400mm lens on a 35mm camera, exposure of one second or longer will cause blurring.

In the evening view left *of White Sands, New Mexico, the moon was actually higher in the sky than it appears here. Two exposures were made: one for the dunes and a second for the moon. Grid lines in the viewfinder were used to position both elements.*

Illuminated only by a full moon in a clear sky, the farmyard scene below, *in California's Napa Valley, required an exposure of 30 minutes at f 3.5 on ISO 64 Kodachrome. Much of this long exposure time was taken up by reciprocity failure.*

CLOUDS

Clouds are the most visible component of weather. In outdoor photography they are by far the most important controlling factors in daylight. As you can see from the photographs on these pages, the variety of cloud effects is enormous, and the usual simple formula given in film tables for adjusting exposure is really not enough for any sophisticated approach to natural light.

Diffusion of light

To make a comparison with studio lighting, clouds act as variable diffusers over the scene, and as reflectors at the same time. Imagine that the full range of these diffusers includes ones of different thickness, texture, extent, at different heights, and capable of being arranged in a number of layers, moving at different rates: the permutations are infinite. The simplest conditions, and the closest to having predictable effects are when the cloud cover is continuous. Overcast skies just diffuse the light, and if they are sufficiently dense that there is no patch of brightness to show the position of the sun, the light is as soft and shadowless as it ever can be. The table on light levels on page 203 gives an indication of how an overcast sky affects exposure.

Even lighting

Medium-to-heavy overcast skies have a reputation for bringing dullness to a scene. To an extent this is true, but not exclusively so. Light comes more or less evenly from the entire sky, so the only shadows are those caused by objects being close to each other; this lack of shadow reduces modelling, per-spective and texture. Most things appear to have less substantial form, and large-scale views appear flat. There is virtually no modulation of light, and the sameness of illumination in all directions makes conditions less interesting. There are none of the lighting surprises that bring so much of the pleasure of photography in changing weather.

Image clarity

Overcast skies are, however, good for certain subjects. The chief characteristic of this kind of lighting is that it is extremely uncomplicated. Hence it is good for giving clear, legible images of subjects that are, for one reason or another, complex. Things with intricate shapes, for example, are prone to appear confusing when direct sun-

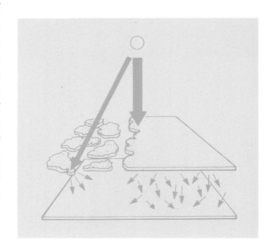

DIFFUSION AND REFLECTION

Clouds mainly diffuse sunlight, but to a lesser extent also reflect it. They reflect most from low white cumulus, adding about ½ stop to direct sunlight. The reading from sunlight reflected through broken cloud might be f16, but f8 from sunlight diffused through solid cloud.

light adds a pattern of shadows. Reflective surfaces make more legible images under diffuse lighting: the reflection of a broad, even light source will cover all or most of any shiny surface. By contrast, in clear weather, the sun appears as a small, bright, specular reflection.

The value of shadowless, overcast lighting, therefore, is in its efficiency rather than in its evocative qualities. It helps to clarify images. We will come across this distinction again when we look at ways of using photographic lighting, particularly in highly controlled studio conditions: efficiency versus character. Much depends on what you see as the purpose of the shot. If the photograph has to remain faithful to the physical, plastic qualities of the subject, this sets certain criteria. Then again, it is possible to say

that certain directions of lighting, types of diffusion, and so on, are better than others. Clarity in the image takes precedence over more expressive qualities.

Total cloud cover

In landscapes and other views that include the horizon, a 100 per cent cloud cover alters the tonal relationship between sky and land. Without cloud, the difference in brightness between the two is usually fairly small; quite often, the subjects are lighter in tone. This is not so when cloud extends all over. Then the cloud covers the light source and, if contained in the view, raises the contrast so high that if the scene includes the horizon, some detail will be lost either in the sky or in the ground. This is particularly so with colour reversal (transparency)

One valuable characteristic of cloudy light is that shadows associated with it are very weak and have soft edges. This is often an advantage in portraiture, particularly when the subject has a richly textured face like the man in the photograph left.

Clouds that have recognizable outlines, such as woolly cumulus or wispy cirrus, become a visual element in a landscape, as in the top photograph right. Indistinct clouds are more important for what they do to the lighting, as in the bottom shot. As well as changing the light level, they also alter the brightness level.

Clouds passing over a landscape create a kind of chiaroscuro – light and shade – effect. This tonal overlay is seen to its best advantage at a distance and from a high viewpoint, as in this aerial view of a southern Philippine port.

film, which has less latitude than negative film. If the subjects or ground are properly exposed, the sky will be white, without any visible texture to the clouds.

The usual answer for this is to use a neutral graduated filter over the lens, aligning the soft edge of the filter's darkened area with the horizon line, so that the sky is made darker. If the final result is a print, another way of adjusting the tones is by different exposures during enlargement (more exposure to the sky if you are printing from a negative, less if from a transparency).

Broken cloud

The lighting conditions are more complicated and less easy to anticipate when the clouds are broken, so that there is a mixture with blue sky (in fact, the complexity extends to situations where there is more than one layer of broken cloud, each different in type). The diagram on page 201 gives an impression of the range of possibilities; even simplified like this, it shows how the intensity, quality and colour of light can vary. On a windy day, these conditions change rapidly, not only from cloud to direct sun, but from one type of weather to another. Watch what happens when a cold front passes over. Between scattered and partial cloud cover, the most noticeable effect is the fluctuation of the light; at the left and right of the scale, conditions are most consistent.

Dramatic lighting

If you are trying to take a particular shot that you have fixed in your mind, scattered cloud on a windy day can be frustrating, to say the least. The light changes up and down, delaying the shooting. However, the

PROJECT: Different cloud conditions
The first project is an exercise in imagination. Overcast weather is generally thought of as being dull and uninteresting for photography, and this in itself is reason enough for working a little harder than usual to find ways of making it work. Look for subjects that have the kind of complexity of form that would look confusing in direct sunlight, and for those with important details that would otherwise be in shadow. For portraits, use subtractive lighting to create modelling: a rigid sheet of black material or black fabric stretched over a frame, placed to one side of the subject, will subtract reflected light from that side. Also, look for subjects that have shiny surfaces and use an overcast sky to give an even, simple reflection.

A more basic project is to shoot pairs of frames to contrast the effects of direct sunlight with those of cloud. The easiest times to do this are when the clouds are moving and there are gaps. Adjust the exposure as necessary, but make a note of how many stops the difference is. Compare the various pairs; notice in particular the effect on colour temperature, on colour intensity and relationships, and on modelling. When shooting landscapes, make a point of looking for interesting patterns and modulations of clouds, and use them in the composition.

sheer variability of broken cloud can produce some of the most interesting, and even dramatic, lighting. To take advantage of it, however, you will need to react quite quickly. Familiarity with the different light levels in any one situation will help; if you have already measured the difference between cloud and sunlight, you can change from the one setting to the other without having to use the meter again. Under heavy cloud with a few gaps, this may be particularly useful, as the sunlight is likely to move in patches across the landscape, and be difficult to measure quickly.

Although light levels are reduced when clouds block the sun, the amount depends very much on the type of cloud. If the clouds are indistinct and spread across the sky, the light loss is on a simple scale from a light haze (as little as ½ a stop less than clear sunlight) through thin high stratus to dark grey low clouds (up to 4 or 5 stops darker, and more in exceptionally bad weather).

Light levels

With distinct clouds, however, such as scattered fair-weather cumulus, the light levels can fluctuate rapidly, particularly on a windy day. Light, white clouds usually cause a simple fluctuation of about 2 stops as they pass in front of the sun from bright to shade in one step. Dark clouds with ragged edges, or two layers of moving clouds, cause more problems, as the light changes gradually and often unpredictably. In the first case, two light measurements are all that is necessary – one in sunlight, the other as a cloud passes – and once this is done, you can simply change the aperture from one to the other, without bothering to take any more readings. with of more complex moving clouds, constant measurement is essential, unless you wait for clear breaks.

The photographs on this page are just three examples of the great variety of cloud formations, and seen together they show the very different effects they can have on a picture. The shot top right reveals weak sunlight filtered attractively through low, dark storm clouds. The photograph right shows scattered cloud cover in fading light and the shot far right illustrates heavy cloud cover in a bright sky.

DISTINCT CLOUDS

Some idea of the visual complexity of definitely shaped clouds is given by the chart below, which plots the brightness of individual clouds – mainly a matter of how thick they are – against the degree of cloud cover. The less the cloud cover, the more the blue of the sky has an effect. The photographs right and below show widely differing types of cloud.

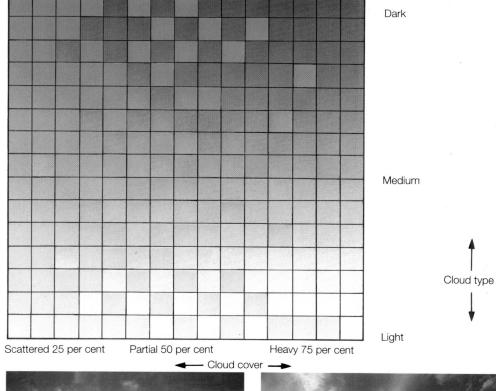

Dark

Medium

Light

Cloud type

Scattered 25 per cent   Partial 50 per cent   Heavy 75 per cent

◀— Cloud cover —▶

Because clouds combine the colour temperature of the sun and sky above, the effect is a slight raising of the colour temperature. The exposure was adjusted for the right-hand shot of the pair below, but the colour is unmistakably bluer.

Clouds can help to reveal the form of a subject or make it less obvious, depending on its surface. The copper roof above shows its shape better on a dull day, but the brickwork, being less reflective, is clearer in direct sunlight.

LIGHT LOSS: EVEN CLOUD COVER	
	f-stops
Clear sun	0
Heavy haze	−1
Light haze	−½
Thin high cloud	−1½
Cloudy, bright	−2
Moderately overcast	−3
Heavily overcast	at least −4

In this pair of photographs of a church steeple in Montreal, there is a marked difference between direct sunlight right hand even a light cloud cover far right. The cloud reduces the intensity of the red, changes the hue by raising the colour temperature, and lowers the contrast. Also, note the effect on the reflections.

	Sunrise/ sunset			Noon summer							
Sun in clear blue sky	4000	4500	5000	5500							
Hazy sky		4500	5000	5500	6000						
Thin cloud (visibly brighter in direction of sun)		5000	5500	6000	6500						
Overcast (completely diffuse)				6500	7000						
50 per cent scattered clouds (sun blocked)					7500	8000	9000				
25 per cent scattered clouds (sun blocked)						9000	10,000	11,000	12,000		
Skylight alone								12,000–20,000			

The height of the sun affects the colour temperature, as does the degree of cloud cover. Each bar in this diagram shows the typical range, in kelvins, from sunrise and sunset at the left to a high midday sun at the right.

HAZE

Haze is the scattering of light by particles in the atmosphere. Fine dust and pollution produce it, as does high humidity. Haze varies considerably, not only in density, but in the wavelengths that are affected. The finest particles scatter the short wavelengths more than most, and produce bluish ultraviolet views over a distance. The haze from humidity, on the other hand, has a neutral colour effect, and looks white from afar.

There are two main visible effects of haze. One is on the view itself, the other is on the quality of light. The effect on a landscape is to make it appear paler at a distance; this is progressive, so that contrast, colour and definition gradually drain away from the foreground to the horizon. This effect is strongest when the sun is in front of the camera (but not necessarily low), and is what contributes most to aerial perspective – the impression of depth due to the atmosphere. To make this work strongly, however, you would need to shoot in such a way that there are at least a few obvious planes of distance in the scene; simply a long view, with no foreground or middle ground, appears pale.

The effect of haze on the lighting is to soften the hard edges of sunlight. The extra scattering reduces contrast and helps to fill shadows. The effect can be an attractive balance between sunlight and diffusion, particularly when the sun is a little in front of the camera, as in the photograph opposite. The amount of haze varies, and in its visible effect, strong haze merges with light continuous cloud.

Reducing haze

Although haze can add to the atmosphere of a view, it can also be unwelcome by hiding detail, colour and crispness. The following are ways of reducing it.

- *Ultraviolet filter* This works on the short wavelengths only, so the effect is unlikely to be total. In addition, with black-and-white film, an orange or red filter has a stronger haze-cutting effect.

When a distant view is required but haze has a noticeable effect on film, as in this series of telephoto views across Canyonlands National Park, Utah, the use of filters can make a substantial improvement in picture quality. In the unfiltered version right the haze appears as a pale blue. At the same time, both contrast and colour saturation have been weakened. Adding an ultraviolet filter below left improves the picture. However, using a polarizing filter below right has the strongest effect of all on the haze.

- *Polarizing filter* This works most strongly at right angles to the sun (in side lighting) and gives an overall improvement.
- *Frontal or side lighting* Either of these are preferable to back lighting, which should be avoided.
- *Avoid distant views* The closer you shoot, the less atmosphere, and so the less haze. For this reason, a wide-angle lens may be better than a telephoto.

The two vertical shots illustrate the marked difference haze can make to a scene. In the horizontal view, clearing early morning mist suggested the use of a 20mm wide-angle lens. At this scale the pastel colours of sky and fields make an attractive combination that would have been lost in a more tightly cropped version.

MIST, FOG AND DUST

Mist, fog and dust can all be so dense as to make even nearby things difficult to see. The droplets or particles are so large that there is no selective scattering of wavelengths, just an overall diffusion. (Dust has its own colour, and tinges the view yellow, light brown, or whatever.) Do not view these as problem conditions: they clear eventually – usually quickly – and meanwhile can make interesting images.

When a fog is dense, or when the sun is fairly high, there is little if any sense of direction to foggy light. If you choose the distance at which you shoot carefully and close to the limits of legibility, the colour and tonal effect will be extremely delicate. Against the light, depending on the density, these conditions produce some form of silhouetting. Close to the camera, the subjects are likely to stand out quite clearly, with good contrast. At a distance, the silhouettes and setting will be in shades of grey. As the conditions shift, thicken or clear, the nature of the images changes significantly. Dust in particular is a very active condition: it needs wind or movement to remain in the atmosphere. Back lighting gives the best impression of its swirling and rising, but there are obvious dangers to the equipment.

Fog filter

There are two ways of creating an impression of mist and fog when neither exists. One, simple but mild in its effect, is to use what is known as a fog filter. This is a grad-

PROJECT: Effects from fog
Fog offers a wide range of opportunities, so on a foggy day, and restricting your shooting to one location, try to create as varied a selection of images as possible. As well as looking for different subjects and viewpoints and experimenting with a range of lenses of different focal lengths, wait until the fog begins to clear to take advantage of the following shifting effects:

● delicate colours illuminated softly by direction-less lighting.
● depth of view with subjects at different distances from the camera, fading progressively towards the distance.
● strong silhouettes against the light.
● pale silhouettes.
● clearing, shifting fog. A wide-angle lens is often the best for showing different thicknesses of fog in one image.
● a view from a high point of a sea of fog with clear air above, ideally with the tops of trees or buildings standing out.

In this early morning shot, taken against the light, the fog hides the background, while the strength of the silhouette is controlled by the camera position: a wide-angle lens let this be only a few yards from the tree.

uated filter on the same principle as the neutral graduated filter shown on page 215, but it shades from clear to diffused. If you use it at a fairly wide aperture, so that the edge between the two halves remains vague, and the diffused area is above, the effect is that of the atmosphere thickening with distance.

The second method, involving much more trouble, is to produce artificial smoke, either from smoke flares or by hiring an oil-based smoke machine. Even a medium breeze is enough to dissipate the smoke as quickly as it is produced, however.

Morning mist gives an overall softness to a Shaker village in Maine, lending an attractive delicacy to the tones and colours. In a situation like this, where there is a clear view of the subject and a choice of camera positions is available, the shooting distance can be selected so as to give different degrees of softness, the focal length being altered as necessary.

Although very damaging to cameras, dust can add considerable atmosphere to a picture. In the shot right swirling clouds of dust churned up by the earth-mover give the vehicle a looming presence. Back lighting from a setting sun makes the most of the subject.

As an illustration of how different lighting conditions affect the same subject, the earth-movers below were photographed, from left to right: in the early morning, the middle of an overcast day, and mid-afternoon.

RAIN AND STORMS

Rain

The speed at which it falls, and the slow shutter setting needed in what is usually poor light, results in rain looking like mist in most photographs. To get some impression of the actual raindrops, the best conditions are backlighting against a dark background, and this is uncommon in rainy weather. The best sense of raininess often comes from the subjects rather than from the light. The levels are usually very low: rain and cloud together easily reduce the light by 4 or 5 stops.

Lightning

As one of the most dramatic features of a storm, lightning can add considerably to the power of a landscape. It is insufficiently strong to take pictures *by*, but you can include it as a subject, provided that the conditions are dark enough. There is no way of synchronizing lightning flashes with the shutter, and the only certain technique is to leave the shutter open in anticipation of a strike. Fortunately, the electrical conditions that produce one lightning flash usually produce a number, often more or less in the same place. At the height of a storm, you should not have to wait longer than about 10 or 20 seconds for the next flash,

Sometimes the most effective image of a storm relies on minimal detail, as in the view below of swirling mist and driving rain on a mountain in Central America.

In the shot right the rain is heavy yet appears like a dull haze. However, the people sheltering beneath umbrellas underline the impression of a rainstorm.

INTERVAL	DISTANCE TO STORM	FILM SPEED (ISO)				
		25	50–64	100	200	400
Under 10 secs	Under 2 miles (3 km)	f8	f11	f16	f22	f32
10–45 secs	29 miles (3–15 km)	f4	f5.6	f8	f11	f16
Over 45 secs	Over 9 miles (15 km)	f2.8	f4	f5.6	f8	f11

Note: the difference between the flash and the thunder is the speed of sound, and 5 seconds equals 1 mile/1.6km.

and it is more likely to be in the direction of the last few flashes than in any other. Nevertheless, lightning in daylight is very difficult to shoot without over-exposure. If there is still light in the sky, estimate the average interval between flashes, and set the camera to allow a time exposure longer than that.

To establish "raininess", some visual clues should be included in the photograph. In the shot below the reflections of car headlights in the wet surface of a Toronto freeway make the point effectively.

Ordinarily, the exposure depends on the intensity of the individual flash, whether it is reflected from surrounding clouds, and how far away it is. You can estimate the last, at least through a group of flashes: count the seconds between the flash and the accompanying thunder, and apply the chart on this page.

Distant lightning over Rangoon below was shot at dusk with a 30-second exposure – long enough to catch a few cloud-to-cloud strikes and one cloud-to-ground strike. The aperture was f2.8 and the film speed ISO 64.

SNOW

A fresh fall of snow is the ultimate in bright surroundings. The studio equivalent is an overhead light and a bright white curved base. When photographing local subjects in a snowscape, such as a portrait, the two most noticeable effects are powerful shadow-fill, particularly from beneath, and frequently bright backgrounds. The reflection that fills the shadows reduces contrast, which is no bad thing for many subjects under a direct sun. Bright backgrounds can create flare, and efficient lens shading is usually necessary. Landscapes and other overall views vary considerably with the quality of the daylight. Contrast is low under cloud, skylight and twilight, but can be high in direct sunlight, particularly with backlighting.

Exposure

In general, exposure is more critical in a snowscape than in most other landscapes. Between a white that reproduces as a muddy light grey and one that is featureless and washed out, there is very little latitude in the exposure setting, and neither over-exposure nor under-exposure looks particularly good. The eye is quick to appreciate a pure white, and equally quick to discover it wrong in appearance. With snow, light measurement and exposure both call for considerable care, but are generally not quite such problems as they are often considered to be.

Extra exposure

The essential thing to remember is that if you take a direct, reflected light reading of white, flat, sunlit snow, you will need to add 1 or 2 stops to the exposure. Reflected readings show how to reproduce the tone they measure as grey. As long as you remember this, there are no great problems, except that the final result is delicate, and it is often wise to bracket exposures, if only by ½ a stop up and down. Incident readings with a hand-held meter are not affect-

All of the photographs on these pages were taken on a single day in one general location – along Hadrian's Wall, the Roman fortification stretching across northern England almost from coast to coast. They are shown in the order in which they were shot, and the first photograph was taken just before sunrise, the last at sunset. Part of the exercise here was to capture as much visual variety as possible from the changing lighting conditions during snowy weather, and in particular exploiting the reflective qualities of the snow. White snow picks up colour more readily than anything else in landscape photography: from the strong blue of a clear sky to the pinks and oranges of a low sun.

1

2

3

4

ed, of course. The project on these pages – a snowscape photographed at different stages of one day – offers more suggestions on how to exploit the effects of snow.

Light reflection

As snow is an efficient reflector, colour or temperature differences in the sky are mirrored, and seem more prominent. Look, for instance, at the two photographs in the skylight example on page 179. In scenic views, this strength of colour is by no means unpleasant, particularly if combined with other colours in the picture.

1 was shot at dawn with a 20mm lens to cover the maximum amount of sky, shading from pink to blue. In 2 a similar colour range is reflected in the snow-covered ridge, shot at right angles to the sun with a 180mm telephoto for contrast. With the sun higher, 3, the shadows are slightly less blue; a 20mm lens gave strong perspective. At the same time of day and with the same lens, aiming at the sun in 4 gives a high-contrast back-lit effect. In 5 a 400mm telephoto was used in the afternoon to compress the elements of a hillside. The sunset in 6 allowed a warm back-lit shot that includes the sun.

5

6

Mountain Light

The height of mountains creates some of their special conditions of light; their relief produces the others, through the frequently rapid changes in local weather. One of the most memorable weather conditions is the clear, crisp air in sunlight that gives high visibility to long views and fine detail. This however, is only one of a variety of types of lighting found in mountains.

Local contrast

The air is thinner at altitude, and is therefore clearer, provided that the weather is fine. Since it is thinner, there are fewer particles to scatter light into the shadow areas, which consequently can be very deep. Local contrast, as a result, is often very high. The skylight in shade is a more intense blue than at sea-level. As usual, this intensity is difficult to estimate without a colour temperature meter, particularly as the values are often unfamiliar.

Ultraviolet rays

The thin air is a less effective screen against ultraviolet rays, and there is a higher component of these short wavelengths. This produces an unusually large difference between what you can see and what colour film will show. Unless you want to make use of the blue cast to demonstrate the distance, use strong ultraviolet filtration. Remember also that, in reacting to the ultra-

The photographs on the opposite page were all taken in the Sierra Nevada de Santa Marta, an isolated part of the northern Andes. The two pictures at the bottom, which were both taken at dawn but on different days, illustrate the difference between adopting a sea-level view and one from a 9000-foot peak.

violet wavelengths, the film receives more exposure, and the distant parts of the scene will look paler than to the eye.

Weather effects

So much for the thinner atmosphere. The interesting part of mountain light comes from the weather, and this is controlled strongly by the relief of ridges and valleys. In particular, clouds become a part of the local lighting, as the project examples show.

At 7000 feet (2000 meters) in the Colombian Andes above, the thinner atmosphere produces a high contrast range in parts of the scene close to the camera. (At greater distances this effect is reduced by haze.) As a result, the contrast range in the foreground of the photograph is about 7 f-stops, giving an almost lunar quality to the rock-strewn landscape. The thin mountain atmosphere also means that there is less screening of ultraviolet rays. The sensitivity of film to ultraviolet light gives a pronounced pale blue cast to distant parts of the landscape, particularly noticeable in the peak in the center of the shot. The lens was unfiltered.

Among shots of the central peaks taken from different viewpoints were two taken at dawn below, one taken from sea-level left and one taken from the air above left.

Another photograph above of the same part of the range as seen left exploits the dramatic viewpoint, complete with low cloud, afforded by a nearby peak.

DAYLIGHT INDOORS

Although there are some technical difficulties with light level, contrast, and the uncertainty of the colour balance, the quality of the light from a window is often both attractive and useful.

Window light

The typical source of indoor natural light is a window set conventionally in a wall. Which way it faces and the view outside control the amount and colour of daylight entering. Look carefully at the view out of the window to determine whether or not there is likely to be a major rise or fall in colour temperature. The walls of neighbouring buildings may have a much greater effect than the sky.

If there is no direct sunlight (or if this is diffused by net curtains, for instance), treat the window as the source of light. This has an important effect on the intensity, as the light, instead of being constant at any distance, falls off rapidly. So, if you are taking a portrait by diffused window light, how close your subject stands to it makes a great difference to the exposure. If you are photographing the room as a complete interior, the level across the picture may be so great

that the contrast must be reduced.

Light from a window is a distinctive mixture of highly directional and broad, so the shadow is even, simple and soft-edged. The combination of qualities makes diffuse window light almost unequalled for giving good modelling, and can be particularly successful for portraits and full-figure shots. This modelling effect is strongest when the window is to one side of the camera's view;

the density of the shadow, and thus the contrast, will depend very much on what happens on the other side of the room: whether there are other windows, how big the room is, and whether it is decorated brightly or not. If the shadow side of the picture is dark and you want to preserve some detail, you can add reflectors.

Shots facing away from and towards the window produce very different effects. With

Daylight through open windows often has an attractive, studio quality. As a fairly large, diffused sidelight, it is particularly suitable for full-length figure shots, as here.

your back to the window, the lighting effect is likely to be very flat, unless beams of sunlight modulate the view. Into the light, the contrast will naturally be high, but flare from the edges of the window can produce a more atmospheric image.

If, however, you feel it is important to be able to see what is going on outside the window as well as the interior of the room, there are special techniques that will help. One is to add lighting to the interior to balance it to the daylight outside, and we deal with this later. A second technique, which needs no other lighting, is to take two exposures on one frame. The first is timed to record the outside scene through the window, then the window is blocked with black cloth or card and the second exposure made using the light from other windows or doorways to record details inside the room.

The side-to-side range of brightness above left is typical of interiors lit by only one window. A neutral graduated filter rotated to shade from right to left evened out the brightness above right.

In the first print below a single exposure, without manipulation, yields a washed-out exterior view. In the second a shorter exposure suited the exterior but made the interior too dark. The third mixes the two exposures, and shading and printing-in techniques gave both the interior and the exterior their best exposure.

ARTIFICIAL LIGHT

The following pages look at artificial light: first tungsten, fluorescent and vapour discharge sources and then flash.

Tungsten lamps are the standard, traditional form of lighting domestic interiors, and this is where nowadays you are most likely to find them. Outdoors, and in large interiors used by the public, they have mainly been replaced by fluorescent and vapour lighting. A tungsten lamp is incandescent – it shines by burning – and its brightness depends on the degree to which the filament is heated. As this in turn depends on the wattage, you can get an idea of the brightness, and the colour, from the rating of the lamp. The colour range, which is between orange and yellow, depends on the colour temperature.

Colour temperature

This is perhaps the first thing to think about when shooting by available light in houses. If you enter a shuttered, tungsten-lit room straight from daylight, you can immediately notice how orange it looks. Usually, however, we see tungsten light at night, and it does not take the eye long to adapt and to see it as almost white.

The first time you photograph a tungsten-lit interior, uncorrected and on regular colour film, you may be surprised at the orange cast: not what you remembered. If you have never done this, take the opportunity now. The table *below* gives the colour temperature values for the usual ratings of domestic lamp, and the filters that you would need to make the lighting appear neutrally white on film. Note that these are for either tungsten-balanced film or daylight-balanced film that has already been filtered to give it the same 3200 K balance.

The temperature of 3200 K is still closer to white than the light from any domestic

TUNGSTEN LIGHT SOURCE	COLOUR TEMPERATURE		FILTERS WITH TYPE B FILM OR DAYLIGHT WITH 80B FILTER	EXPOSURE AT 3 FEET (1M) ISO 400 FILM WITH FILTER ATTACHED	f STOPS WEAKER THAN MIDDAY SUNLIGHT
	KELVIN*	MIREDS*			
Candle flame	1800	555	80A/80B	3 seconds at f2	About 12
40-watt domestic lamp	2760	362	82C	1/15 second at f2.4	About 8½
60-watt domestic lamp	2790	358	82C	1/15 second at f2.8	About 8

The figures in the columns marked with an asterisk are readings taken from particular light sources and may vary slightly according to the age and make of the lamp and the voltage applied to it.

A typical lighting situation with tungsten, flames and other incandescent lamps is when the light source appears, as in the shot left. It is best to overexpose the lamp so that the illuminated parts of the scene record adequately.

The photographs opposite were taken under the same tungsten lighting at a display of classical dance in Java. The near shot was taken on tungsten-balanced film, the other on daylight-balanced film. The value of correcting the colour temperature is here a matter of taste.

bulb, but it makes a sensible start. This colour temperature, as we will see later in the section on photographic lighting, is normal for photographic tungsten and tungsten-halogen lamps. In its visual colour effect, tungsten-balanced film goes almost the whole way to correcting the colour cast. However, the complete answer is not a purely technical one. The ultimate criterion is what *looks* right, not what measures perfectly. The project on the next page is designed to help you work out the necessary compromise.

Mixed lighting

Another important consideration concerning the colour temperature is whether the tungsten lighting covers the entire picture area, or whether it is isolated in a scene that has other illumination. This consideration applies to all kinds of available light, and is bound to affect your decisions on filtration and correction. Here, we will treat local lighting as a distinct situation, and deal with it a little later, as mixed lighting.

The intensity of light available is always a problem, as with all non-photographic artificial lighting. This deserves qualification, but in terms of the mixture of image quality and ease of taking pictures, the ideal standard would allow you to use a fine-grained film, say ISO 64, at shutter speeds of around $\frac{1}{125}$ second with a choice of apertures around the middle of the range for a standard lens: something in the order of *f* 8. Give or take a couple of stops of light, this constitutes the right lighting conditions for trouble-free hand-held photography. Available tungsten lighting falls short of this by several stops, and so needs extra care

and camera-handling skills in almost every technical area of shooting. We could deal with these almost anywhere in this section of the book, but the problem affects fluorescent and vapour lighting also, which are discussed below.

Inverse Square Law

Unlike daylight, tungsten and all other forms of artificial lighting operate under the Inverse Square Law, which must be borne in mind when making calculations about the light level. This says that light falls off with the square of distance, which means that doubling the distance from a light source means quartering the illumination. This effect is even stronger with domestic tungsten lamps than with other kinds of artificial lighting, because the light source is so concentrated, and explains the pooling effect of lamps in a room. Most domestic interiors are far from evenly lit; each lamp tends to create a pool of light around it, with intervening darker shadow areas. The eye senses this less than film because human vision adapts rapidly to different light levels, even in one scene.

Fluorescent light

Fluorescent lamps have a discontinuous spectrum, producing a greenish colour cast. A fluorescent lamp works by means of an electric discharge passed through vapour sealed in a glass tube, with a fluorescent coating on the inside of the glass. These fluorescers glow at different wavelengths, and have the effect of spreading the spectrum of the lamp's light. Visually this is an improvement over vapour lamps because the spectrum can be evened out to appear more

like that of daylight, but the deficiencies that remain are usually significant.

If these deficiencies were consistent, it would be a simple matter of using one standard correction filter. However, as the chart on this page shows, fluorescent lamps vary in the visual effect that the manufacturer tries to produce. Some are slightly green when photographed, others very much so. The practical difficulty is in telling how much of a green cast will appear just from looking. The descriptions of the different types of lamps are, as you can see from the recommended filtration, meaningless for photography; a result of the difference in response between the eye and film to different wavelengths.

In shooting by available light, the usual response of most photographers is to want to correct the green cast to a neutral white

illumination. A large part of the problem aesthetically is that an overall bias towards green is considered unattractive by most people, except in special and occasional circumstances. If you go back for a moment to the section on tungsten lighting, you can see how a shift to orange is tolerated.

The same is not true of green. Whereas orange is a colour of illumination that is within our visual experience (e.g. firelight, rich sunsets) and has, on the whole, pleasant associations of warmth, green is not a natural colour of light. Nevertheless, although this is a fairly good reason for wanting to make corrections, you should, as a first step, think about whether you can make some use of the green cast, or indeed, whether the colour will make any important detrimental difference to the image.

Recommended filters for fluorescent light

TYPE OF FLUORESCENT LAMP	DAYLIGHT-BALANCED FILM	TYPE B FILM	TYPE A FILM (KODACHROME 40)
Daylight	40M+40Y +1 stop	85Br40M+40Y +1⅔ stops	85B+40R +1⅓ stops
White	20C+30M +1 stop	60M+50Y +1⅓ stops	40M+30Y +1 stop
Warm white	40C+40M +1⅓ stops	50M+40Y +1 stop	30M+20Y +1 stop
Warm white de luxe	60C+30M +2 stops	10M+10Y +⅔ stop	No filter
Cool white	30M +⅔ stop	60R +1⅓ stops	50M+50Y +⅔ stop
Cool white de luxe	20C+10M +⅔ stop	20M+40Y +1⅓ stops	10M+30Y +⅔ stops

Vertical strip-lights cast the usual greenish light in the shot left *of Bangkok's Emerald Buddha. Filtration would have made the green statue appear duller.*

Used as illumination for the façade of a building, the colour of fluorescent lighting is quite acceptable.

Given time, it is always possible to make full correction for fluorescent lighting, provided it is the only light source. A safer method is prior testing on film. In the shot above *a test showed that the CC30 Magenta used here was the best. Filtration, however, reduces the light reaching the film and so a tripod is often necessary.*

Acceptable colour cast

One reason why it may not be important to make a correction is sheer familiarity. Fluorescent lighting is used so much in large interiors, like supermarkets and offices, and so many uncorrected and under-corrected photographs are regularly published, that viewers are to an extent accustomed to seeing the greenish cast. For this reason alone, it is rarely a disaster. Another reason is that, in scenes that combine differently coloured light sources, the green of the fluorescent lamps will be localized. Offset by, for example, the orange of tungsten lighting, it will not dominate the picture. Indeed, the positive side of mixed lighting is that the colour combinations can be intrinsically attractive, and contribute to the image. Then again, the unattractive

associations of green light may be exactly what you need if you intend to convey a particular kind of atmosphere. Institutional settings, such as the emergency reception area of a hospital, a seedy bus terminal or subway, are likely to look more effective if the fluorescent lighting is left uncorrected. This is something you can test for yourself without difficulty.

Colour correction

If, however, you do want to correct the lighting, there are several options. The simplest and most usual technique is to use a filter of the opposite colour over the lens. This is straightforward provided that you know the strength and exact hue of the colour cast. If you have a three-way colour temperature meter, you can measure this

directly and immediately, but it must be the type of meter that will measure colour shifts outside the strict amber-to-blue range of colour temperature.

Filters for fluorescent light

Three-way colour temperature meters are perhaps something of a luxury. Without one, the most accurate alternative is to try and identify the type of lamp, and use the filters recommended in the table on page 218. Be warned, however, the manufacturing standards as regards the spectrum are not particularly consistent, and that in any case age can change the colour of the lamp. Moreover, one interior may have different types of lamp.

However, if you compare the different filter recommendations, you can see that most are quite close to one basic value: CC30 Magenta. If you have neither the time nor the means to find out exactly what the filtration should be, using either a Kodak Wratten CC30 Magenta or its equivalent will usually work. At the least, it will make an improvement. Specialist filter manufacturers produce a specific fluorescent light correction filter in glass or plastic which is virtually the same, but more convenient for quick use if you buy it in a screw-mount to fit your lenses. Certainly, as the table on selecting filters shows, the lack of red in fluorescent lighting is closer to the colour balance of regular daylight film than it is to either Type B or Type A films.

The exact tint of green depends on the type of fluorescent lamp, but most fluorescent-lit interiors can be made to appear almost neutral by using a magenta filter of about CC30 strength. In these two shots the colour-corrected version left, below was shot with one.

In a planned location shot with preparation time available, a professional photographer would normally test the colour cast well before time by photographing the setting on the type of film to be used, varying the filters on different frames. You may wish to use the recommended filtration in the table as a starting point, and filters could be added and subtracted in strengths of CC10. The processed film would then show which single filtration to use for the principal photography. Even without going to this effort, you could borrow from this technique and bracket the filtration as you shoot: CC10, CC20, CC30 and CC40 Magenta versions will improve the chances of one corrected image. Incidentally, none of the Polaroid colour films are of any use for testing fluorescent lighting, being unlike normal colour films.

Film choice

The film you choose will, in any case, make a difference. Colour reversal film produces its final image in one step, so the filtration you select at the time of shooting must be accurate if you are going to use the results as slides. Colour printing, however, gives one more chance to adjust the filtration. If you are using colour negative film, filtering at the time of shooting is less critical. You will, however, have no reference for adjusting the print unless you include a standard colour chart in one of the shots (see page 245); the print enlargement will have to be filtered by eye, and if you leave this to a colour laboratory, you should send the negative with specific instructions.

A final alternative which does not involve adding any lighting of your own is to filter the fluorescent lamps at source. The problems of assessing the colour shift are the same as with choosing a filter for the lens, and each tube must be filtered. Use lighting filters of the type sold for stage lighting and cinematography, available in sheets and rolls in non-flammable material. This is normally effective only if the fluorescent tubes are concealed. The special advantage of this technique is when the fluorescent lighting is mixed with other sources, such as daylight, tungsten or photographic lamps. A reliable but difficult alternative to this is temporarily to replace the existing tubes with fluorescent lamps that are specially corrected for photography. The difficulty here is in matching the size of the fittings.

The intensity of fluorescent lighting is relatively weak, and the filters will reduce the exposure even further. On ISO 100 film, the typical level in a supermarket, for instance, would be $f2.8$ at $\frac{1}{30}$ second without any filtration or plus $\frac{2}{3}$ stop with a CC30 Magenta filter. In any case, you should try to keep the shutter speed no faster than $\frac{1}{30}$ second, because of the way a fluorescent tube works. It is a pulsating light source; in an old lamp you can often see the flicker. If you move a pencil rapidly backwards and forwards in front of a fluorescent light source (such as a light box) you can see a strobe effect which corresponds to the cycle of the lamp.

Photographic lamps

The other technique for balancing fluorescent lighting is to use photographic lamps. The standard location for fluorescent lamps is overhead, in the ceiling, and this can create shadow difficulties with portraits and some foreground areas in an interior view.

This alone may make it worthwhile introducing fill lighting. One method is to use the same type of fluorescent tube, but close to the camera, and filter as above. A more portable alternative is to add a greenish gel filter over the head of a portable flash to give it the same colour as the ambient light; again, filter as before.

Tungsten with fluorescent lighting

Another lighting possibility makes use of the colour opposition between fluorescent and tungsten lamps. Green and orange are not exactly opposite, but in its general visual effect, the combination of the two is acceptably normal in most circumstances. A technique well worth trying, therefore, is to aim one or more tungsten lamps directly up into the fluorescent lamps. The tungsten lighting adds some of the missing spectrum. To do this, you must be able to hide the tungsten lamps, their stands and cables, from view.

PROJECTS: Correcting and using colour casts

Practise basic correction by bracketing filtration. The importance of choosing the precise filters depends to a large extent on what results you are prepared to accept. Make a test from CC10 Magenta to CC30 Magenta or CC40 Magenta and decide for yourself from the processed film whether or not the differences seem important. Use only transparency film for this project. After photographing a number of scenes lit by fluorescent lamps, ideally on one type of film, compare the uncorrected frames of each. This will give some idea of the range of colour casts.

Another project is to find ways of using the colour cast of fluorescent lighting to enhance the photograph. Try this with scenes that could benefit from appearing shabby, unfriendly or deserted.

Vapour discharge light

While vapour discharge lamps are much less common than fluorescent or tungsten, being more powerful they are often used for large public areas, particularly outside. The three principal types of lamp are sodium, which looks yellow in photographs, mercury, which looks bluish-white and photographs between that and strongly blue-green, and multi-vapour, which is reasonably well balanced for colour photography. Sodium lamps are typically used for street-lighting and for flood-lighting buildings, mercury lamps in large warehouses and industrial plants, and multi-vapour lamps in sports stadiums, where television cameras need good colour balance.

Multi-vapour lighting

The emissions of vapour discharge lamps peak strongly in very narrow bands of the spectrum, and are completely lacking in many wavelengths. Only multi-vapour lamps produce a colour quality that is close to normal, and being able to distinguish them from mercury vapour sources is not always possible. As a guide, however, all sports stadiums that have television coverage will almost certainly have multi-vapour lighting, for this reason.

Filtration

Without the benefit of a coating of fluorescers to spread the output over other parts of the spectrum, the effects of vapour discharge lamps are very difficult to control by filtration. Sodium lamps are notorious for this, emitting only in a yellow-green wavelength. The only substantial effect that filtra-

In this East Malaysian oil refinery the blue-green lights are mercury vapour, the yellowish sodium. But from this distance it is not worth using colour correction, as the lights are only a small element in the composition.

tion has is to make the image darker. Mercury vapour lamps have more than one peak, and can benefit from red and orange filters, but results are difficult to predict. If the circumstances allow it, you should take test photographs beforehand.

The only realistic advice is to accept the colour that you get. If you are shooting in close-up, and more balanced colours are really necessary, provide photographic lighting that will overwhelm the existing vapour lamps; this means either relatively powerful tungsten lamps used close, or, with less difficulty, flash at the highest synchronization setting.

Unfiltered mercury vapour lamps in a hangar used for assembling the main fuel tank of the Space Shuttle produce a typical blue-green cast. Compare this with the fluorescent-lit hangar on page 220. Some correction with filters is possible, but the discontinuous spectrum prevents a completely neutral result.

To take a wide-angle photograph of fireworks in a setting, use the start of the display to judge the height and position of the bursts, and frame the shot accordingly. With the camera locked on a tripod, vary the exposure times to include single and multiple bursts. This shot was taken in New York at the centenary celebrations of the Statue of Liberty. The focal length was 35mm, and the aperture f2.8 with ISO 64 film.

CITIES AT NIGHT

The light sources available outside at night are the same types as those we have just looked at, but in different proportions. Vapour lamps are used much more extensively outdoors than indoors, because of their higher output; this is particularly true of street lighting and flood-lighting.

Tungsten as street lighting is increasingly less common, but can be seen in shop and other windows and as car lights.

Although the light sources are the same as those used to illuminate interiors, their effect is very different. The scale of the usual type of outdoor shot is greater, and the surroundings do not give the same degree of reflection as do interior walls and ceilings. As a result, there is much more pooling of light: in a typical scene there are many lights, and they are localized. Only very rarely are there enough lights in a concentrated area to give the impression of overall illumination.

In most night-time city views, however, there is either one well-lit area, such as a flood-lit building, or a pattern of small lights. In many ways, this causes fewer difficulties than an interior, and there are fewer occasions when you might need to decide on the principal light source and correct the colour with filters. The impression of a colour cast occurs when most of the picture area is affected; when there are other lights in the image, colour balance becomes much less important.

Localized light
The localization of the light sources makes

For the flood-lit shot of the Federal Reserve Building in Washington DC left, a spot meter was used, and the exposure based on the reading from the darker of the pair of outspread wings.

In the top photograph above taken well after dusk, the shape of the buildings is lost. The other shot, taken towards the end of dusk, reads much more clearly because residual daylight is mixed with the artificial light.

SUBJECT	ISO 64–100	ISO 160–200	ISO 320–400	ISO 800	ISO 1000	ISO 1600
Normally lit street	½–1 sec, f2.8	¼–½ sec, f2.8	⅛–¼ sec, f2.8	¹⁄₁₅–⅛ sec, f2.8	¹⁄₁₅ sec, f2.8	¹⁄₃₀–¹⁄₁₅ sec, f2.8
Brightly lit street	¹⁄₁₅ sec, f2.8	¹⁄₃₀ sec, f2.8	¹⁄₆₀ sec, f2.8	¹⁄₆₀ sec, f4	¹⁄₆₀ sec, f4.5	¹⁄₆₀ sec, f5.6
Downtown nightclub/theater district	¹⁄₃₀ sec, f2.8	¹⁄₆₀ sec, f2.8	¹⁄₆₀ sec, f4	¹⁄₆₀ sec, f5.6	¹⁄₆₀ sec, f6.3	¹⁄₆₀ sec, f8
Neon sign	¹⁄₃₀ sec, f2.8	¹⁄₃₀ sec, f4	¹⁄₃₀ sec, f5.6	¹⁄₃₀ sec, f8	¹⁄₃₀ sec, f9	¹⁄₃₀ sec, f11
Shop window	⅛–¹⁄₃₀ sec, f2.8	¹⁄₁₅–¹⁄₆₀ sec, f2.8	¹⁄₃₀–¹⁄₆₀ sec, f2.8	¹⁄₃₀–¹⁄₁₂₅ sec, f4	¹⁄₃₀–¹⁄₁₂₅ sec, f4.5	¹⁄₃₀–¹⁄₁₂₅ sec, f5.6
Floodlit building	½ sec, f2.8	¼ sec, f2.8	⅛ sec, f2.8	¹⁄₁₅ sec, f2.8	¹⁄₁₅ sec, f3.5	¹⁄₃₀ sec, f2.8
Subject under street light	½–1 sec, f2.8	¼–½ sec, f2.8	⅛–¼ sec, f2.8	¹⁄₁₅–⅛ sec, f2.8	¹⁄₁₅–⅛ sec, f2.8	¹⁄₃₀–¹⁄₁₅ sec, f2.8
Distant city lights	1–10 secs, f2.8	½–5 secs, f2.8	¼–2 secs, f2.8	⅛–1 sec, f2.8	⅛–1 sec, f2.8	¹⁄₁₅–½ sec, f2.8
Firework display over city	¼–2 secs, f2.8	¼–2 secs, f4	¼–2 secs, f5.6	¼–2 secs, f8	¼–2 secs, f9	¼–2 secs, f11
Aerial firework display	1–4 secs, f4–f5.6	1–4 secs, f5.6–f8	1–4 secs, f8–f11	1–4 secs, f11–f16	1–4 secs, f14–f19	1–4 secs, f16–f22
Lightning over city, 4–10 miles (6–16 km) away	Open shutter f5.6	Open shutter f8	Open shutter f11	Open shutter f16	Open shutter f19	Open shutter f22
Flames, large fires	¹⁄₆₀–¹⁄₃₀ sec, f2.8	¹⁄₃₀–¹⁄₁₅ sec, f2.8	¹⁄₆₀–¹⁄₃₀ sec, f2.8	¹⁄₁₂₅–¹⁄₆₀ sec, f2.8	¹⁄₁₂₅–¹⁄₆₀ sec, f3.5	¹⁄₁₂₅–¹⁄₆₀ sec, f4
Subject lit by fire	¼–½ sec, f2.8	⅛–¼ sec, f2.8	¹⁄₁₅–⅛ sec, f2.8	¹⁄₃₀–¹⁄₁₅ sec, f2.8	¹⁄₃₀–¹⁄₁₅ sec, f3.5	¹⁄₆₀–¹⁄₃₀ sec, f2.8
Floodlit stadium	¹⁄₃₀–¹⁄₁₅ sec, f2.8	¹⁄₆₀–¹⁄₆₀ sec, f2.8	¹⁄₁₂₅–¹⁄₆₀ sec, f2.8	¹⁄₂₅₀–¹⁄₁₂₅ sec, f2.8	¹⁄₂₅₀–¹⁄₁₂₅ sec, f3.5	¹⁄₂₅₀–¹⁄₁₂₅ sec, f4
Open-air rock concert	¹⁄₃₀ sec, f2.8	¹⁄₆₀ sec, f2.8	¹⁄₁₂₅ sec, f2.8	¹⁄₁₂₅ sec, f4	¹⁄₁₂₅ sec, f4.5	¹⁄₁₂₅ sec, f5.6
Car headlights/tail-lights at motorway (streaked)	10 secs, f11–f16	10 secs, f16–f22	10 secs, f22–f32	5 secs, f22–f32	3 secs, f22–f32	2 secs, f22–f32
Subject lit by car headlights at 20 feet (6m)	½ sec, f2.8	¼ sec, f2.8	⅛ sec, f2.8	¹⁄₁₅ sec, f2.8	¹⁄₁₅ sec, f3.5	¹⁄₃₀ sec, f2.8
Oil refinery	2 sec, f2.8	1 sec, f2.8	½ sec, f2.8	¼ sec, f2.8	⅛ sec, f2.8	¹⁄₁₅ sec, f2.8

measurement difficult. A spot meter is the most useful meter to have, but the table above is more practical under a variety of conditions. Use it as a guide rather than as a completely accurate recommendation, and bracket exposures around the figures given. For many night-time scenes the accuracy of the exposure is not, in fact, very critical. However, one thing that often makes overall cityscapes unsatisfactory is that the large number of lights does little to show up the setting, and remains as a pattern of dots. For this reason it usually helps, in making this kind of shot, to take the photograph at dusk, because at that time there is just a little residual daylight.

Fireworks

Firework displays, like lightning, make their own exposure. Light intensity apart, there is little point in trying to use a fast shutter speed: the effect of a bursting firework display is created by the streaking of the lights, even to the eye. A short exposure simply shows less of the display. Conversely, provided that the sky is really black, leaving the shutter open will *not* cause overexposure, but add more displays to the image.

Judging exposure times

For the best effect of the bursts, exposure times are usually between half a second and four seconds, but you can judge this for timing them from the moment the rockets reach their bursting height. This allows fairly slow, fine-grained film to be used successfully: f2.8 is a reasonable aperture with ISO 50 or ISO 64 film. In any case, the exposure is not critical: try making a variety of exposures to determine this for yourself.

For a view that includes the setting, as in the photograph on page 224 lock the camera firmly on the tripod, and make sure that the framing and the focal length are right for the height of the displays. Check this and the location of the fireworks by watching a few through the viewfinder before shooting. For a close view of a single burst, try this technique: use a medium telephoto lens and the tripod head partially loosened (enough so that you can move the camera, but still sufficiently tight to hold it when you stop). Pan upwards to follow the rocket as it ascends, and as soon as it bursts, stop and open the shutter.

PROJECT: Neon displays

Although these are fluorescent lights, the colours of the displays overwhelm the greenish colour cast typical of fluorescent lighting. There is usually little point in trying to make any compensation with filters. For this project, find a suitably interesting and attractive display, and set up the camera on a tripod. Most displays are high up – well above street level – and the easiest technique is usually to stand back, across the street or further, and use a telephoto lens. For one exposure, use a CC30 Magenta or fluorescent-correction filter, just to be able to see what difference it makes. Apart from this, take a series of different exposures, using the figures recommended in the table on page 218. As you are using a tripod, fast film is not necessary, and in any case you will need to keep the shutter speed at 1/30 second or slower, to compensate for the tendency of fluorescent lamps to pulsate.

Which exposure looks best is usually a matter of taste, and the range of what is acceptable is quite wide. In comparing the results later, you should notice that short exposures give more intense colours, reproduce the tubes as thin lines, and show nothing or very little of the surroundings. Longer exposures give a thicker appearance to the display, which characteristically also appears paler in colour.

For backlit displays like the sign outside a Las Vegas hotel above, read the light level of the sign and then reduce the exposure by 1 or 2 stops.

Although the range of exposure settings below covers 4 stops, each shot is acceptable. The TTL meter reading was that used for the second lightest version.

PHOTOGRAPHIC LIGHT

If you were to undertake a wide-ranging exploration of illuminated studio and location photography, you would eventually find a use for all the sources of photographic lighting covered in this section of this book. However, for cost if nothing else, most photographers commit themselves to one type of lighting, at least until they have gained some experience.

Portable flash

While portable flash has its uses on location, it does not have quite as many as its manufacturers would like you to believe: it is essentially convenience lighting for hand-held shooting, and offers few possibilities to exercise full lighting control. Its basic drawback is that it is nearly always camera-mounted, and offers little chance to manipulate lighting quality.

The majority of the photographs shown as examples in this section of the book have been made with equipment that is mains-powered and designed for use not as naked lamps, but with fittings that change the quality of the light. Essentially, then, the choice of lighting equipment lies between mains flash and mains tungsten; a few other specialized sources are also dealt with for the sake of comprehensivity, but basic photographic lighting falls into one of these two categories.

System compatibility

As with other photographic equipment, such as cameras, there are many competing systems, and these are often not compatible. This is particularly the case with mains flash, in which the power units, collectors and flash-heads cannot normally be interchanged. Before buying anything, make all the comparisons you can, and anticipate your future needs. You might, for instance, eventually need several identical lamps, or a set of specialized lights – one for still-life main illumination, and others for backgrounds, and so on. Also, if you expect to shoot on location as well as at home or in the studio, the weight and transportability of the equipment will be important.

Some makes of lighting system are designed with certain characteristics that are relevant to the type of photography for which they are to be used. One well-known professional range, for instance, comprises flash-heads already fitted into different sizes of area lights expressly for still-life photography.

Lighting quality control

What will be stressed throughout this section of the book is the importance of controlling the quality of lighting. This may seem an obvious point to make, but if you are used only to portable flash, for instance, the sheer quantity of materials, time and effort that go into full lighting control may be a surprise. In still-life shooting, studio portraits, room sets and other controlled situations, convenience and simplicity are low priorities. Precise lighting takes time to plan and construct, and can be untidy and complex when set up.

Conflicting lighting

In terms of equipment, what must always come first is the means to produce as full as

The main sources of light designed specially for photography are flash and tungsten. Here three kinds of flash represent the range available: a mains-powered unit for studio and controlled location work, an on-camera portable flash and the less common but powerful flash bulb, blue-tinted to match daylight's colour. At the top is a 1000-watt quartz-halogen light designed for portability.

possible a range of directions, diffusion, concentration and all the other qualities that define a particular type of illumination. Often, this will take a lot of effort, and introduce you to a special class of lighting problem. Typical of this sort of difficulty is the need to reach a satisfactory compromise between conflicting lighting qualities. For instance, diffusing a lamp in such a way that it suits one object in a group may cause an unwanted spill of light onto another. The main light and background light may (and often do) conflict, and separating the effect of each on the other may call for some ingenuity in managing and placing the equipment.

Choice of lamps

The most important decision at this stage is the choice of the basic lamps. Although they can hardly ever be used satisfactorily alone as direct lights, most of the rest of the equipment you will need for modifying the light does not have to be bought – you can make it yourself. Indeed, some of the diffusers and reflectors shown later are not even available commercially. For mechanical precision, light fittings do not compare with most other photographic equipment, and because of this and the variation in individual requirements there is every reason to design your own to suit your own particular tastes in lighting effects.

PORTABLE FLASH

In the range of photographic lighting, portable flash is principally a convenience, and it is important to appreciate its limitations. Portable units are designed to be small and easy to use; with these as priorities, quality and variety of lighting take second place.

A typical portable electronic unit is powered by several dry-cell batteries, mostly either rechargeable or multiple 1.5 volt AA size, and made to be used attached to the camera (usually 35mm). The attachment is either into a standard hot-shoe, which provides synchronization, or into a fitting peculiar to each camera model, with multiple contacts to the exposure control system and viewfinder display. The latter, known as dedicated flash, is increasingly the norm. If the flash is used off-camera, the synchronization or dedicated connections must be made by cable.

The batteries charge the capacitor and this, when the contact is made, releases the full charge almost instantaneously through the flash tube, ionizing the gas inside. The intensity of the light output depends on the size of the capacitor and on the square of the voltage at which the unit operates; the duration of the flash depends on the size of the capacitor and the resistance of the circuit, but is typically between $\frac{1}{1000}$ and $\frac{1}{50,000}$ second. Although this duration is faster than any shutter speed, there are mechanical limitations to synchronizing the two with a focal plane shutter. What is called the flash synchronization speed for any camera is in

The great value of portable flash is that it makes it possible to take at least some kind of photograph in situations where there is insufficient light. Direct, on-camera flash pictures usually work best when the subject has strong tones or colours, as here.

Many portable flash units have some means of swivelling the head so that it can be directed upwards to provide bounced flash. The picture below was taken with the on-camera flash shown right.

The simplest alternative to direct, on-camera flash is to bounce the flash light off a nearby light-toned surface, such as the ceiling of a room. In the photograph below bounced flash provides most of the illumination, but an exposure of ¹⁄₁₅ second allowed some of the ambient light to register.

effect the maximum shutter speed; the flash can also be used with any slower setting. Focal plane synchronization speeds vary, depending on the model of camera.

Synchronization with a leaf shutter in the lens is easier, and works at all speeds.

Second-curtain synchronization

Flash is normally synchronized to fire when the shutter opens. This means that if you want to take a picture (using flash) of a car with the tail lights appearing as red trails behind, you will need to photograph the car moving *backwards* – not an easy thing to do on the motorway. With second-curtain synchronization, the flash fires just as the shutter is about to close at the end of a long exposure, solving the problem.

The measure of flash output is BCPS (beam candlepower-second), but the more commonly used value is the guide number, as this enables the photographer to calculate the aperture setting from the distance between flash and subject. Manufacturers publish the BCPS output of their units, which varies according to the film speed rating, but the conditions under which it is established are not consistent. If the output is calculated when the flash unit is being used in a small room with light-coloured walls and ceiling, it will be higher.

The guide number is a more practical measurement of output, and is also published by the manufacturer. It also varies with the film speed rating, and is the product of the aperture (in *f*-stops) and flash-to-subject distance. Under the old ASA film speed rating system, the distance is in feet, but with the DIN rating it is in meters. If

Without flash, the averaged meter setting of 1/125 second at f8 showed little of the grapes above left. The normal flash setting would have been f8, but this was changed to f16, and the shutter speed to ¹⁄₃₀ second, to fill in the shadows above right.

For cameras that accept dedicated flash, special extension cables are available. An off-camera flash set-up can be extended by adding a second (or more) flash unit(s). If the first flash is connected by a dedicated cable, subsequent units need only a regular sync. cable.

only one guide number is given, you can assume that it has been calculated in feet unless stated otherwise (some manufacturers, for instance, quote guide numbers as "ISO/ft" or "ISO/m"). Hence, for what the manufacturer considers to be a good normal exposure, a flash unit with a guide number of 80 would have to be used with an aperture setting of $f8$ if the subject were 10 feet (3 m) away. So, if the flash unit is set to manual – for maximum output – the exposure can be set by dividing the guide number by the subject distance.

In most circumstances, however, this is not necessary as the majority of units have an automatic system for controlling the exposure. In the simpler and older method, a photo-cell measures the light reflected back from the subject, and a thyristor circuit responds extremely rapidly to quench the flash discharge. This is satisfactory up to a point, but a more sophisticated method, dedicated flash, incorporates a number of improvements. As the name implies, dedicated flash is the use of a camera and flash unit that are designed specifically to work together. The two units then function in a totally integrated way. Typically, a dedicated flash unit creates a display of functions in the camera's viewfinder: a "sufficient light" signal appears as long as the exposure does not totally drain the capacitors of the flash, and a ready light comes on in the viewfinder when the flash has recycled. In a few models, dedicated flash units meter exposure from the film's surface during exposure by means of a photocell incorporated into the camera body.

The on-camera flash position is at least extremely convenient. It helps, therefore, to know what subjects and settings do well under this kind of hard, frontal lighting. Referring back to pages 188-9, the similarities with frontal sunlight are obvious. You should, however, become familiar with the two or three standard techniques for altering the quality of portable flash lighting. One is to remove the unit from the camera and aim it from a different direction. This is particularly simple with dedicated flash, because the automatic exposure is set independently of the position of the light; but it does require a specific multi-core cable.

When using a unit off-camera, remember that the shadows will be larger and the contrast very high unless you use a reflector or a second flash unit opposite. Off-camera flash is easiest with the help of someone else to hold the flash unit.

Bounce-lighting

The second technique for modifying the light is to bounce it off a nearby reflecting surface. One of the most available is the ceiling of a room, and most flash units are designed to tilt upwards and to make use of this. Portable flash does not allow you a preview of the lighting effect, so it is important to practise bounce-lighting so that you can be confident of the results when you need to use it. The light intensity is reduced drastically, and a normal problem is that it is reduced too much and there is not enough light for the photograph. In such a case, consider using a slower shutter speed so as to add the existing room lighting. As the photograph on page 230 demonstrates, this also produces a more natural image. There are not many ways of calculating the intensity of the bounced light as it reaches the subject beyond using a flash meter. One thing that you can do with a dedicated flash unit, however, is to fire the flash a few times, adjusting the aperture until you find the setting at which there is just enough light. At this setting the output is full, and just sufficient.

Filling in shadows

Another method of using portable flash that goes beyond the simple direct frontal use is as fill-lighting for shadows. This can be done from any direction, but the most common way that it is used is facing sunlight, to show detail in foreground shadows. Many dedicated flash units now offer this lighting choice automatically. The camera's meter system measures the ambient light then adds the appropriate amount of flash. Alternatively, work it out for yourself. Fill-lighting is intended to be substantially less than the main lighting it faces. The best way to plan this is to think of the ratio of the fill to the principal light – 1:2 is strong, 1:4 is natural, 1:6 and less is weak (these are rough judgements).

The technique is first to frame the shot and to set the exposure for the ambient lighting (leaving the shadows dark). Then, with the flash set on manual, work out from the guide number or the table on the back of the unit what the flash-to-subject distance ought to be to give the ratio you want at the chosen aperture setting. If this step seems complicated, think of it like this: the guide number or table will show you easily enough what the distance ought to be for normal, full lighting: for a 1:2 ratio, read off the distance against 1 f-stop smaller, for a 1:4 ratio 2 f-stops smaller and so on. Then, either take the flash off the camera and use it from the indicated distance, or move the camera and flash back together.

STUDIO LIGHTING

In the following pages we look first at studio flash and then other forms of studio lighting. Compared with portable on-camera flash, the mains-powered flash used in the studio is built to perform on a much larger scale. Simply being able to draw continuously available power at a much higher voltage makes it possible to use capacitors that will discharge enough energy to meet virtually any conceivable demand in photography. The light can be diffused, reflected or redirected in all kinds of ways, and still reach the subject at a sufficiently high

Used alone, with no shadow fill and against a black velvet background, a 2 foot square (0.6m) area light gives strong modelling to the hawk eagle left. With a moving subject, flash is essential to avoid blur.

level to allow a small aperture and good depth of field.

To make use of the extremely high output of the mains flash capacitors, the flash tubes are considerably larger than those in portable units. As a result, the peak flash duration is much longer than that of a portable flash unit. Instead of thousandths of a second, mains flash duration is measured in hundredths of a second: between $\frac{1}{200}$ and $\frac{1}{500}$ second is typical of units in the 200-800 joule range.

Mains flash operation

Basically, a mains flash unit works as follows. As the power supply is in the form of an alternating current in a relatively low voltage, the first part of the circuitry is a transformer and associated rectifier (or more than one in the case of larger units). The transformer steps up the voltage and the rectifier converts the alternating current to a direct current (AC to DC). This unidirectional high-voltage source then supplies the capacitor (or banks of capacitors) which store the charge. On command, the high-voltage output in a capacitor is discharged through the flash tube.

Studio flash design

There are two main kinds of construction. In one, now reserved for high-output units, the power-pack and controls are in a separate housing, with the flash heads connected by cable. In this design, the power-pack

Food photography, particularly the cooking process, often involves movement. For the shot of chili crab being cooked left, a $2\frac{1}{2}$ x $3\frac{1}{2}$ft (0.8 x 1m) area light was suspended overhead, so that its light would be reflected in the liquid.

Over large lighting distances, such as in the car museum right, the only way of increasing flash exposure beyond a certain level is to make several flashes. With tungsten lighting, as used here, increasing the time exposure is usually simpler and more straightforward.

The two principal types of photographic lighting used in the studio are electronic flash and tungsten, and there is very little other choice. Each has particular advantages over the other, and these characteristics are set out in the comparative checklist below.

	FLASH		TUNGSTEN		FLUORESCENT
	Portable	Mains	Mains	Battery portable	
Light output	Low, individual pulse sets limit	High, but individual pulse sets limit	Fairly high; no limit to quantity reaching film if time exposure is used	Low, but time exposure increases level	Low, but time exposure increases level
Compatibility with other sources	Colour-balanced for daylight, otherwise use filters. Mixed exposure calculations with ambient lighting a little difficult		Needs filtration to make compatible with any other source. Continuous, so easy to judge effect and measure exposure with other, ambient lighting		If tubes are those corrected for photography, colour-balanced for daylight. Exposure calculation easy with ambient lighting
Controlling quality of light	Only a few possibilties (and then with flash removed from camera). Shadow fill very convenient, however.	The most possibilities: many fittings available, including enclosed boxes	Many possibilities, but cannot be enclosed without cooling fans	Limited	Limited, but excellent for diffused area light
Portability	Excellent	Difficult	Quite difficult	Good	Quite difficult
Weight and complexity	Lightweight	Heavy, complex, expensive	Moderately heavy, simple, moderately inexpensive	Fairly simple and uncomplicated, but battery needs care	Simple, uncomplicated
Heat output	Negligible	Little	High, damaging to some subjects	Low to moderate	Very little
Treatment of subject movement	Freezes action	Freezes all but the fastest action	Blurs action	Blurs action	Blurs action

has more than one outlet to supply different heads at the same time, and the power ratio can be varied between them The second design is the integral unit, in which a single housing contains everything: controls, capacitors, flash heads, etc. Although individually heavier as a head, the integral design is easier to carry and use, and needs fewer cables.

The controls in this basic system are partly automatic and partly selected by the photographer. The main choice offered to the user is in output, and most units offer a selection of levels up to the maximum. For instance, a stepped control might offer, for example, quarter-power, half-power, three-quarter-power and full power, or the control may be stepless (the quarter-power to full-power range is still the most common). Input from the mains is controlled automatically so that the capacitors store just the charge necessary for the selected output. The capacitor voltage tends to decay naturally, and in a typical flash unit an amplifier will cut in when the voltage has decreased by about 5 per cent, and top up the level.

Multiple flash heads

In flash units that have the power unit and control console separate from the flash head, there is usually a facility for supplying several heads at the same time, and of selecting the amount of charge passed to each. Normally, this is in the form of a ratio selector, so that, for example, half the total output may be passed to one head and a quarter each to two others.

Once the flash has been fired, either by a triggering switch or by the synchronization cable attached to the camera, the capacitors are recharged automatically. Often this is

arranged in such a way that there is an initial surge, which may last for a fraction of a second, until this is reduced by a limiting circuit to a lower current. With a large flash unit, you should check that the initial surge does not exceed the fusing of the mains circuit. The time taken to charge up the capacitors is known as the recycling time, and this varies between makes. It also, understandably, depends on the output, and if you select a lower output, the flash will be ready for firing again in less time than if it is switched to maximum. Recycling times typically vary between ¾ second and 4 seconds at full charge.

Level of charge

Switching up or down on the output control, or cross-switching between outlets on a separate power-pack, requires a change to the level of the charge stored in the capacitors. In switching up, there is a short delay while the amplifier tops up the level; in switching down, the extra unwanted charge must somehow be bled off. On some units a bleed circuit does this; on others, there is a dump switch, which effectively discharges a flash manually. Natural decay will, in any case, bring the level down eventually, although this may take between several seconds and anything up to a minute or two.

Safety

When using mains-powered flash, always be rigorous about safety, for in this case it is your own. Always earth the equipment correctly, and never, ever, make any connections or disconnections with the mains supply attached (for instance, if you need to remove the flash tube, or when plugging in and out of the outlets on a separate power-

pack). It should also go without saying that it is dangerous to use water close to one of these high-voltage units, so that if you need, for instance, to spray a still-life set, take care to shield the power-pack and flash head.

Many units incorporate a safety circuit that bleeds off power once the unit is switched off at the mains, but if not, the circuitry inside can remain live for up to a minute, depending on the make of the unit. This alone is a good enough reason for leaving the works inside the housing. Unless you are completely confident about what you are doing, always leave electrical repairs of this kind to an expert.

Area lights

The speed of the flash discharge results in a low heat output; unless the flash head is fired rapidly and continuously, there is more heat produced by the modelling lamp than by the flash tube or internal electronics. The implications of this go well beyond being able to photograph ice-cream without melting it, and such like. The relative coolness of a flash head means that it can be used right next to almost any kind of material suitable for modifying the light quality. In particular, it can be enclosed, and this seemingly simple fact was responsible many years ago for a major revolution in studio lighting. The area light is a product of mains-powered flash, and from the late 1960s onwards changed the appearance of still-life photography. Area lights are precise diffusers, but at least one manufacturer produces area lights not as attachments but as basic lighting equipment. These are the exceptions to the normal practice of building flash equipment as raw light sources.

The most powerful studio flash systems, such as the one illustrated here, are of 1000 joule output or more, and tend to have flash heads that are separate from the power-packs. The size of the capacitors makes this the only practical construction.

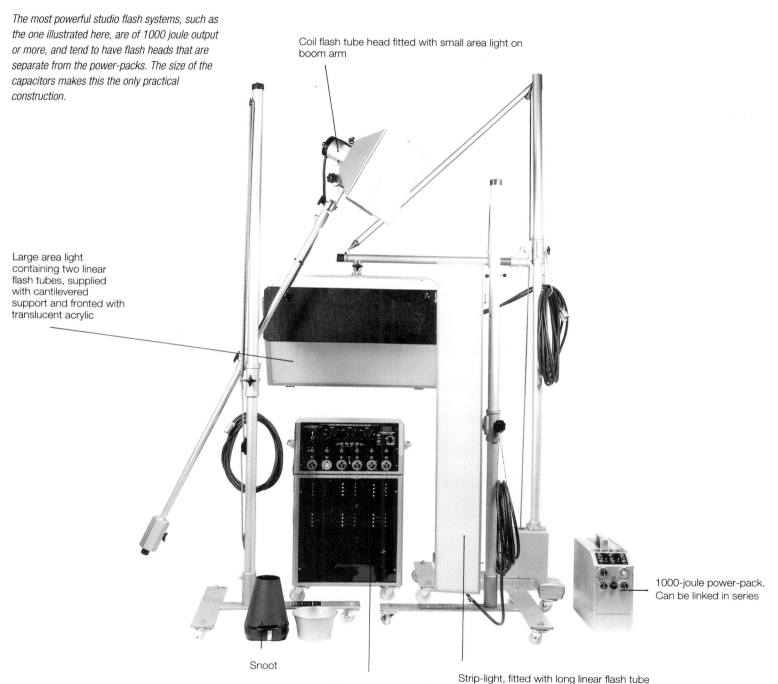

Coil flash tube head fitted with small area light on boom arm

Large area light containing two linear flash tubes, supplied with cantilevered support and fronted with translucent acrylic

1000-joule power-pack. Can be linked in series

Snoot

5000-joule power-pack and console

Strip-light, fitted with long linear flash tube

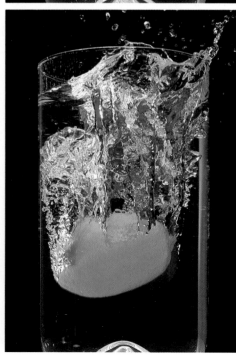

Rapid movement introduces two extra difficulties to using studio flash. One is synchronizing the exposure with the right movement in the action; the other is that the flash duration in a large flash tube is relatively long, and may not be fast enough to freeze the subject. In the photographs on this page, a lemon was shot as it was dropped into a glass of water. Try this for yourself, dropping the lemon and triggering the camera manually. Note the crucial delay between pressing the shutter release and the discharge of the flash. On the developed film, see how much blurring there is.

Flash versus tungsten

If you compare the available ranges for flash equipment with those of tungsten lighting, you can see one noticeable difference in the heads. Although most of the tungsten units have built-in reflectors, often adjustable, most flash tubes are backed with the absolute minimum of reflective dish, usually no wider than the dimensions of the basic head. Essentially, flash units are made to be used with attachment fittings. While beam control is normal in tungsten lighting, it is not standard in flash.

There are two practical reasons why flash manufacturers avoid this. One is that the beam of the flash tube is never visible for long enough to judge by eye, and the nearest you can get to seeing what it will look like is the light from the modelling lamp. The second reason is that a flash unit is structurally more complex than most tungsten lamps, with integral units now more popular than ever. As a result, there are more complications in trying to make the flash tube move in and out of the housing to adjust the spread of light.

Studio tungsten

Tungsten lighting is incandescent, created by burning a tungsten filament at a controlled rate in a sealed transparent envelope (glass in the case of traditional lamps, a quartz-like material in the case of more efficient tungsten-halogen lamps). Regular photographic tungsten lamps work on the same principle as ordinary domestic lamps but have much higher wattages, between 200 and several thousand. Their light output is therefore much higher, and the colour temperature is controlled, at 3200 K (312 mireds) in nearly every design. This stan-

dardized colour temperature is also that of Type B colour film, and this is the material of choice for colour photography with tungsten lighting. If regular daylight-balanced film is used, a blue 80A conversion filter is needed: this has a mired shift of −131, the difference between 3200 K and 5500 K. Some lamps are available with a blue coating to the glass, giving a colour temperature that approximates that of daylight. These are intended more for use in mixed lighting conditions, such as combined with daylight, than for straightforward studio use.

Traditional photographic tungsten lamps are available with wattages ranging from 275 to 1000 at their rated voltages (110, 120, 220 or 240); their light output is in proportion. Of those commonly available for still-life photography, most have standard screw or bayonet fittings for use in a variety of holders and reflectors.

Photofloods

Although they have similar fittings and a similar appearance, photofloods have shorter lives than tungsten lamps – often as little as eight hours. They have a colour temperature of 3400 K, very slightly bluer than other tungsten lamps and matched to the now uncommon Type A colour film. With Type B film, an 81A filter gives the necessary correction (or an equivalent lighting filter can be fitted to the lamp), although the difference is sufficiently small for many photographers to ignore it. As with photographic lamps, be careful about using them in ordinary domestic fittings which may not be able to tolerate high temperatures. These uncomplicated traditional tungsten lamps are inexpensive, but blacken with use as the burnt tungsten redeposits on the glass;

their light output and colour temperature becomes lower. They are now seldom used in professional studios.

Tungsten-halogen lamps

The more efficient version of tungsten lighting is the tungsten-halogen lamp. This uses the same coiled tungsten filament but it burns at a much higher temperature in halogen gas. As a result, these lamps maintain virtually the same light output and colour temperature throughout their life; they also last longer than traditional lamps and are smaller for their equivalent wattage. Available wattages range from 200 to 10,000, although the most powerful are intended for cinematography; the highest normal wattage for still photographic lights is 2000. The light output is the same as that from a new tungsten lamp of traditional design of the same wattage.

The design of tungsten-halogen lamps varies to suit the different makes of lighting unit, but the two main types are both 2-pin: single-ended, which is intended to be used upright, and double-ended, which is used horizontally. It is important for safety and for the life of the lamps to use them *only* in these positions.

There are other important precautions. Never touch the quartz-like envelope with bare fingers as the greasy deposit will cause blackening and shorten the lamp's life. Instead, use paper, cloth or a glove. If you do accidentally touch the surface, wipe the finger-marks immediately with spirit. If you travel with tungsten lights and carry two sets of lamps for different voltages (110/120) and 220/240), be careful to identify the ones fitted before switching on: using a lower voltage lamp on a higher voltage circuit will immediately burn it out and may cause damage if it explodes. Not all lamps carry the voltage information on them, so make sure they are in clearly-marked containers if you store them away from the fitting.

Operating temperature

These lamps have high operating temperatures because they are very efficient, and can set fire to flammable materials, such as wood, paper and fabrics. Keep a careful eye on the position of the light, and keep it at a distance from anything that might be damaged (in particular, the light's own cable: certain parts of the housing can melt it through to the core, which would be extremely dangerous). If in doubt about damage to something, keep touching it to see if the heat builds up. Never enclose a tungsten-halogen lamp in order to modify the light; it needs good ventilation, because of the high operating temperature. Many light housings have folding doors that can be closed to protect the lamp when not in use (open, some act as reflectors, others as barn doors); never operate the light with these doors closed or even partly closed.

Beam control

All tungsten light housings incorporate some kind of reflector behind the lamp, partly to make use of all the light radiated (and so increase the light falling on the subject), and partly to control the beam. The deeper and more concave the reflector, the more concentrated the beam. As it is more difficult to spread a beam that is already tight when it leaves the housing than it is to concentrate a broad beam, most general-purpose housing have reflectors that give a

spread of between about 45° and 90°. Light that gives tighter concentration is for more specialized use.

Many housings allow some change to the beam pattern by moving the lamp in and out of the reflector, or by moving reflector doors. Barn doors fitted to some housings have a slightly different effect: they cut the edges of the beam rather than concentrate it. The beam patterns from most housings show a fall-off from the center outwards; even with a well-designed reflector, there is still an intense concentration of light in the lamp's filament. One method of reducing this fall-off in the design of the housing is to cover the lamp from direct view with a bar or a spiller cap. If the reflector dish is large as well, the result is a degree of diffusion. Even softer, but less intense, light is possible if the inside of the dish is finished in white rather than bright metal.

Filtering

Used alone in the studio, tungsten lamps normally need no colour filters, as long as the appropriate film is used. However, tungsten lighting is frequently used on location, in interiors, and this is often in combination with existing lighting, like daylight and fluorescent light. As a result, lighting filters are often needed for converting the colour temperature or for correcting the colour to that of fluorescent lamps.

The most common filters are blue, to match daylight; full blue is −131 mireds, half-blue −68 mireds and quarter-blue −49 mireds. They are available as heat-resistant gels (actually plastic film), glass and dichroic. Dichroic filters are partial mirrors, reflecting red back to the lamp and passing blue; they are not always consistent, and

ideally should be checked with a colour temperature meter.

Some housings have built-in filter holders; others are used with frames attached in front. With frames there is a danger of spill from the gap between them and the light. This can either cast reddish patches of light on the scene, or else reduce the overall colour temperature. You may need to flag this spill, or to wrap more gel around the gaps (but be careful of heat damage).

Positioning lights

The usefulness of a light is in proportion to how easily and securely it can be supported. A few large, sophisticated lights are self-supporting – they are supplied with their own means of positioning – but most need additional support. The first, essential function of any such fixture is to hold a light, and whatever fittings it needs to control the quality, in the right position. It is pointless having a good lighting system and then needing to make compromises in the photograph just because you cannot get the lighting direction that you would like. Certain lighting angles are difficult, particularly when you are using large diffuser fittings, but if this is what the photograph needs, you should try to find a practical way of providing support.

Apart from being able to aim the light in the right direction and from the right height, there are a few other factors that you should consider before buying any supports. One is that it should be safe and secure. The heavier and larger a light, the more important this is. The lamps themselves usually cause few problems, and if they sit on an appropriate size of conventional stand, none at all.

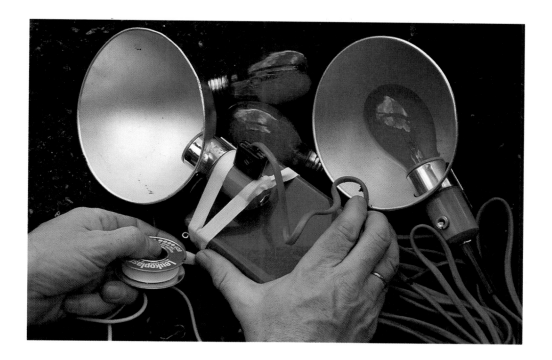

High-power flash bulbs above are at their most useful in situations where a strong output is needed to cover a large area, yet there is no mains electrical supply. In the example below the location was a large cave in Borneo where birds' nests are collected. Flash bulbs were used from the ground and by one of the collectors.

Most lamps used in still photography are fitted either with a spigot or a socket, in either case ⅝ inch (16mm) in diameter. The same is true of most stands. The spigots fit into the sockets, and double-ended separate spigots are available to convert sockets if necessary. Some very heavy tungsten lights, not normally used in still photography, have 1⅛ inch (29mm) spigots, and some lighting systems use, inconveniently, individual proprietary methods of attachment.

SOFTENING LIGHT

Softening the output of a lamp is the most basic procedure in lighting. It cuts hard shadows and makes the illumination more even. There are two ways of doing this – diffusion and reflection.

Diffusion

You can diffuse a light by shining it through a translucent material; the important effect of this is to increase the area of the light source. Think of the naked lamp, whether flash or tungsten, as the raw source of light, small and intense. Unless there is a lens and a beam focusing mechanism, the pattern of light will be intense in the middle, falling off rapidly towards the edges. The beam may also be uneven in shape, depending on the construction of the lamp and built-in reflector. Check this for yourself by aiming the light directly at a white wall from fairly close, then stand well back and look at the spread of the beam.

Placing a sheet of translucent material in front of the lamp makes this sheet – the diffuser – the source of light for all practical purposes. Try this for yourself with a lamp on a stand, aimed horizontally. From in front, the light is intense and small; this is why the shadows that it casts are deep and hard-edged. Now take a rectangle of translucent acrylic of the type similar to that used for light boxes. Hold it in front of the lamp; if it is very close, or very large, you

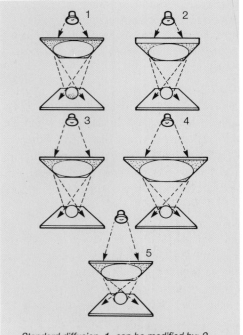

Standard diffusion, 1, can be modified by: 2, using a thicker diffuser, which gives a more even area of light; 3 , moving the light farther away; 4, using a larger sheet of diffusing material, which increases the area of the light source; and 5, moving the diffuser closer.

Diffusion softens shadows and highlights left.

The most often used diffuser is a translucent umbrella below. *The beam test checks a light's illumination pattern* below center. *Almost any translucent material can be used as a diffusing screen* below right.

The lighting for this still-life of Leonardo da Vinci's surgical sketches used a diffuser smaller than the subject and at a distance. The result is the soft shadow edges typical of diffused lighting, but with fairly strong contrast.

will see a bright center grading outwards to darker edges: exactly the same as when the lamp was aimed at a white wall. Move the sheet away from the lamp and towards you until it looks fairly evenly illuminated. This is efficient diffusion, and the source of light is now the acrylic sheet.

The area of the light is larger, and so the shadows it casts have soft edges and are less intense overall. One side-effect is that the intensity of the light is reduced, and this is more or less in proportion to the degree of diffusion. The greater the thickness of the diffusing material, the more light it absorbs, and if the diffusion is increased by moving the light further away, natural fall-off will reduce the intensity.

Degree of diffusion

Three factors control the degree of diffusion; three ways in which you can increase it or decrease it. The first is the thickness of the diffusing material (two separated sheets have the same effect as one single, thicker sheet). For any given distance between the light and the diffuser, the optimum thickness of the diffuser occurs when it absorbs any fall-off from the center of the beam. In other words, the diffuser needs to be sufficiently thick to give the effect of a thoroughly even coverage, from corner to corner. If it is thinner, the light will appear brighter in the center and darker towards the corners – the area of the light will be, as a result, a little smaller. However, if the dif-

One of the best uses of reflected lighting is boosting the overall level in an interior when daylight is visible through a window. Here a 1000-watt halogen lamp, filtered with a full blue gel (see page 240) was sited behind the camera, pointing up and back, to give a shadowless increase in lighting.

fusing sheet already projects an even light, increasing its thickness will only lower the intensity, not create any more diffusion.

Distance

The second factor is the distance between the light and the diffuser. The greater this is, the wider the spread of the beam, and the less noticeable the fall-off from center to edge. This, therefore, also increases the area of the diffused light, although as long as the illumination is even across the sheet, moving it further from the light does nothing to help.

Turning now from the light source to the subject, the amount of diffusion in the light it receives depends on the third factor, size. The larger the area of light appears from the position of the subject, the greater its diffusing effect. Imagine yourself as the subject underneath a typical area light. If the rectangular area light is small or far away, it occupies only a small part of the "sky", and the shadows it casts will be fairly hard-edged and deep. If it is replaced with a larger rectangle, or is brought closer, it fills more of your view. The light reaches you from a greater angle, and this weakens the shadows and softens their edges.

Relative apparent size

The important measurement is the relative apparent size, a combination of the size of subject, size of area light, and the distance between them. One way of combining these elements in one measurement is to take the angle of view from the subject to the light, making allowance for the size of the subject. As a general guide, as long as the light appears the same size as the subject or larger, it is diffuse.

The extreme of diffusion occurs when the light surrounds the object from all visible sides (the qualification of "visible" is important; light from opposite the camera contributes nothing). To achieve this, the diffus-ing sheet must be shaped to wrap around the subject.

Diffusing materials have other qualities which are not always noticeable but affect the construction. One is texture, apparent in fabrics, netting and corrugated plastic. To some extent, this texture actually helps the diffusing effect by scrambling the light that passes through it, making the diffuser more efficient. However, if any part of the subject or setting is highly reflective – a polished surface, perhaps, smooth metal or a liquid –

there is always a possibility that the diffused light will appear as a reflection; if so, any texture in the diffusing screen will be visible, and this may spoil the image.

Another quality is the shape of the diffuser; this also becomes important when its reflection can be seen, but even with non-reflective subjects. it may matter if you use the diffused light to cover only a part of the scene. The fall-off from a diffused light is soft and gradual, but if you need it to occur precisely, following a line, the diffuser must have an appropriate shape. The simplest and least obtrusive shapes are rectangular, and are the staple lighting for still-life work. Portraiture rarely needs this kind of precision and umbrellas are more usual.

Allied closely to the shape of the diffuser is control over the amount of spill from the sides. The space between the diffuser and the lamp allows direct light to escape, and this will reflect off any bright surroundings, including the walls and ceiling of the room and equipment used close to the set. Often this may not matter, but there is a danger in forgetting that occasionally it might.

Shading

One basic method of limiting the spill is to shade the lamp with barn doors or flags, angled so as to limit the beam of light as much as possible to the diffuser. A more efficient method is to seal the gaps entirely, effectively enclosing the light. This design of light fitting is known as an area light or window light, and is very popular for still-life photography. There are several possible designs, all box-like. Ideally, the interior of the fitting helps to control the beam so that the front translucent panel is evenly lit: most such fittings are shaped to act as

reflectors and have reflective surfaces either in bright metal or white.

Enclosing a light like this is only safe if the heat output is low, and this is a good time to consider the relative merits of flash and tungsten for diffusion. Tungsten lamps, particularly the highly efficient tungsten-halogen variety, generate a great deal of heat, and the majority of diffusing materials, if not actually inflammable, can warp and discolour if placed close. Fittings that enclose create a build-up of heat, and cannot safely be used with tungsten lamps unless they have a built-in electric fan or ventilation. For choice of diffusion, flash has major advantages over tungsten.

Testing for neutral colour

Although it is normally safe to assume that the basic light source, if purpose-built for photography, is colour-balanced, there is usually no guarantee that the diffusing material will not add a cast. In practice, most of the materials are neutral: if a material looks white to the eye, it will probably transmit the light without altering any of the wavelengths. Nevertheless, you should test the materials that you finally choose. Use colour transparency film to be able to judge the results accurately.

This is not as wide-ranging a colour test as the kind you would do for a new film; if the diffusing screen makes any difference at all, it will be very small, within CC10 on the colour compensating filter scale, and likely to affect all colours in the subject. To check for very fine differences, use a neutral grey card, something familiar (like your hand), and the shadow of the neutral object on a white surface. Between them, these three should show up any differences. Take one

shot with no diffusion, and then however many others are necessary to test the different screens that you have.

PROJECT: Diffused light and subject
Measure the light loss at normal working distances from fitting a variety of diffusing screens. Use a hand-held incident meter, making one reading of the naked light and others of the different screens. Before you decide which screens to use, and before constructing any special fittings, like area lights, make sure that the output is sufficient for the kind of photography, film and lens apertures that you will normally use.

Vary the relative sizes of diffusers and subjects to see the difference in effect on the shadows and contrast.

Reflection

Bouncing light off a bright surface is mainly an alternative to diffusion. Its effects are very similar, both in principle (it increases the area of the light) and in the way it softens shadows and lowers contrast. Although it is difficult to control bounced light as precisely as diffusion can be controlled, and so is not as useful for still-life shooting, reflective lighting can be very easy and convenient. Suitable surfaces are commonly available, and photographic lamps can often be used naked, without any fittings at all.

In the basic arrangement for lighting by reflection, the light is aimed directly away from the subject towards a white surface. You can see the potential problems for controlling the light in such a set-up. The silhouette of the lamp and stand appears in view, the beam is not even and does not have precise limits, and changing the direction of the lighting would involve moving both the light and the reflecting surface separately (which is not possible with a wall).

CONCENTRATING LIGHT

Concentration is concerned with the area of light that falls on the subject – its size, shape and the sharpness of its edges. Light from a diffuser can, to an extent, be concentrated on a small area, although it is easier to work with the beam from a small light source because it is more manageable. Light can be concentrated at various points in the beam: by shaping the reflector behind the lamp, by using a focusing lens, by flagging the light at the sides, and by masking it close to the subject (including placing a black card with an aperture cut into it in front of the light).

Circle of light

The most efficient method by far is to use a lens, and this is how focusing spots and luminaires work. This makes it possible to produce a sharp-edged circle of light on the subject; its size can be varied. If a card cut to shape is placed at the focal point of the lens, the circle can be altered to an aperture of any other shape. Although focusing spot fittings are available for flash units, they are mechanically simpler for tungsten lighting, as the focus can be judged by sight (the modelling lamp in a flash unit is usually in a slightly different position and has a different shape from the flash tube, and focusing the modelling lamp will not always have exactly the same effect on the flash.

This is extreme concentration, and not needed very often in most studio photography (although it is very useful for rim-lighting effects, such as highlighting hair in a beauty or portrait shot). The basic kind of light concentration is created by shaping the reflector of the lighting unit itself. This has a different kind of focusing effect. Except in those lamps (usually tungsten) that contain a control for moving the relative positions of the lamp and reflector to alter the beam, all the standard reflector fittings are designed to give what is considered to be a normal beam: in the region of 60° to 90°. This is quite concentrated, but additional reflector fittings narrow the beam still further. The most effective reflector design is parabolic.

Apart from using reflection to concentrate the beam, other methods work subtractively – by cutting off the light at the edges, leaving just the central part – with the result that the beam loses some intensity. Fittings on the light include a snoot, or cone, and various types of mask such as flags and barn doors. Any other masks, such as black card, can be used closer to the subject.

Standard dish reflectors come in various shapes for use with tungsten photoflood lamps. They produce beam angles of between 60° and 90° – the wider the reflector, the less intense the light. This mild concentration of light is more effective than using a tungsten lamp without an attachment.

Snoots and lenses give tight beams. The two upper units left are snoots, while the lower spot has adjustable condensers to focus the light.

For the strongest spot-lighting effect, concentrated lights like those at the bottom of the opposite page generally need to be positioned at some distance from the subject.

To isolate the desk and typewriter above from the surroundings, a 400-joule flash fitted with a snoot was suspended from a boom close to the ceiling.

TRANSPARENT SUBJECTS

Of all the possible physical qualities of an object, transparency needs the greatest care in lighting. A transparent object simply most of the other qualities, but transparency is visible whether you like it or not. A transparent object simply shows its background. As a result, it is the lighting of the background that needs major attention, and the most common method of photographing something transparent is to make the light the background. This involves some kind of backlighting in most situations. Although it is hardly a rule, there is rarely any other way of showing the transparent qualities of an object and yet keeping the image simple and legible. If the transparent object has to

Lit conventionally, the translucent jade figure far left is dull and dark. Backlighting, however, reveals a rich, glowing green. It is usually necessary to retain some frontal or side lighting to convey the basic shape.

feature strongly in a photograph, then it needs some variety of lighting to show through it. The most obvious and cleanest technique is trans-illumination. For this, the light source should be broad and fairly even – a light box beneath the subject is ideal.

Things that are completely transparent, such as clear glass bottles and jars, set an extra problem: that of making a clear, legible picture. The edges of an object define its shape, but in a transparent material there is always a danger that these edges become lost to view. To get the maximum definition of outline in, say, a bottle or glass, mask down the area of the back light as much as possible. The masking must be behind the transparent object. There are two methods for this; to use black cards or flags, or simply to move the light source further back.

With a broad backlighting source, treat the background as a highlight. This gives you two fairly simple methods of measuring the exposure. One is to take a direct meter reading, either with the TTL meter in the camera or a hand-held meter pointed directly towards the object with its reflected light fitting. The reading you get will then be between 2 and 2½ stops brighter than average, so simply add that amount of exposure to the camera setting. The second method is to use a hand-held meter with its reflected-light dome, with the sensor pointing directly towards the back light. This will give an exposure setting that will be within ½ a stop of a good exposure.

To show the translucency of the shell shown here, strong backlighting was used and all surrounding light cut by means of a mask. A close-up view was chosen for the final shot below to make the most of the pattern of different thicknesses.

TEXTURE

Texture is the tactile quality of a surface; of the skin of an object rather than its body. It is mainly, but not entirely, a matter of local relief, with rough and smooth as the two extremes. This in turn depends on how closely you look at a surface: from a few inches, a block of concrete appears, and feels, rough, but seen as part of a building from a distance, it looks completely smooth. A girl's skin may be smooth enough in a head-and-shoulders portrait, but if you shoot a close-up of just the lips, you will find that an enlargement will show all kinds of imperfections.

Coarseness range

What we can call the coarseness range of texture has upper and lower limits. The upper limit is when the relief is so strong that it affects the actual shape of the object; it is no longer a quality of the surface, but of the thing itself. The lower limit is the point at which the surface appears smooth. From the examples mentioned at the start, you can see that this is entirely relative. At some degree of magnification, the smoothest surfaces have a strong texture. It is also subjective; there is no measurement that you can apply.

Side lighting

Strictly speaking, even a mirror-like finish is a texture of sorts. Experience of natural lighting shows what the most effective studio conditions should be. Go back for a moment to side lighting on pages 184-5, and in particular to the photograph of the paper lantern. As a general rule, a naked lamp at a raking angle to the surface is the classic treatment to give strong texture.

However, the actual angle should depend very much on the coarseness of the texture. If the relief is strong and deep, a very shallow angle may lose detail unnecessarily. One technique you should consider is to add a reflector opposite the light to lighten the shadows and preserve this detail. If you move a lamp to an increasingly acute angle, there comes a point at which most of the surface falls into shadow, and texture suddenly becomes lost (this, of course, is what happens at sunset). Strong texture can

The classic lighting technique for revealing texture at its strongest is at an acute angle and with a direct (that is, undiffused) source. The sun in a clear sky is the hardest light source available, and almost parallel to the wrought-iron grille in the photograph below, it makes the subject's texture dominate the image.

accommodate some degree of diffusion. Texture may not be the only quality that you want to bring out, and the best lighting may be that which only just reveals the essential texture and no more.

Finally, some surfaces may combine two or more layers of different texture. A wrinkled fabric, for instance, has the texture of the weave and the texture of the wrinkles. The lighting angle that suits one may be less satisfactory for the other.

Exploiting texture

The first step in working texture into the design of a photograph is to recognize it. We are accustomed to thinking of texture at relatively small scales – on the kind of objects that might be used in a still-life shot – but it is a good idea to make a practice of looking for texture at all scales. Look for the texture in a landscape, or the texture of the

On the slightly curved fragment of the pre-Colombian pot right, the texture is that of the granulated surface. Partially diffused light aimed from an angle that grazed this surface gave a very strong impression of texture.

surface of the sea. Anything that appears sufficiently level to qualify as a surface has a texture.

Texture is a quality of structure rather than of tone or colour, and so appeals principally to the sense of touch. Even if we cannot physically reach out and touch the subject's texture, its appearance works through this sensory channel. This explains why texture is revealed through lighting – at a small scale, only lighting reveals relief. Particularly important are the direction and quality of the lighting.

PROJECTS: Experimenting with texture

As a basic exercise in discovering texture, take a surface with distinct, hard-edged relief, such as a rough brick or the crust of a loaf. Experiment with the two basic lighting variables, angle and diffusion. Vary each, and from the results decide which gives the strongest and clearest impression of texture. Hard light from a small naked source and an acute angle to a flat surface will always make textures seem strong, but this may be at the expense of legibility.

Then collect the following surfaces, or those of them that you can find easily, and produce the best textural photograph that you can for each: silk, leather, glazed ceramic, fur, a metal grille, gravel. Note the different adjustments that you need to make to the position of the light, its diffusion, and the position of the surface.

By comparison with the photograph above, see how the same principle of a hard light source shining at an acute angle brings out texture on a much larger scale. The view right, which was taken from an aircraft and shows petrified trees and sand-dunes in Australia's Pinnacles region, reads clearly in late afternoon sunlight.

SILHOUETTES

When you are shooting towards or into the sun, contrast is high (see pages 188-9). But if instead you choose a viewpoint that produces a silhouette, hiding the sun, there is no need to reduce contrast. For silhouettes work *because* of high contrast, and depend on shape and the co-ordination of two principal tones, black and the light background. Beyond establishing a dark silhouette and sufficient brightness behind it, there is little the exposure can do for the image.

Exposure problems

Silhouettes taken directly into the sun normally hide the image of the sun itself, as the shot of a dock-side crane shows. In a clear sky, the brightness around the sun is highly localized, so that severe underexposure, particularly with a wide-angle lens, will

make the sky quite dark towards the edges of the frame. This will lose any silhouette outline away from the center. If the silhouette is small in the frame, and you use a telephoto or macro lens, you can outline an object against the sun's disc itself.

The other type of silhouette is against the sun's reflection, usually in water. One advantage here is that, unless the water is perfectly calm and flat, it will have a slight diffusing effect on the sunlight. Instead of a concentrated patch of brightness, the background is larger and more even. With a telephoto lens, as in the shot of the moose, this background can fill the frame, and the outline of the silhouette appears clean, sharp and obvious. A further advantage is that the necessary higher camera viewpoint gives a view slightly down, and it is often easy, as in this example, to isolate the image of the silhouette completely. This is usually more legible than having the silhou-

Silhouettes show little detail, so the exposure can vary and still be acceptable, within limits. But overexposure gives a flared effect, as in the back-lit shot above right.

ette merge with an equally dark ground-level base.

Off-axis backlighting can give considerable atmosphere to a photograph, with a glow softening the high contrast. This glow is in fact a mild flare, and so needs to be kept under control. Flare is by no means always something to avoid, but you should be certain that the effect you get is really what you want rather than a lowering of image quality. The special condition of off-axis lighting is rim lighting. This needs a dark or fairly dark background to show up the subject's edges.

PROJECT: Silhouette exposure

Make all the practical light readings that you can for a silhouette shot, and then bracket the exposure widely, shooting several frames. The normal criteria for judging exposure do not apply here. In a high-contrast silhouette shot there is no mid-tone area that needs legible exposure. The subject is the silhouette, and so the clarity of the outline is the standard. The absence of a mid-tone actually gives a certain freedom of choice in the exposure, which is why you should bracket very widely, over at least 5 stops, possibly more. You will probably find that more than one exposure looks acceptable. The upper limit on exposure is usually when the density of the silhouette weakens noticeably into grey and when the edges of the outline begin to lose definition due to flare. The lower limit is when the background becomes dim, obscuring the silhouette's outline. However, you might find that overexposure in some situations gives an attractive effect.

With the sun directly behind the subject, as in the shot above, there are no stray highlights to confuse the outline, but the exposure must be kept short.

The silhouette left was shot with a macro lens at ½ x magnification, and at full aperture. At a smaller aperture the diaphragm blades' shape deforms the sun far left.

Colour

If you make confident and good use of it, colour can be by far the most powerful element in a photograph. It can be immediately striking, as in the two pictures here, or it can be delicate and subtle. You could, of course, say the same about many graphic techniques, but colour plays a different role in our perceptions. We respond to colour in a complex way that goes beyond a simple visual response. Colours evoke reactions at an emotional, subjective level.

If colour has been used powerfully in an image *and* at the same time it strikes a sympathetic chord in the viewer, it can be the very essence of the picture. In this, it differs from other graphic elements. The ways in which you can arrange lines in a photograph may, for instance, create a sensation of movement or stability, but colour can create deeper responses, including some that are not always possible to describe. Nevertheless, the difficulty of finding exact ways of talking about colour does not lessen the importance of what Gauguin called its "inner force".

More than one artist has insisted on the need to experience and feel colours. One of the great teachers of the art of colour, Johannes Itten, wrote that colours "have a mystical capacity for spiritual expression, without being tied to objects". In other words, *you* can make colour the reason for and the subject of a picture.

Colour works on three levels. Sometimes we respond to all three at once, at other times just to one or two. They are: *Visual* – this is the objective, immediately obvious level; *Expressive* – the emotional level, evoking sensations that are often subjective and non-visual; *Symbolic* – the cultural level, where certain colours and combinations are associated with things that we have been brought up with.

Before we go into this multi-level sensation of colour, we should look, briefly, at the theory of colour relationships. the starting point is the palette of pure colours, and these begin with three primary hues. There are different sets of these, but they qualify to be called primaries when all other colours can be made from them. For

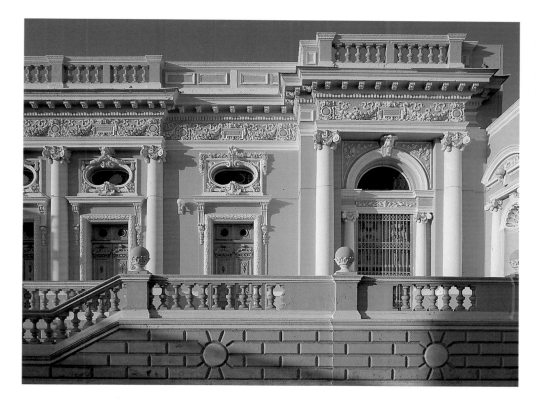

The façade of this colonial mansion in the Mexican city of Mérida appears all the more vivid because of the choice of lighting. Early morning sunlight gives high colour and shadow contrast on the richly textured stucco.

painters, the three primaries are yellow, red and blue. In photography the more commonly used primaries are red, green and blue. In printing they are magenta, yellow and cyan (blue). Here, I will use the more traditional painters' primaries, because they are the ones which best fit the psychology of colour.

When two primaries are mixed, the result is a secondary colour. There are three of these: orange (made from yellow and red), green (from yellow and blue) and violet (from red and blue). If these secondaries are then mixed with their nearest primaries, we get another set of six colours – which are referred to as tertiary – yellow-orange, red-orange and so on.

At one level, the idea of mixing colours is an irrelevance in photography, and unless you are working in a studio or other really controlled conditions, you will only rarely have an opportunity to adjust colour values and balance their proportions. in nearly all cases, using colour in photography is a matter of selection – of choosing what is available from real life. However, this is not to say that only painters can control the colours they use. Photography offers all kinds of opportunity for rearranging the colours of an image: change of viewpoint, different framing, moving the subjects, altering the lighting, and careful choice of filters. One of the special advantages that photography enjoys is that it records ready-made

colours; it takes very little effort to capture striking combinations.

Studying colour will help you to refine your discrimination and judgement. It is too easy to judge colour relationship subjectively, on a scale of "like/don't like". Certainly, most people *do* think about colour in this way, but they miss out. The analogy is enjoying music without having any musical training or background – while the lack does not inhibit the pleasure of listening, having some knowledge will definitely enhance it. If you want to become skilled in creating powerful colour effects, studying it will give you the means. Although colour evokes a subjective response, it also works according to definite principles.

THE QUALITIES OF COLOUR

A colour can be defined in terms of its hue, its brilliance and its saturation. Hue is very much the prime quality of a colour, and is what gives the colour its uniqueness. In photography, the two main ways in which you can influence a hue are by using a different colour of light (for instance, waiting for the orange cast at sunset instead of the neutral white light from a midday sun) and by using a coloured filter over the lens. In either case, however, it is only possible to change the overall hue, not that of individual objects.

The two other qualities, brilliance and saturation, are a matter of degree of a hue. Brilliance is the lightness or darkness of a colour; white and black are the extremes of this scale. It is sometimes a little difficult to distinguish brilliance from saturation, but it may help to remember that, in varieties of brilliance, the colour remains pure and unadulterated.

The actual range of lightness and darkness differs between hues, and this can cause difficulties in matching the brilliance. Yellow can only vary between a medium tone and very light; there is no such thing

Hue is the most obvious quality of colour, and vivid differences, as among the rowers below, normally cause a photograph to be described as "colourful".

A flag fluttering between light and shade above shows the difference in brilliance in the blue. To varying degrees, colours can be light or dark.

as a dark pure yellow. Red becomes pink when very light, and so loses its main qualities. Blue, however, covers the full range. Orange does not have dark pure versions, because of its closeness to yellow, but the range of greens is affected more by the blue component than by the yellow, and can be very light or quite dark. Violet changes its character at either end of the scale, becoming lavender when light, but hard to distinguish from deep blue when dark.

Saturation

Saturation is a variation in the purity of a colour. At one end of the scale are the pure, intense colours of the colour circle. As they become less saturated, they become more grey, less "colourful", and dirtier. Colours become unsaturated when they are mixed with white, black, grey or their opposite colours. Although this has no immediate practical concern for the photographer, it has a direct bearing on his material, since most colours in nature are saturated. Most photographic subjects are things found rather than built by the photographer, so adulterated or broken colours are the staple palette. In nature, greys, browns and dull greens predominate, and it is for this reason that the occasional pure colour is often prized and made the feature of a colour photograph when found. Rich colours are therefore more often seen as desirable by the majority of photographers than are pastel shades. There is no judgement intended here – rich combinations and pale combinations can make equally powerful images.

Saturation defines the purity of colour, but early morning haze desaturates the telephoto shot of Florence left.

PRIMARY COLOURS

Understanding the personality of each of the primary colours – yellow, red and blue – and the secondary colours formed from them, lays the foundation for exploiting the wide range of colour relationships in photography.

Yellow

Yellow, the brightest and lightest of all colours, does not exist in a dark form unless it is degraded; the darkest pure yellow is still brilliant compared with all other colours. As it is usually found against darker tones, yellow often seems to radiate light in a picture. Matching its brilliance with other

The strong yellow of these autumn leaves is helped by the fact that they are back-lit, and so show the full colour undiluted by surface reflections, and also by the shadowy backdrop. As the colour squares show, a bright colour like yellow receives energy from a dark setting.

Varieties of yellow are found in gold surfaces. The purer the gold, the yellower the hue, but this is always modulated by the surroundings that the metal reflects.

colours is difficult: a similar blue, for example, would have to be quite pale. There is very little latitude in yellow: to be pure it must be an exact hue, while even a hint of yellow-green is obvious. As gold, yellow tends slightly towards orange and has a metallic look. Yellow (and every other colour) expands, contracts and changes when seen against other colours. It is most intense against black, and most insipid against white. Out of orange and red it extends the spectrum in the direction of brightness. When it is seen against violet and blue it is strong.

Expressively, yellow is vigorous and sharp, the opposite of placid and restful. It can even be thought of as astringent, and would rarely be considered as a suitable setting for a food photograph, for example. Other associations are mainly aggressive or cheerful. There is no clear line separating the expressive and symbolic associations of yellow. Much of its vigour derives from the source of its most widespread symbolism: the sun. (The sun when high appears white rather than yellow, but it is too strong to look at. When it is low enough in the sky to see without discomfort it is usually yellow.) Yellow also symbolizes light, and strong light in particular.

Pure yellow is not common on any large scale in photography. Certain objects are customarily painted yellow, for example school buses in North America and road warning signs in some countries. Some autumn vegetation, such as aspens, are yellow, as are lemons, melons, and star-fruit. Gold-painted and gilded objects can be yellow, as is anything bathed by a low sun. This can be emphasized by shooting into the sun, particularly with a telephoto lens which is allowed to flare.

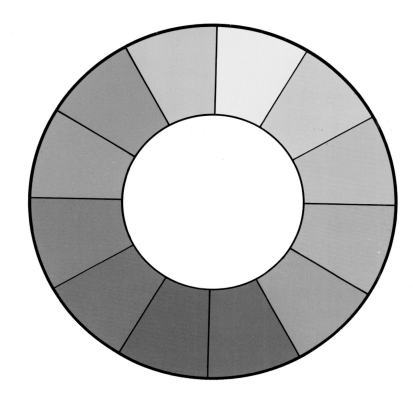

The three primary colours are combined as follows to form the secondary colours: yellow + red = orange, red + blue = violet, yellow + blue = green right. In the 12-hue colour wheel above right the secondaries are mixed with their adjacent primaries to form the six intermediate colours known as tertiaries.

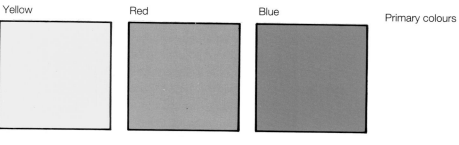

Yellow   Red   Blue   Primary colours

Primary + secondary colours

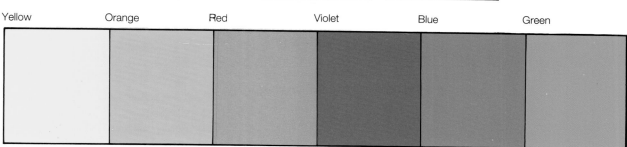

Yellow   Orange   Red   Violet   Blue   Green

A clear sky is the most accessible source of blue for photography. In the picture right *it is also reflected in the plate-glass façades of office buildings. The modulation of the colour across the sky is due to the use of a wide-angle lens; the intensity peaks near the zenith, becoming paler near the sun and the horizon. Note that the blue loses nothing of its essential character even when it becomes closer to cyan in the light part of the image.*

Blue

Blue recedes visually, being much quieter and less active than red. Of the three primaries, it is the darkest colour, and it has its greatest strength when deep. It has a transparency that contrasts with red's opacity. Although pure blue tends towards neither green nor violet, it has a considerable latitude, and is a hue that many people have difficulty in discriminating.

Identifying a pure, exact blue, is less easy than identifying red or yellow, particularly if there are no other varieties of blue adjacent for comparison. One of the interesting parts of this colour project is assembling different transparencies which were taken on different occasions, all of which were of things you considered to be one colour. The variations in hue are often a surprise; without colour training, the eye tends to imagine that hues are closer to the standard of purity than they really are.

Coolness

Expressively, blue is, above all, cool. Used in decoration, it even produces the sensation that the actual temperature is lower than it is. The contrast with red also occurs in other ways: blue has associations of intangibility and passivity. It suggests a withdrawn, reflective mood. The primary symbolism of blue derives from its two most widespread occurrences in nature: the sky and water.

Photographically, pure blue is one of the easiest colours to find. A clear daytime sky is blue, as are its reflections (in the form of shadows and on the surface of the sea and lakes). Water absorbs colours selectively, beginning at the red end of the spectrum, so that underwater photographs that are taken in clear, deep conditions display a rich, deep-blue cast.

Red

In complete contrast to the restrained qualities of blue, red is visually one of the most insistent, powerful colours, and immediately attracts attention. When set against cooler colours, green in particular, red advances towards the viewer. It has considerable kinetic energy, and produces some of the strongest vibration effects against other colours, as we will see later.

Density

In contrast to the transparency and luminosity of yellow, red is relatively dense and solid. In terms of its characteristic of redness, it has considerable latitude; in other words, it can move a way towards orange or towards violet and still be seen as essentially the same colour. At the far end of its bluish range, it produces a variety of exotic hues, including magenta and purple. Even when adulterated towards russet, and when dark, red remains recognizable because of its characteristic intensity.

Energy

While yellow can be felt to radiate light, red radiates the most energy. Emotionally, red is vital, earthy, strong and warm – even hot. By extension, red can connote passion in one direction, and in the other, the infernal. If we add the obvious association with blood, there are connotation of warfare and fiery destruction.

These temperature associations have obvious origins, and indeed, red is commonly used as the symbol for heat. Perceived as a very powerful colour, it is a symbol for warning and prohibition, such as to indicate "stop" at traffic lights. Red has also, from its expressive associations with blood and war, been a symbol of political revolution. During the Chinese Cultural Revolution some traffic lights were left unused because of the supposedly negative use of red!

Widespread colour

Red is fairly abundant for photography. It is relatively popular as a paint finish on buildings, vehicles and signs. In nature, many flowers are red, and display interesting varieties of hue.

Embers and other burning things glow red at a certain temperature, and the richest of sunsets and sunrises, when the sun is extremely low, are red, lighting clouds to the same colour.

The power of red can be demonstrated in a paired exercise like the one below. The red arrow is tiny, but against blue it attracts the attention like a magnet.

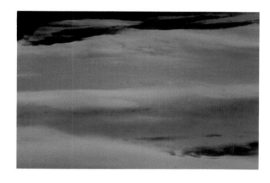

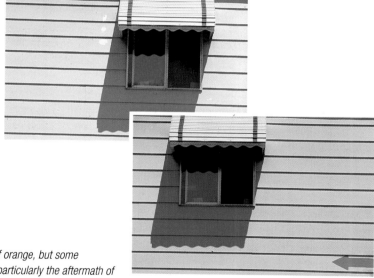

Most sunsets are varieties of orange, but some conditions favour rich reds, particularly the aftermath of a tropical storm, as in the photograph above left.

Objects bathed in red-filtered artificial lighting take on a peculiar tonal quality, as in the shot left. Deep shadows become virtually black, but highlights remain red and do not lighten as would be normal in a full spectrum.

SECONDARY COLOURS

Orange

Orange is the mixture of yellow and red, and absorbs some of the qualities of both. It is brilliant and powerful when pure and, since yellow radiates light and red radiates energy, it is by association very much a colour of radiation. When lighter, as pale beige, and darker, as brown, it has a neutral warmth. Orange is the colour of fire and of warm late afternoon sunlight. It has associations of festivity and celebration, but also of heat and dryness. Symbolically, it is interchangeable with yellow for the sun, and with red for heat.

In nature, pure orange can be found in flowers, and in a slightly adulterated form in the light cast by tungsten bulbs and other sources of low (less than 2000 K) colour temperature. The 85B standard filter used with type B film (film adapted for tungsten light) in daylight is a slightly dull orange, to compensate for the blue cast of the film.

Violet

The mixture of blue and red stands out among colours as being the most elusive of all. Many people have great difficulty distinguishing pure violet, often selecting a purple instead. The difficulty in recognizing violet is compounded in photography by the problems in recording it. The dye response in some colour films and papers is

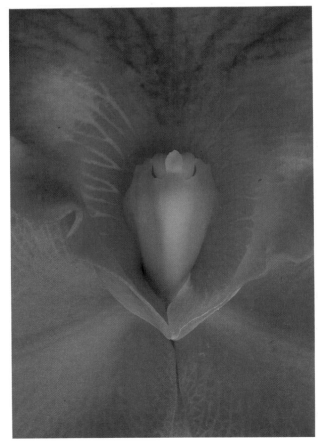

Although it is not completely faithful to the loveliness of the original bloom, the close-up view of an orchid right contains similar varieties of violet.

The vibrant mass of garlands on a Delhi flower-stall depicted in the photograph opposite produces a typically strong, brilliant orange. Most colour reversal (transparency) films reproduce this colour clearly and brightly. In this case the film was Kodachrome, slightly underexposed for extra intensity.

particularly unsuccessful with this colour. Pure violet is the darkest colour. When light, it becomes lavender, and when very dark it can be confused with dark blue and blue-black. If reddish, it tends towards purple and magenta; if less red, it simply merges into blue.

Violet has rich and sumptuous associations, but can also create an impression of mystery and immensity. A violet landscape can contain suggestions of foreboding and other-worldliness. By extension, purple has religious and superstitious connotations. Violet symbolizes piety in Christianity, and in magic and astrology. It is a relatively difficult colour to find for a photograph. In nature, some flowers are violet, but are often difficult to record accurately on film. The wavelength of ultraviolet used as "black light" appears on film as pure violet. Under certain conditions, the light before dawn and after sunset can appear as a reddish version of violet.

Green

Between yellow and blue, green has the widest distinguishable range of effects. It

The photograph below shows green chilis shot in daylight. The sky was overcast, and so reasonably neutral in colour, but even so, a slight coldness comes through – evidence of the sensitivity of green to slight colour differences.

can take on many different forms – depending on how yellowish or bluish it is – with distinct characteristics. Although of medium brightness, green is the most visible of colours to the human eye: at low levels of illumination, we can see better by green light than by any other wavelength.

Green is the main colour of nature, and its associations and symbolism derive principally from this. Plants are green, so it is the colour of growth; by extension it is a

and progress. For the same reasons, yellow-green has spring-like associations of youth. Symbolically, green is used for the same purposes as its expressive associations – youth and nature, with plant-life in particular. In nature at least, greens are very common. Pure green, however, is not easy to find, as you see by taking a number of images in this colour and comparing them with a standard reference, such as a Wratten 58 green filter.

BROKEN COLOURS

In traditional colour theory, pure colours have prominence, and painters are trained to construct hues from the primaries and secondaries. In contrast, photography deals almost exclusively with the colours found in the real world, and its colour priorities are consequently different. As we have seen through cataloguing the principal hues, they are not particularly common in nature. Most found colours are broken: that is, they are seen as a mixture of hues that gives a deadened, unsaturated effect.

Subtle palette

Such broken colours are, however, very rewarding to work with, because of the great variety of subtle effects. Colour theory gives an artificial stress to the pure primary and secondary colours, as these are the foundations of all others; it would be a mistake to infer that pure hues are inherently more desirable in a picture. The differences between broken colours are on a much narrower range than the pure colours, and working constantly with them trains the eye to be more delicate in its discrimination, and to prize rare colours.

Natural colours

Russet, sienna, olive green, slate blue – these and an almost limitless variety of others, including the chromatic greys, make up the basic palette of colours available for photography. This is one of the important differences between photography and other graphic forms: the choice of colour in photography is mainly limited to what is naturally available.

PROJECT: A unifying colour theme
If you are taking a set of pictures that are intended to be displayed together, there may well be an advantage in linking them graphically. There is hardly ever any point in trying to force this, but one opportunity that sometimes arises is colour. The subjects may have a particular range of hues, or, quite often, the setting may have certain colours characteristic of it. The example here will give you a better idea of how this can work.

In the case the subject was a hill-tribe from the Golden Triangle in south-east Asia. One thing that became apparent once the shooting was under way was the predominance of browns. The earth, the buildings of wood and bamboo, even the skin tones were in a variety of shades of brown. Although not an insistent characteristic, it was prevalent in most of the locations and seemed relevant to the life of these people, emphasizing visually the close relationship they have with their environment. A small point, but valuable because it helped to give a unity of design to the shots.

In practice, the way of exploiting such a colour theme is a matter of editing and selection, cropping the shots in such a way that colours outside the chosen range are excluded. This was hardly possible in all situations, but once having recognized the possibility, it became a stylistic addition to the photography. Clearly, this is a project that you can reasonably expect to do only when there is a genuine colour characteristic in the setting. Also, it lies very much within the realm of broken colours, partly because these are the most commonly found hues, and also because their modulation is quieter and less overpowering than that of pure colours.

Browns and chromatic greys make up the earth colours of the landscape in Andalusia, southern Spain, in the photograph below.

The warm browns of the hill-tribe villages in the Golden Triangle seen in the shots opposite *create a visually unifying element for a long photographic assignment.*

The leaden finish of the imposing Javanese statue right appears metallic because of its particularly strong reflective qualities. The textured surface and diffused light from an overcast sky produce a relatively even gradient of tone.

In the photograph left the gilded bas-relief figures which decorate the doors of a temple in Thailand contain distinct but soft-edged highlights on the convex parts of their surface. The effect is typical of light falling on a reflective metallic surface.

Special Colours

Apart from the primary and secondary colours described on the preceding pages, there are various kinds of colours that might be referred to as special for one reason or another. A particularly interesting example for photographic purposes, and a group that has unique characteristics, is the metallic colours. What distinguishes these colours is the special gradient of shading towards the highlights, and the extremely subtle shift of hue which accompanies it.

In particular, metallic surfaces have a fairly high reflectivity and so pick up the tones and colours of their environment. As this is overlaid on the inherent colour of the metal, the effects can be interesting and dynamic. The type, quality and direction of the light source makes all the difference, and if you have sufficient control to alter any of these factors, you can experiment with the variety of effects.

The reflections of direct artificial lights over a parking lot are intense and concentrated in the polished metal of the cars below. Note the slight colour shifts that accompany the variation in tone.

Interference colours

A special assembly of colours exist through a naturally occurring phenomenon known as interference. Interference effects are seen when a material slows some of the light rays passing through it or reflecting off it, and when these interact with other rays to create a play of colours. In the same way that a prism, or drops of water in the area of a rainbow, split light into the colours of the spectrum of which it is composed, so interference colours are also produced by a variety of substances, including oil slicks, ordinary soap bubbles, pearl and mother-of-pearl.

BLACK AND WHITE

Although they lack all hue, the three neutral shades of black, white and grey are essential components of colour photography. Not only do they exist as counterparts and settings for the colours just described, but they are mixed with these pure hues in varying degrees to make adulterated browns, slates, and other subdued colours.

Black

Black, being the extreme of density and solidity, needs the contrast of another shade or colour in order to make any kind of picture. As a result, it is used in images mainly as a background, as a shape (such as in a silhouette), or as a punctuation. In photography, black is produced as the maximum density on film and paper: D-max, as it is known. Black can never be too dense; indeed, the limitations of emulsion and photographic paper are sometimes such that it appears weak, like very dark grey. This slight weakness is particularly unsatisfying in a black, which ought to represent a solid anchor for all the other colours and shades, wherever it occurs in a picture. Over-exposure, fogging, or altered processing will create this weakness in the D-max.

Where black shades to grey, the grey is very sensitive to its neutrality or otherwise. Any slight hint of a colour cast is immediately recognized, and then inferred to be a part of the blackest areas. Certain colour emulsions do actually have a slight cast in their maximum density.

The neutrality of black outweighs most of its associations and symbolism, but where it appears extensively in an image it can be heavy and oppressive. Depending on how it is used, it can be either dense, like a solid wall, or empty, as in featureless space.

Photographically, black is the absence of light. Partial shading, using a mask held in front of the lens, can therefore blacken areas of the image. If you want to guarantee that an area reproduces as black, you may need to take precautions, since the eye is sensitive to even a slight lightening of tone. For instance, black paper is *not* likely to

In an image such as that of the lens right the density of the black depends critically on the exposure. An incident-light or substitute reading is usually necessary. The key tones in an essentially black image are the grey highlights – in this case these are found in the raised rubber rectangles on the left side of the lens grip.

produce an adequately dense background in a straightforward studio still life. Black velvet is the material of choice.

White

White is the absence of any tone whatso-ever: clear film in a transparency or unex-posed printing paper (negative/positive). Nevertheless, just as a black object must contain tonal highlights and modelling in order to be recognizable, so a white image needs at least the modulation of pale greys or off-whites. These slight modulations are very susceptible to colour cast, however – even more than with black.

Photographically, white needs care in exposure. Slight underexposure makes it appear muddy; slight overexposure destroys the hint of detail and usually gives a washed-out effect. Although its neutrality robs white of strong expressive association, it generally symbolizes purity.

Grey

The number of greys is almost limitless, ranging between black and white, but also varying in hue depending on slight colour casts. If a colour is heavily unsaturated, it becomes a grey rather than a greyish hue.

In its purest form, grey is the essence of neutrality, deadening the sensation of colour in proportion to its area in the picture. For this reason, it may be desirable to have any grey slightly tinted in a colour photograph in order to give it some life.

Without any qualifying description, grey is assumed to be mid-grey, and this has a special place in photography. Mid-grey is exactly halfway between black and white, and reflects 18 per cent of light falling on it. Hence an 18 per cent grey card, as it is

known, is sometimes used for exposure cal-culations; it is the standard for an average subject. A through-the-lens reading of 18 per cent grey gives exactly the same expo-sure value as a hand-held incident meter.

Pure grey has leaden, mechanical associa-tions, with connotations of being uninterest-ing (the word is used this way to describe people). Bluish grey expresses coolness; reddish and orange-grey warmth. Grey is the colour of stone, and so also borrows associations of solidity and weight. As a group, greys are very common, not only in nature (rocks, dark clouds, water on an overcast day) but in man-made environ-ments (concrete, plaster, streets, buildings, smoky atmosphere). Pure neutral grey is difficult to record, however, because of the eye's sensitivity to colour bias. Under-exposure of white produces any shade of grey; neutral density filters are pure grey.

Shooting in monochrome exploits the abstract qualities of both black and white. The image shot on colour transparency film, above, *is a completely natural, realistic version of the subject. Most viewers would concentrate on the attitude of the lioness and cub, rather than on the graphic treatment. The black-and-white image, lacking colour, is more abstract, and the lioness's shape and line become more important to the overall effect.*

BLENDING COLOURS

It is not quite enough to say that certain pairs and combinations of colours are harmonious. Each colour has an intrinsic brightness, so complete balance requires that the combinations are seen in certain proportions. In photography, this is complicated by the details of texture, shape, and so on. The colour in photographs is enmeshed in the structure of the subject.

Basic colour combinations

As a start, however, we can look at the basic combinations of primaries and secondaries. The complementary for each primary colour is a secondary: red/green, orange/blue, yellow/violet. However, we have already seen something of the differences in brightness among these six colours, and the strength of each in combination follows this. In descending order, the generally accepted light values, determined by Goethe, the German poet, playwright and amateur scientist, are yellow 9, orange 8, red and green 6, blue 4 and violet 3. When they are combined, these relative values must be reversed, so that violet, for example, occupies a large enough area to make up for its lack of strength. The areas needed for these colours are, therefore: violet 9, blue 8, red and green 6, orange 4 and yellow 3.

The principle of this system applies to any colour, whether intermediate on the colour circle, a mixture, or poorly saturated.

Colour harmony is weaker when the red and green are not pure. In the shot below *the main relationship is seen as being between the palm and its shadow.*

In the picture below, *the strength of the red of the barn roof is out of proportion to the space it occupies. Despite its size, the "colour accent" demands attention.*

Orange and blue arranged so that the orange dominates possess colour harmony, but produce a more dynamic effect than when the blue is dominant (see page 272). In the shot right *eye is drawn towards the blue sashes in an attempt to restore the expected colour proportions.*

Although the limited extent of the orange and blue combination in the photograph below *produces nothing like the harmonious relationship seen in the orange and blue examples above and on page 272, it helps to move the eye diagonally across the image between the two patches of the sculpture and the sky.*

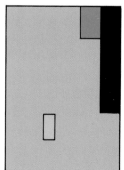

The brightness or darkness of the hue also affects the proportion.

Intuitive use of colour

Although exact harmonious proportions could be worked out for any colour image, the exercise would be quite pointless and impractical. Under no circumstances should these proportions be followed rigidly. Although the principles exist, and it is important to be familiar with them, design should never follow rules. If you want to create harmony in a photograph, intuitive judgement of the balance of colours is sufficient; it is the only method which allows an imaginative approach. The principles of harmony should not be neglected, but are for preparation only.

Red/green harmony

Pure red and pure green have the same luminosity, and so combine harmoniously in equal proportions. This, however, presupposes that both colours are pure and exact, and as this rarely happens, in practice there is little point in measuring the areas precisely. As a project, look for red/green combinations, but the furthest that you need to go is to keep the proportions approximately equal: a quick judgement by eye alone is sufficient. In nature, red/green combinations are mainly limited to plant-life; although green is abundant in many landscapes, red is much less so.

Red and green, with their same luminosity, produce a special colour effect known as vibration. The edge between the two colours seems to be optically unstable; if you stare at it for long enough you can see a light and dark fringe. This optical vibration makes pure red/green combinations unsettling to look at for long, and even irritating. Nevertheless, the effect is eye-catching and dynamic.

To a greater or less extent, vibration occurs between any two brilliant colours, but nowhere is the effect as strong as it is between red and green. This is because they are complementary as well as naturally having the same luminosity. Blue against red and blue-green against orange-red are the next most energetic combinations. Unless you shoot freshly painted man-made combinations, it is not particularly easy to achieve very strong vibration in photographs; as we have already seen, saturated colours are relatively uncommon in nature. In this respect urban settings offer more variety.

As you might expect, changing the proportions weakens the harmony. However, when the balance is extreme, the smaller colour acquires extra energy. As you can see in the aerial photograph of the farm buildings, the red roof, far from being overwhelmed by the green of the fields, draws attention to itself insistently. Instead of a colour combination, we have a colour accent. The effect is stronger when red is on a green background than vice versa, because of the tendency of warm colours to advance while cool colours recede.

Orange is twice as luminous as blue, so that the best balance is when the blue is twice the area in a picture. Compared with red/green combinations, this makes for less

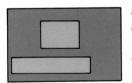

In the shot below, *Balinese ceremonial parasols make a strong contrast with the blue of the sky. Being brighter, they produce the best equilibrium when the area they cover is roughly half that of the sky in the frame.*

The orange light from a setting sun enhances the colour of the cliffs below. *In this colour combination, the large area of sky makes it easy to adjust the proportions: by changing viewpoint, focal length and framing.*

optical confusion about which colour is the background. It also drastically reduces the vibration, so that orange and blue are generally more comfortable to look at.

Of the three classic colour harmonies, orange/blue is probably the easiest to find photographically. Orange and blue lie very close to the ends of the colour temperature scale, so that they can be found in many common lighting conditions. A low sun, candle light, and low-wattage tungsten light bulbs are some of the sources of orange – not pure, but close enough. A clear sky, and the light from it, is a ubiquitous blue. The photograph of cliffs at sunset is an easy example. As well as contrasting in brightness, orange and blue have the strongest cool/warm contrast of any primary/secondary complementary pair.

The center of the violet above contains the colour harmony of yellow and violet. By closing in with a macro lens, the proportions can be adjusted.

The dawn view of fishing boats left *benefits from an attractive yellow-violet harmony. Although the two hues are pale, the persistent harmony creates a calm feeling.*

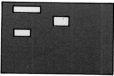

The classic primary combination is of the three pure colours red, yellow and blue, shown right on coloured balloons. The areas of the three colours are roughly equal, and the combination of colours gives a satisfying effect as opposed to an exciting one.

PROJECT: Proportion

One practical method of dispelling the idea that the traditional balance proportions are "correct" is to take a situation which allows you to vary the proportions of two complementary colours. The easiest circumstance is a single-colour back-ground and an object of manageable size: one that you can move, walk around, and shoot from differ-ent distances and viewpoints. here, I have taken the most readily available complementary pair – orange and blue – in an easy form. We start with a composition which organizes the two colours in approximately balanced proportions – 1:2 in favour of orange – and then change the viewpoint, lines and designs progressively. The object of this exercise is less to improve the image than to understand the variations in tension and balance.

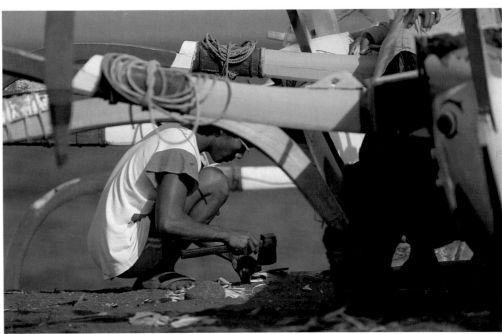

Even though they are distributed among other, for the most part, neutral hues, and scattered throughout the image, the intensity of the three pure primary colours punches through the photograph of painted Balinese fishing boats right. No other combination of colours possesses quite the same intensity.

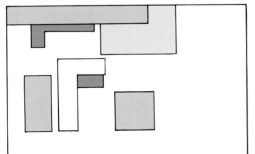

Yellow/violet harmony

This third complementary pair combines the brightest and darkest of all the pure hues. As a result, the contrast is extreme and the balanced proportions need to be 1:3, with the yellow occupying only about a quarter of the image. At these proportions, the yellow is almost a spot of colour, and the sense of a relationship between the two is correspondingly weak.

The relative scarcity of violet in subjects and settings available for photography makes yellow/violet an uncommon combination, particularly as in the ideal proportions the violet must occupy a large area. One of the few reliable natural combinations is in flowers; the close-up of the center of a violet is a classic example.

Multi-colour combinations

While red/yellow/blue is the most powerful mixture of pure hues, other combinations of unbalanced colours can have similarly impressive effects. As you can see from the pictures on these and the following two pages, there is a major difference between groupings of strong, bold colours and those of delicate, pastel shades. Pure hues fight intensely for attention, and the strongest combinations are those of three colours. Even a fourth introduces excess competition, so that instead of building each other up, the colours dissipate the contrast.

Wherever you can find groups of pure colours, they make easy, attention-grabbing shots. Being unbalanced in their positions around the colour circle, they do not mix to

In the diagram below left, the three primary colours, evenly spaced around the colour circle, form an equilateral triangle. Together they cancel each other out, mixing to produce a neutral grey. In the diagram below right, the secondary hues, also evenly spaced around the circle, balance each other in exactly the same way as the primaries.

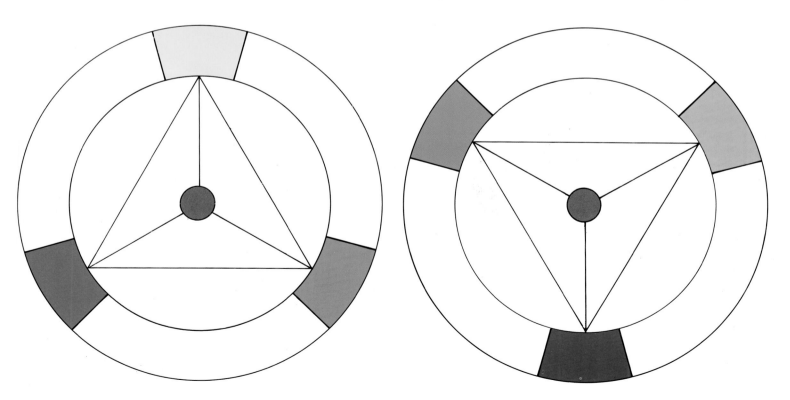

grey in the visual cortex, and so contain the element of tension missing from the examples of primary and secondary mixes on these pages. Considered as part of an overall programme of shooting, strong colour combinations are the short-term, straight-between-the-eyes images. They fit well into a selection of less intense pictures as strong punctuation, but several together quickly become a surfeit.

Three-way colour balance

We can extend the balancing principle of complementary pairs to three and more colours. Going back to the colour circle, three equally spaced colours mix to give a neutral colour (white, grey or black depending on whether light or pigments are mixed). The most intense triad of colours is,

There is a hidden consistency in the four-way combination above. The dominant green acts as a setting for the limited areas of the three classic primaries.

In the picture below, apart from the contrast of hue, the colours green, blue and orange share a similar quality of desaturation. This helps to make a coherent image.

Despite the extreme subtlety of the colours in the shot below, the original hues from they derive are fairly close to the primary triad of yellow, red and blue.

as you might expect, primary red, yellow and blue. The colour effect in a photograph depends very much on how saturated they are and on their proportions: equal areas give the most balanced result.

Soft colours

Diminishing the range of colour intensity has the interesting effect of refining the eye's discrimination. The differences in hue between unsaturated colours are less obvious than with fully saturated colours, and the eye pays more attention in assessing the differences and relationships. The precise colours are usually inherently more interesting because they are less familiar than the pure primaries and secondaries. Appreciating these more subtle colour relationships takes a little longer, so that in terms of viewing, this kind of photograph is normally a slow starter, but lasts. There are more opportunities for exploring colour relationships with pastel hues.

Colour contrast

There are natural associations between temperature and colour. Flame and things glowing with heat are either orange, or close to it on either side on the colour circle (that is, yellow-orange, or towards red). The hottest colour as perceived by most people is, in fact, orange-red. Its complementary, opposite on the colour circle, is blue-green, and this gives the coldest effect (these temperature associations are real; for example, a room decorated in shades of blue-green does feel physically colder than one in orange-red, even if both are identical in temperature).

The colour circle can be divided in half, between cold and warm. The centers of the two half-circles are blue-green and orange-red respectively. These two poles always have temperature associations, but the colours on either side depend on context for the strength of their effect. Green, for instance, may appear cool if contrasted with a distinctly warm colour like orange, but will not generate this impression if combined with yellow-orange.

Distance

This cool/warm contrast, an additional way of dividing the colour circle, can affect the other qualities of colours (the individual qualities of particular hues, the harmonious effects of proportions). One particularly important association is the suggestion of distance. Cool colours recede, warm colours advance; blue-green and its neighbouring colours are associated with backgrounds and distance. If the colour of a subject is warm, and that of its background cool, the impression of depth will be heightened. This is a different depth sensation from the one created by light/dark contrast, but if the two are combined (a pure orange against a deep blue, for example), the impression is slightly stronger. As a result, a small area of a warm colour set in a larger cool-coloured frame always looks appropriate.

Coolness and warmth

Cool/warm contrast has other associations, also related to our experience. Cool colours suggest transparency and airiness. This comes in part from the blue colour of a clear sky, in part from the pale blue of things seen at a distance through atmospheric haze. The opposites for warm colours, opacity and earthiness, are not such strong associations, but exist by virtue of the contrast. Also, cool colours, blue-green in particular, suggest wetness – a natural association with water – while orange-red and similar hues suggest a dryness – from the effects of heat. Cool/warm contrast occurs frequently in both natural and artificial lighting conditions. The contrast between sunlight and blue sky, which is also the contrast between sunlight and shadow, occurs everywhere, and when the sun is low is exaggerated. At dusk, the colours in the direction of the setting sun are warm; in the opposite direction they are cool. Twilight gives a particularly cool background. Artificial lighting produces even stronger opposites. Tungsten lighting is yellow-orange on daylight-balanced film, and the lower the wattage and the dimmer the lamp, the more orange it appears. Fluorescent lighting appears greenish to blue-green when photographed on daylight-balanced film, and strongly blue-green when shot on type B film.

Colour circle

Most of the above are colour temperature effects, and it is important to understand the differences between this scale and the cool/warm contrast of the colour circle. They are similar, but not identical. For instance, the colour temperature scale goes from hot (orange) through white hot to extremely hot (blue). This is physically accurate, but outside our normal experience. On the contrary, we associate blue with cool things, not with extreme heat. The second difference, although it is a small one, is that the range of colour temperature is not along a scale of pure colours; both the orange and blue at either end are a little dull in comparison with those of the colour circle.

GLOSSARY

Aberration General term for the failure of a lens to focus a sharp, accurate image. Aberrations, which include astigmatism, coma, field curvature and diffraction, may have very different causes. Compound-lens design is one of the principal methods of reducing aberrations.

Accessory shoe Fitting on the body of a camera that is designed to accept accessories and portable flash units. *See also* **Hot shoe**.

Additive colour The method of producing different hues by combining light. Three primary colours added together in equal proportions give white light.

Aerial perspective The visual effect of depth in a scene created by atmospheric haze, which makes the more distant parts of the view appear lighter in tone, paler in colour and have less contrast.

Angle of view The angle, measured from the lens, that takes in the full view projected onto the picture format.

Aperture The approximately circular opening inside a lens that can be enlarged or reduced to control the amount of light passing through.

Aperture priority In-camera metering system in which the photographer selects the aperture and the camera meter adjusts the shutter speed accordingly. *See also* **Program mode**.

ASA *American Standards Association* Arithmetically progressive rating of the sensitivity of a film to light. Although superseded by the **ISO** system, the latter makes use of ASA, and in practice, the ratings are the same. ASA 200 film, for example, is twice as fast as ASA 100 film.

Asymmetry Lack of symmetry or proportion; off-centeredness.

Autofocus Camera system in which the lens is focused automatically, either passively by measuring the contrast in part of the picture, or actively by responding to an ultrasonic or infra-red pulse emitted by the camera.

Automatic exposure Camera system in which a photo-electric cell measures the light reflected from the scene, and adjusts the amount allowed to reach the film.

Available light Artificial lighting that is not specifically designed for photography. Tungsten, fluorescent and vapour-discharge lighting are the main sources. Also known as existing light.

Average reading Exposure measurement made from all the light reflected by a scene.

Backlighting Lighting from behind the subject directed towards the camera position.

Barn doors Adjustable masks fitted to the front of a photographic lamp to prevent light from spilling at the sides.

Base lighting Lighting from beneath the subject, directed up.

Bellows A light-tight flexible sleeve, usually concertina-like, connecting the lens panel to the rest of the camera. Used where there is a need to move the lens, such as extending or tilting it. Fitted to view cameras, some rollfilm cameras and close-up extenders.

Between-the-lens shutter Shutter located inside a compound lens; it works by means of opening and closing a circular aperture.

Bit-mapped image Electronic image composed of a pattern of **pixels**. The resolution depends on the devices used – for input, display and output – and cannot be re-sized or edited without distortion. This is the normal form of a scanned photograph.

Blur Unsharpness in an image caused by movement – either the subject or the camera – or by inaccurate focusing.

Bounced light Technique for softening light by aiming a lamp towards a large reflecting surface, such as a white wall or ceiling.

Bracketing Technique in which the same picture is photographed several times at different exposures in order to guarantee that at least one is accurate. Mainly used when the lighting conditions are uncertain.

Brilliance (of colour) The brightness or tone of a colour.

Broken colour *See* **Degraded colour**.

Burning-in Photographic printing technique in which selected areas of the image are given additional exposure to alter the density in just those areas. *See also* **Dodging**.

Cable release Flexible cable that attaches to the shutter release button. Used for firing the shutter without the risk of vibration at slow speeds caused by moving the camera.

Camera angle The direction in which a camera points, particularly with reference to the horizontal.

Camera movements Mechanical adjustments to the position or angle of the lens and the camera's film back. Usually refers to movements other than straightforward focusing, such as tilts and shifts which make changes to the shape and position of the image. Most view cameras but very few smaller formats allow camera movements.

Cassette Metal or plastic film container in which the film is wound on a spool, unwinding from a slit when loaded in the camera. Used for 35mm film and some rollfilm formats.

Catadioptric lens *See* **Mirror lens**.

CCD array A silicon chip connected to electronic circuitry containing tightly packed sensors known as charge-coupled devices (CCDs). In a **digital camera** or scanner, a lens focuses an image on the array, and each sensor converts light falling on it from one small part of the scene into an electronic impulse. The image is thus digitized, the image quality depending largely on the number of CCDs in the array.

CD Compact disc, on which digitized information is recorded, for later reading by optical means. Originally developed for recording sound, CDs are now also used for storing other kinds of digitized information, including images, for which their high capacity makes them well suited. Varieties of CDs include CD-ROM (commercially prepared discs that can be read but not altered), Photo CD (a proprietary Kodak format used for storing images scanned from photographs), and CD-R (recordable CDs on which images and other information can be written using a desktop recorder).

Center of curvature The center of a notional sphere of which a lens surface is a section.

Center-weighted exposure Method of measuring the light reflected from a subject used in **TTL metering**. Extra value is given to the center of the frame, because this is typically where most people place the main subject.

Chroma The intensity, or saturation of a colour.

Chromatic Coloured; having to do with colour. A chromatic grey is intrinsically neutral but with a touch of colour.

Circle of confusion The appearance of a point when it is projected by a lens, and so a measure of sharpness. If it is not in focus, it appears as a small disc. The circle of least confusion is the smallest image of a point created by focusing a lens at a given aperture.

Click stop The graduation of the lens aperture control ring that allows the steps from one *f*-stop to another to be felt and heard.

Clip test A test development of a short length taken from the end of a roll of film; made to see whether the entire film needs adjusted processing.

Close-up In general terms, a close, frame-filling image of a subject. Specifically, the scale of photography between the point at which exposure compensation is needed because of the lens extension (about 1:7) and life-size (1:1).

Colour balance The relationship between the principal colours – either red, green and blue, or cyan, magenta and yellow – in an image.

Colour bias/colour cast Overall tinting of an image towards one hue.

Colour compensating filter Coloured filter designed for making corrections and adjustments to an image, such as when making duplicates or to compensate for **reciprocity failure**. Available in red, green, blue, cyan, magenta and yellow, in varying strengths.

Colour harmony (1) combinations of colours that balance each other, in the sense that if they were mixed the result would be neutral. (2) Pleasing combinations of colours – this is the common use, but is, by definition, subjective.

Colour circle The arrangement of distinct colours in a ring for ease of calculating colour relationships and effects.

Colour reversal film Colour film that carries a positive, transparent image when developed. During processing, the tones and colours of the recorded negative image are reversed so that the final image is produced from the unexposed areas, hence the name. Also known as transparency or slide film.

Colour temperature The temperature at which an inert substance glows at a particular colour. In photography, the important range of colour temperature is from 2000K (reddish colours) through 5000K-5500K (white) to above 6000K (bluish colours).

Colour transparency film *See* **Colour reversal film.**

Complementary colours The colours which, were each to be mixed equally with a **primary colour**, would produce a neutral hue. hence the complementaries of red, yellow and blue are, respectively, green, violet and orange. On the colour circle, complementaries lie opposite their primaries.

Compound lens Lens constructed from two or more elements. Different shapes and curvatures make it possible to correct certain aberrations with a compound lens.

Concave lens Lens element in which the surfaces curve inwards towards the center. This makes light rays passing through it diverge. *See also* **Convex lens.**

Contact sheet A print of all the frames of a roll of film. Usually made by exposing printing paper in direct contact with the negatives or transparencies.

Contrast The subjective appearance of the difference in contrast between different tones in an image. Colour contrast is the subjective impression

of the difference in intensity between adjacent colours.

Contrast range The range of tones, from darkest to lightest, in an image.

Convergence A perspective effect in which parallel lines in a subject appear to slope towards each other in a photograph, caused by viewing the lines at an angle. The eye compensates for the effect in real life, but notices it in an image.

Convex lens Lens element in which the surfaces curve outwards from the center. This concentrates light rays passing through the lens, and makes it possible to bring parallel rays to a common focus. *See also* **Concave lens**.

Covering power The maximum diameter of good-quality image that a lens can project. It must be at least as wide as the diagonal of the film format, and significantly wider if camera movements are used.

Cropping Reducing the image area by closing in one or more sides of the frame. Usually performed at the stage of printing a photograph or preparing it for display.

Cyan A mixture of blue and green, and one of the three subtractive primary colours – the others are magenta and yellow.

Darkslide Metal or plastic sheet that protects film from exposure to light in a camera that has a detachable film holder. It is withdrawn once the holder is in place in the camera. Used with view cameras and some rollfilm cameras.

Daylight film Colour film balanced for use with daylight and electronic flash – that is, between 5000K and 5500K.

Dedicated flash On-camera flash unit designed for use with a specific camera, linking directly with the camera's internal circuitry.

Depth of field The distance between the nearest and farthest points in a subject that appear acceptably sharp in an image. The smaller the lens aperture, the greater the depth of field.

Depth of focus The distance that the lens can be moved towards and away from the film and still give an acceptably sharp image. The smaller the aperture, the greater the depth of focus.

Developer Solution of a chemical compound that converts silver halide crystals into black metallic silver, The main component is the developing agent, to which is added alkali, preservative and other ingredients.

Diffraction Lens aberration in which light rays are scattered by the sharp edge of the aperture, causing unsharpness.

Diffuser Material that scatters transmitted light, so increasing the area of illumination and softening the light.

Digital camera Camera that uses a **CCD array** in place of conventional film to record the image focused by its lens.

Digital A way of representing data as a number of distinct units. A digital image needs a very large number of units so that it appears as a continuous-tone image to the eye; when it is displayed these are in the form of **pixels**.

Digitize To convert a continuous-tone image into digital form that a computer can read and work with. Performed by a scanner.

Diminishing perspective The impression of perspective created by a series of obviously similar objects appearing smaller with distance.

DIN (*Deutsche Industrie Norm*) German speed rating for film, being logarithmically progressive.

Direct reading *See* **Reflected light reading**.

Distortion An image or part of an image that is twisted out of shape.

D-max (*Maximum density*) The maximum possible density in a photographic material.

Dodging Photographic printing technique in which selected areas of the image are given less exposure to alter the density in those areas alone. *See also* **Burning-in**.

Dolly A rolling trolley to support a camera tripod or a lighting stand. The wheels can usually be locked for stability.

Double exposure Making two separate exposures on one frame of film.

DX coding A type of bar code on a film cassette that is read electronically by contacts inside an automatic camera. It gives information about the film, including its ISO speed, that the camera can use to set certain controls.

Dynamic The quality of apparent movement in an image, created by various techniques of composition.

Dynamic balance The sense of balance in an image created by the opposition of visual elements that each have a feeling of movement.

Dynamic tension The sense of forces pulling in opposite directions when looking at certain images. Contains a feeling of potential movement.

Effective aperture The diameter of a lens aperture when seen from the front of the lens.

Electronic flash Pulse of light produced by passing an electric charge at high voltage through an inert gas in a sealed transparent envelope.

Electronic shutter Camera shutter timed and operated by electronic rather than the traditional mechanical means.

Electronic imaging The recording of images on an electronic medium, such as tape, disk or CD. This may be either in digitized form (such as by using a scanner or a CCD array in place of film) or analogue (as in still video). Electronic imaging is used directly with a digital or still video camera, or secondarily, with a scanner to convert a conventional photograph.

Emulsion Light-sensitive substance composed of halides suspended in gelatin, used for photographic film and paper.

Exposure In photography, the quality of light that reaches the film. It is a product of the intensity of the light and the amount of time it is allowed to fall on the film.

Exposure latitude The amount of over-exposure or under-exposure that can be given to a film and still make an acceptable image with standard processing.

Exposure meter Instrument for measuring the amount of light falling on a subject or reflected from it. Most meters are built into cameras, but there are separate hand-held models.

Exposure value (EV) A value for the amount of light. Used in exposure measurement, it links shutter speed and aperture. A single EV number can represent, for example, 1/60 sec at $f5.6$ *and* 1/250 sec at $f2.8$.

Extension ring/extension tube Rigid tube that fits between the lens and camera body to allow greater magnification. Available in different thicknesses.

Eye-line The implied line in a picture suggested by the direction in which a person (or animal) photographed is looking.

f **number/f-stop** The standard way of describing the relative aperture of a lens. Calculated as the lens's **focal length** divided by its **effective aperture**. It makes it possible to compare the aperture settings of different lenses. The standard series – $f1$, $f1.4$, $f2$, $f2.8$ and so on – is in steps of a factor of two: each higher number represents half the amount of light being passed.

Fast film Film that is more sensitive than average to light, and so can be used in dim lighting conditions. *See also* **Slow film**.

Fast lens A lens with greater than normal light-gathering power. *See also* **Lens speed**.

Fill light/fill-in light Illumination of just the shadow areas in a view.

Film plane The plane at the back of the camera in which the film lies and on which the image is focused.

Film speed The sensitivity of film to light, now measured as its **ISO** rating.

Filter Transparent sheet of glass or plastic attached to the lens – usually coloured or tinted to modify the light reaching the film. In electronic imaging, a filter is software included in an image-editing program that alters some image quality of a selected area.

Filter factor The number by which the exposure must be multiplied to compensate for the amount of light absorbed by a filter.

Fish-eye lens Extreme wide-angle lens in which the curvilinear distortion is left uncorrected to give greater coverage.

Fixer A solution of sodium thiosulphate or other silver halide solvent which removes the silver halides in film that have not been exposed to light. It converts them to soluble salts, which are then removed by the washing stage of processing. Fixing halts any further darkening in the image.

Flare Non-image-forming light. Caused by scattering and reflecting inside the lens, it degrades image quality. The two most common occasions are when a bright light shines directly on the lens, and when a large area of the view outside the picture frame is bright.

Flash A source of light that operates in a pulse. **Electronic flash** is now normal, but the more old-fashioned expendable flash bulbs are still available and occasionally used.

Flash bulb Transparent bulb containing a substance (wire or paste) that ignites with a brilliant flash when a low-voltage charge is passed through it. Expendable; now largely superseded by electronic flash.

Flash synchronization System for making the pulse of light from a flash coincide with the opening of the shutter.

Floating lens elements Individual elements in a compound lens that move in relation to the others during focusing. Used particularly in zoom lenses, to make the optimum correction of lens aberrations.

Floppy disk Removable electronic medium for use in computers to store information.

Fluorescent light A pulsating artificial light created by passing an electrical charge through vapour, which excites phosphors coated on the inside of a sealed tube.

Focal length Distance between the rear **nodal point** of a lens and the **focal plane** when the lens is focused on infinity. The standard way of classifying lenses by how much they magnify the image.

Focal plane The plane that is perpendicular to the **lens axis** and at which the image is sharply focused.

Focal plane shutter Camera shutter system consisting of blinds immediately in front of the **focal plane**. The blinds open and travel across the plane.

Focal point Point on the lens axis where light rays from a subject meet.

Focusing Changing the distance between the lens (or some lens elements) and the film plane to make the image sharp.

Focusing screen Glass or plastic screen mounts in the camera either at the film plane or at an equivalent off-axis distance, to allow accurate composition and focusing.

Fog The darkening of a negative or print that is unrelated to the image – a fault caused either by exposure to light or to certain chemicals.

Fog filter A type of diffusing filter used in front of the lens to simulate mist or fog.

Follow focus Manual focusing technique in which the focusing ring on the lens is turned at a rate that keeps pace with the approach of a moving subject, to keep the image focused the whole time.

Format Size and shape of the film or picture area. 35mm is the most common format, measuring 24x36mm.

Fully automated diaphragm (FAD) System in an **SLR** camera that allows full-aperture viewing up to the moment of exposure, stopping the lens down to a preselected aperture when the shutter is triggered.

Gelatin filter Thin filters for use in front of lenses, made from dyed gelatin sheet.

Golden Section Division of a line or a rectangle (such as a picture frame) according to fixed proportions, so that the ratio of the smaller part to the larger is the same as that of the larger to the whole. Widely regarded as being aesthetically satisfying, particularly in Classical Greek culture and during the Renaissance.

Grad/graduated filter Glass or plastic filter which shades from clear to a tone, either neutral or coloured. It can be used, for instance, to darken the image of a sky. Despite its name, its shading is smooth and not in steps.

Grain An individual light-sensitive crystal in an emulsion.

Graininess The subjective impression of **granularity** in a photograph. At normal viewing distances, the effect is created by clumps of grains, not individual ones.

Granularity A measure of the size and distribution of grains in an emulsion.

Grey card Card that reflects 18% of the light striking it. This is equivalent to the mid-tones of an average subject, and it can be used for making substitute **reflected light readings**. *See also* **Substitute reading**.

Ground-glass screen Sheet of glass finely etched on one side for use as a **focusing screen**.

Guide number Measurement of light output used to describe the power of a flash unit. When the guide number is divided by the distance (in feet or meters) to the subject, it gives the aperture setting for a given film speed.

Heat filter Transparent screen used in front of a photographic lamp to absorb heat without reducing the light output.

High key Type of image made up of light tones only.

Highlight The brightest area of a subject or image.

Hot shoe Fitting on the body of a camera similar to an **accessory shoe**, but containing the electrical contacts needed to trigger a flash unit when the shutter release is pressed.

Hue The quality of colour that is defined by its wavelength; the most obvious and commonly cited distinction between colours.

Image file format The form in which an image is handled and stored electronically. There are many such formats, each developed by different manufacturers and with different advantages according to the type of image and how it is intended to be used. Some are more suitable than others for high-resolution images, or for object-oriented images, and so on. Examples are TIFF, PICT and EPS.

Image-editing program Software for a computer that makes it possible to enhance and alter a scanned image.

Incident light The light that falls *on* a subject, as opposed to the light reflected *by* it.

Incident light reading Exposure measurement of incident light, usually made with a translucent attachment to a hand-held meter. This kind of reading is independent of the tone and colour of the subject.

Infinity (∞ on the lens distance scale) The distance from which light rays reach the lens parallel to each other.

Integral masking The addition of orange dyes to colour negative film at the manufacturing stage to compensate for deficiencies in the image-forming dyes.

ISO (*International Standards Organisation*) The current internationally accepted **film speed** rating, made up of the older **ASA/DIN** ratings but commonly abbreviated everywhere except German-speaking countries to the ASA rating.

Joule Unit of electrical output, equivalent to one watt-second. Used to describe the power of studio electronic flash units.

Kelvin (K) The standard unit of thermodynamic temperature, calculated by adding 273 to °C. In photography, used to measure the **colour temperature** of light.

Key light The main light source.

Key reading Exposure reading of what is judged to be the most important tone for the photograph.

Kilowatt Unit of electrical power, equivalent to 1000 watts.

Latent image The invisible image formed by exposing an emulsion to light. Development renders it visible.

Latitude *See* **Exposure latitude**.

LCD (*Liquid Crystal Diode*) Solid-state display used to show information in the camera viewfinder and in display panels on the body. The surface of the display changes from transparent to black when an electrical charge is applied.

Leaf shutter *See* **Between-the-lens shutter**.

LED (*Light-Emitting Diode*) A small battery-powered light used in the viewfinder displays of some cameras.

Lens axis Line through the **center of curvature** of the lens, in the direction of the **angle of view**.

Lens shade Attachment to the front of the lens to shield it from flare.

Lens speed The quantity of light that a lens can transmit from a scene to the film, usually expressed as its *f* **number**.

Light balancing filter A filter used to convert the **colour temperature** of light to the type of film used.

Light meter *See* **Exposure meter**.

Linear perspective The impression of perspective created by the **convergence** of lines towards a vanishing point.

Long-focus lens Lens with a focal length longer than that considered to give normal perspective. In practice, for 35mm format, longer than 50mm.

Luminance The amount of light reflected or emitted by a subject.

Macro lens Lens specifically designed to give the best image quality at magnifications close to life-size.

Magenta A mixture of red and blue; one of the three subtractive primary colours. The other two are cyan and yellow.

Magnification The size relationship between a subject and its image. If the image were twice the size of the subject, the magnification would be x2.

Manual operation Camera operation in which the photographer overrides or by-passes the normal automatic systems such as metering and focus.

Megabyte (MB) Unit of information capacity in a computer, standing for 1000 bytes. A byte is the individual digital unit. Large computer files, such as image files, are measured in megabytes.

Microprism Patterned array of small prisms used on certain focusing screens as a focusing aid.

Mid-tone Average level of brightness, mid-way between highlight and shadow, equivalent to a reflectance of 18 per cent. *See also* **Grey card**.

Mired (*MIcro-REciprocal DEgree*) Measurement of colour temperature that allows the strength of light balancing filters to be added and subtracted. Equivalent to one million divided by the **kelvin** value.

Mirror lens Design of lens, usually long-focus, that uses mirrors to reflect light back and forth and so reduce the physical length of the barrel.

Mixed light Different types of light source combining to illuminate a scene.

Mode *See* **Program mode.**

Modelling lamp A continuous-light lamp (usually tungsten or fluorescent) fitted next to a flash tube in a large electronic flash unit, to give a preview of the lighting effect.

Monorail camera View camera construction in which the operating parts are supported on a single rail.

M-sync Synchronization system for using a camera with flash bulbs.

Multiple exposure Making several separate exposures on one frame of film.

Multiple flash Firing a flash unit several times during one exposure to increase the amount of light reaching the film.

Neutral density filter Grey filter for use in front of the lens that reduces exposure to the film without altering the colour.

Nodal plane The plane perpendicular to the **lens axis** that passes through the **nodal points**.

Nodal point One of two points in a **compound lens** at which light rays entering converge (the front nodal point) and light rays leaving diverge (rear nodal point).

Non-substantive film Colour film in which the colour-forming dyes are not present in the film as manufactured, but added during processing. Kodachrome is the best-known example.

Off-the-film (OTF) metering A through-the-lens (TTL) metering system in which measurements are made at the moment of exposure, as reflected off the surface of the film.

Opalescent The milky or cloudy white translucent quality of some materials used as diffusers.

Opaque Impermeable to light.

Optical axis *See* **Lens axis.**

Optimum aperture The aperture setting that gives the highest image quality for a given lens and conditions – a balance between conflicting lens aberrations.

Orthochromatic film Any photographic film (black-and-white) that is insensitive to red. It can be handled under a red safelight.

Over-exposure Giving an emulsion more light than is needed to form an acceptable image. In a transparency, or in a print from a negative, the result is lower contrast, weaker colours, pale shadows and lost highlights.

Oxidation Reducing chemical reaction caused by prolonged exposure to air or to chemicals that add oxygen, remove hydrogen or remove electrons. In film development, the exhaustion of a solution.

Paint program Computer-image-management software which enables pixels and groups of pixels to be altered and manipulated electronically.

Panchromatic film Any photographic film that is sensitive to all colours of the spectrum.

Panning Swinging the camera to keep a moving subject centered in the frame.

Panoramic camera A camera that produces a film format longer than 1:3 for a wide field of view.

Parallax The apparent movement of objects in relation to each other when the viewing position is changed.

Pentaprism Five-sided prism used in the viewing system of an **SLR** camera to turn the image the right way up and right way round. *See also* **Prism.**

Perspective The appearance of objects, relative to one another, in terms of position and distance. Strictly speaking, perspective changes only with viewpoint.

Photoflood A tungsten photographic lamp run at higher than normal voltage to give more light output. Its life is consequently short.

Photomacrography Photography at magnifications greater than life-size (1:1) that can still be made without resorting to a microscope.

Photomicrography Photography at extreme magnifications, using the optical system of a microscope.

Picture area The area of the *subject* that fills the picture frame of the camera.

Pixel The smallest unit of area of a digitized image, normally a square. The number of pixels in which the image is recorded determines its resolution.

Point source A source of light that appears as a point, without dimension.

Polarization Restricting the random vibration of light waves to a single plane.

Polarizing filter Filter that polarizes light entering the lens.

Primary colours Any three colours that can be mixed in proportions to make any other colour. Each therefore covers approximately a third of the visible spectrum. In painting, the primaries are considered to be red, yellow and blue. In combining light (and therefore the dyes used to make film), the primaries are red, blue and green. In printing they are cyan, magenta and yellow.

Printing-in *See* **Burning-in**

Prism Transparent optical element with flat surfaces shaped to refract light. *See also* **Pentaprism, Refraction.**

Process lens A lens designed to produce its best image quality when photographing flat objects.

Program mode One of several ways in which an automatic camera can be set to operate by the photographer so that different priorities can be selected. *See* **Aperture priority** and **Shutter priority.**

Pulling The under-development of film, to compensate for over-exposure and/or to reduce contrast.

Pushing The over-development of film, to compensate for under-exposure and/or to increase contrast.

Rangefinder Device for measuring distance by optical triangulation, fitted to traditionally designed non-reflex cameras.

Reciprocity failure At very short and very long exposures, the **reciprocity law** fails to hold true, and extra exposure is needed. With colour film, the three dye layers are often affected differently, causing a colour cast.

Reciprocity law Exposure = intensity x time. In other words, the amount of light reaching the film is the product of the lens aperture and the time the shutter is left open. Halving one and doubling the other gives the same exposure.

Reflected light reading Exposure measurement of the light reflected from a subject – the normal method of TTL systems.

Reflector A sheet or surface used to reflect light towards a part of the subject. Its texture, colour and tone affect the quality of the reflected light.

Reflex camera A camera design that allows a direct view of the image through the lens, by means of a mirror between the lens and a focusing screen.

Refraction The bending of light rays as they pass through a transparent medium.

Reproduction ratio The relative proportions of a subject and its image. If the image were twice the size of the subject, the ratio would be 1:1.

Resolution The ability to image detail. A common measurement is lines per millimetre — the number of lines that can be separately imaged over a width of one millimetre. In electronic imaging, pixels per inch and dots per inch are common measurements.

Ring flash Electronic flash unit in the shape of a ring that fits around the front of the camera lens. Its effect is almost shadowless lighting.

Rollfilm Film rolled on a spool, usually with a dark paper backing. The most common type is 120, which gives a maximum image width of 6cm.

Saturation The purity and intensity of a colour.

Secondary colours *See* **Complementary colours**.

Shadow fill *See* **Fill light/fill-in light**

Selenium cell Photo-electric cell which generates its own electrical charge in proportion to the light striking it.

Serial flash *See* **Multiple flash**.

Shading *See* **Burning-in**.

Shadow detail The darkest visible detail in a subject or image. Often used to set the lower limit for exposure.

Sheet film Film used in the form of flat sheets rather than rolls or strips, and usually for large formats, such as 4 × 5-inch and 8 × 10-inch. Normally loaded individually into film holders.

Shift Movement of the lens or the film holder in a camera perpendicular to the lens axis – that is, up, down, or to one side.

Shutter priority In-camera metering system in which the photographer selects the shutter speed and the camera meter adjusts the aperture accordingly. *See also* **Program mode**.

Silver halide A light-sensitive compound of silver and bromine, chlorine, iodine or other halogen. Silver halide crystals are the main active component of photographic emulsions, and after they have been exposed to light and adequate development they convert to visible, black metallic silver.

Single-lens reflex (SLR) Camera design in which the lens that exposes the image can also be used for viewing. *See also* **Reflex camera**.

Skylight Light reflected from the atmosphere – blue on a clear day, making shadow areas outdoors appear bluish in colour photographs.

Slave trigger A remotely operated device for triggering additional flash units without a cable connection. The normal method is a photo-cell that reacts to the pulse of light from the main flash unit.

SLR *See* **Single-lens reflex**.

Slow film Film with low sensitivity to light, usually producing a fine-grained image.

Slow lens A lens with less than normal light-gathering power. *See also* **Lens speed**.

Snoot A black cylinder, straight-sided or slightly tapered, that fits in front of a photographic lamp to concentrate the light into a circle.

Soft-focus filter A filter that deliberately reduces image sharpness in a controlled way.

Spectrum Range of frequencies. The spectrum of light is the range of visible radiation, from dark red to violet.

Speed *See* **Film speed** and **Lens speed**.

Spotlight A photographic lamp with a focusing system that concentrates the light into a narrow, adjustable beam.

Spot meter Exposure meter that measures **reflected light readings** from a very narrow angle, as little as 1°.

Spotting Small-scale retouching on a print or film.

Standard lens Lens with a focal length that produces an image with a perspective similar to that of the unaided eye. For 35mm format, 50mm is usually considered to be the standard lens.

Static balance Sense of balance in an image created the opposition of visual elements that are themselves statically placed.

Still video Electronic imaging system that uses video (camcorder) technology to capture still images. Still video is analogue, not digital.

Stop bath Chemical solution that neutralizes the action of the developer on the emulsion, effectively stopping the development.

Strobe (abbr. for stroboscopic light) A rapidly repeating electronic flash unit. Used to give a multiple image of a moving subject.

Substitute reading Exposure measurement of a surface that has the same reflective characteristics as the subject. *See also* **Grey card**.

Supplementary lens Lens that can be attached to the prime lens to change its characteristics, notably its focal length.

Swing Rotating movement of the lens or film holder around a vertical axis. Used to alter the shape of the image or its distribution of sharpness. *See also* **Camera movements**.

Symmetry The equal distribution of points, lines or shapes around a center or central division in a picture.

Tele-converter A **supplementary lens** that fits between the prime lens and the camera body, to increase the focal length.

Telephoto lens Design of **long-focus** lens in which the distance between the lens and film is less than the focal length – a means of making the lens more compact.

Tertiary colours Colours derived from the mixture of primaries and adjacent complementaries on the colour circle – the third stage of creating colours from primaries.

Through-the-lens (TTL) meter Exposure meter built into the camera, measuring light from the subject that passes through the lens.

Time exposure An exposure of several seconds or more.

TTL *See* **Through-the-lens (TTL) meter**

Tungsten light Form of artificial light that is created by heating a filament of tungsten wire electrically until it glows.

Tungsten-halogen lamp A type of tungsten lamp, more efficient than normal, in which the tungsten filament burns at a very much higher temperature in halogen gas.

Type B film Film designed for use in tungsten light. Gives a blue cast of used in daylight.

Under-exposure Giving an emulsion less light than is needed to form an acceptable image. In a transparency, or in a print from a negative, the result is lower contrast, dark tones, lost detail in the shadows and muddy highlights.

View camera A traditional design of camera, normally used for large format, in which the image is viewed on a **ground-glass screen** in the position of the **film plane**. After viewing, the film is inserted and exposed.

Viewfinder Optical aid to viewing and framing, normally found on a non-reflex camera.

Viewpoint Camera position relative to the subject.

Vignetting Fall-off of illumination at the edges of an image.

Visual weight The visual importance attached to an element in an image by the viewer. Psychological associations often play an important part.

Wide-angle lens Lens with an angle of view wider than that of a **standard lens** for the **format**.

Zoom lens Lens with a continuously variable focal length over a certain range.

Zoom flash An automatic on-camera flash feature in which the angle of the beam of light varies according to setting of the **zoom lens** fitted.

INDEX